# DIETRICH BONHOEFFER WORKS, VOLUME 5

*Life Together*

and

*Prayerbook of the Bible*

D0880205

This series is a translation of
DIETRICH BONHOEFFER WERKE
Edited by
Eberhard Bethge, Ernst Feil,
Christian Gremmels, Wolfgang Huber,
Hans Pfeifer, Albrecht Schönherr,
Heinz Eduard Tödt†, Ilse Tödt

DIETRICH BONHOEFFER WORKS

General Editor
Wayne Whitson Floyd, Jr.

# DIETRICH BONHOEFFER

# Life Together

# Prayerbook of the Bible

*Translated from the German Edition*
*Edited by*
GERHARD LUDWIG MÜLLER AND ALBRECHT SCHÖNHERR

*English Edition*
*Edited by*
GEFFREY B. KELLY

*Translated by*
DANIEL W. BLOESCH AND JAMES H. BURTNESS

FORTRESS PRESS        MINNEAPOLIS

**DIETRICH BONHOEFFER WORKS, Volume 5**

First Fortress Press paperback edition 2005

First English-language edition with new supplementary material published by Fortress Press in 1996. Originally published in German as *Dietrich Bonhoeffer Werke Bande 5* by Christian Kaiser Verlag in 1987.

Dietrich Bonhoeffer Works, Volume 5, copyright © 1996 Augsburg Fortress. For permission information regarding this volume, see pp. 2, 142.

Cover photo: Dietrich Bonhoeffer. Used by permission of Archive Photos/DPA.
Jacket design: Cheryl Watson
Internal design: The HK Scriptorium, Inc.

ISBN 0-8006-8325-0

---

*The Library of Congress has cataloged the hardcover edition as follows:*

Bonhoeffer, Dietrich, 1906–1945.
   [Works. English. 1996]
   Dietrich Bonhoeffer works / [general editor, Wayne Whitson Floyd, Jr.].—1st English-language ed. with new supplementary material.
      p.   cm.
   Translation of: Dietrich Bonhoeffer Werke.
   Includes Bibliographical references and index.
   Contents:—v. 5. Life together ; Prayerbook of the Bible
   ISBN 0-8006-8305-6 (v. 5 : alk. paper)
   1. Theology. I. Floyd, Wayne W. II. Title.
BR45 .B6513 1996
230'.044—dc20                                       95-38988

---

The paper used in this publication meets the minimum requirements of American National Standard for Information Sciences—Permanence of Paper for Printed Library Materials, ANSI Z329.48-1984.

Manufactured in the U.S.A.

09    08    07    06    05    1    2    3    4    5    6    7    8    9    10

# CONTENTS

# GENERAL EDITOR'S FOREWORD TO DIETRICH BONHOEFFER WORKS

Since the time that the writings of Dietrich Bonhoeffer (1906–1945) first began to be available in English after World War II, they have been eagerly read both by scholars and by a wide general audience. The story of his life is compelling, set in the midst of historic events that shaped a century.

Bonhoeffer's leadership in the anti-Nazi Confessing Church and his participation in the *Abwehr* resistance circle make his works a unique source for understanding the interaction of religion, politics, and culture among those few Christians who actively opposed National Socialism. His writings provide not only an example of intellectual preparation for the reconstruction of German culture after the war but also a rare insight into the vanishing world of the old social and academic elites. Because of his participation in the resistance against the Nazi regime, Dietrich Bonhoeffer was hanged in the concentration camp at Flossenburg on April 9, 1945.

Yet Bonhoeffer's enduring contribution is not just his moral example but his theology. As a student in Tübingen, Berlin, and at Union Theological Seminary in New York — where he also was associated for a time with the Abyssinian Baptist Church in Harlem — and as a participant in the European ecumenical movement, Bonhoeffer became known as one of the few figures of the 1930s with a comprehensive and nuanced grasp of both German- and English-language theology. His thought resonates with a prescience, subtlety, and maturity that continually belies the youth of the thinker.

In 1986 the Christian Kaiser Verlag, now part of Gütersloher Verlagshaus, marked the eightieth anniversary of Bonhoeffer's birth by issuing the first of the sixteen volumes of the definitive German edition of his writings, the *Dietrich Bonhoeffer Werke*. Preliminary discussions about an English translation began even as the German series was beginning to emerge. As a consequence, the International Bonhoeffer Society, English Language Section, formed an editorial board, initially chaired by Robin Lovin, assisted by Mark Brocker, to undertake this project. Since 1993 the *Dietrich Bonhoeffer Works* translation project has been located in the Krauth Memorial Library of the Lutheran Theological Seminary at Philadelphia, under the leadership of its general editor — Wayne Whitson Floyd, Jr., the director of the seminary's Dietrich Bonhoeffer Center — and its executive director — Clifford J. Green of Hartford Seminary.

*Dietrich Bonhoeffer Works* provides the English-speaking world with an entirely new, complete, and unabridged translation of the written legacy of one of the twentieth century's most notable theologians; it includes a large amount of material appearing in English for the first time. Key terms are translated consistently throughout the corpus, with special attention being paid to accepted English equivalents of technical theological and philosophical concepts.

The *Dietrich Bonhoeffer Works* strives, above all, to be true to the language, style, and — most importantly — the theology of Bonhoeffer's writings. Translators have sought, nonetheless, to present Bonhoeffer's words in a manner that is sensitive to issues of language and gender. Consequently, accurate translation has removed sexist formulations that had been introduced inadvertently or unnecessarily into earlier English versions of his works. In addition, translators and editors generally have employed gender-inclusive language, so far as this was possible without distorting Bonhoeffer's meaning or dissociating him from his own time.

At times Bonhoeffer's theology sounds fresh and modern, not because the translators have made it so, but because his language still speaks with a hardy contemporaneity even after more than half a century. In other instances, Bonhoeffer sounds more remote, a product of another era, not due to any lack of facility by the translators and editors, but because his concerns and his rhetoric are, in certain ways, bound to a time that is past.

Volumes include introductions written by the editors of the English edition, footnotes provided by Bonhoeffer, editorial notes added by the

German and English editors, and afterwords composed by the editors of the German edition. In addition, volumes provide tables of abbreviations used in the editorial apparatus, as well as bibliographies which list sources used by Bonhoeffer, literature consulted by the editors, and other works related to each particular volume. Finally, volumes contain pertinent chronologies, charts, and indexes of scriptural references, names, and subjects.

The layout of the English edition has retained Bonhoeffer's original paragraphing, as well as his manner of dividing works into chapters and sections. The pagination of the German critical edition, the *Dietrich Bonhoeffer Werke,* is indicated in the outer margins of the pages of the translated text. At times, for the sake of precision and clarity of translation, a word or phrase that has been translated is provided in its original language, in normal type, set within square brackets at the appropriate point in the text. All biblical citations come from the New Revised Standard Version, unless otherwise noted. Where versification of the Bible used by Bonhoeffer differs from the NRSV, the verse number in the latter is noted in the text in square brackets.

Bonhoeffer's own footnotes — which are indicated by superscripted numbers in square brackets — are reproduced in the form in which they appear in the German critical edition, complete with his idiosyncrasies of documentation. In these, as in the accompanying editorial notes, existing English translations of books and articles have been substituted for their counterparts in other languages whenever available. When non-English titles are not listed individually in the bibliographies (along with an English translation of those titles), a translation of those titles has been provided within the footnote or editorial note in which they are cited.

The editorial notes — which are indicated by plain, superscripted numbers — provide information on the intellectual, ecclesiastical, social, and political context of Bonhoeffer's pursuits during the first half of the twentieth century. These are based on the scholarship of the German critical edition; they have been supplemented by the contributions of the editors of the English edition. Where the editors or translators of the English edition have substantially added to or revised a German editors' note, the initials of the person making the change(s) appear at the note's conclusion. When any previously translated material is quoted within an editorial note in an altered form, such changes should be assumed to be the responsibility of the translators.

Bibliographies at the end of each volume provide the complete information for each source that Bonhoeffer or the various editors have mentioned in their work. References to the archives, collections, and personal library of materials that had belonged to Bonhoeffer and that survived the war — as cataloged in the *Nachlaß Dietrich Bonhoeffer* — are indicated within the *Dietrich Bonhoeffer Works* by the initials NL followed by the appropriate reference code within that published index.

The production of any individual volume of the *Dietrich Bonhoeffer Works* requires the assistance of numerous individuals and organizations, whose support is duly noted in the respective editor's introduction. A special note of gratitude, however, is owed to all those prior translators, editors, and publishers of various portions of Bonhoeffer's literary legacy who heretofore have made available to the English-speaking world the writings of this remarkable theologian.

This English edition depends especially upon the careful scholarship of all those who labored to produce the critical German edition from which these translations have been made. Their work has been overseen by a board of general editors — responsible for both the concept and the content of the German edition — composed of Eberhard Bethge, Ernst Feil, Christian Gremmels, Wolfgang Huber, Hans Pfeifer, Albrecht Schönherr, Heinz Eduard Tödt†, and Ilse Tödt.

The present English edition would have been impossible without the creative and untiring dedication of the members of the editorial board of the *Dietrich Bonhoeffer Works:* Mark Brocker, James H. Burtness, Keith W. Clements, Clifford J. Green, Barbara Green, John W. de Gruchy, James Patrick Kelley, Geffrey B. Kelly, Reinhard Krauss, Robin W. Lovin, Michael Lukens, Nancy Lukens, Paul Matheny, Mary Nebelsick, and H. Martin Rumscheidt.

The deepest thanks for their support of this undertaking is owed, as well, to all the various members, friends, and benefactors of the International Bonhoeffer Society; to the National Endowment for the Humanities, which supported this project during its inception; to the Lutheran Theological Seminary at Philadelphia and its Auxiliary who established and help support the Dietrich Bonhoeffer Center on its campus specifically for the purpose of facilitating these publications; and to our publisher, Fortress Press, as represented with uncommon patience and *Gemütlichkeit* by Marshall Johnson, Rachel Riensche, Pam McClanahan, and Lois Torvik. Such a collaboration as this is fitting testimony to the spirit of Dietrich Bonhoeffer, who was himself always so attentive to the creative mystery of community, and that ever-deepening collegiality which is engendered by our social nature as human beings.

Wayne Whitson Floyd, Jr. , General Editor
January 27, 1995
The Fiftieth Anniversary of the Liberation of Auschwitz

# Abbreviations

| | |
|---|---|
| *AB* | *Act and Being* |
| *CC* | *Christ the Center* (U.K. Title *Christology*) |
| *CD* | *The Cost of Discipleship* |
| *CF/T* | *Creation and Fall/Temptation* |
| *CS* | *The Communion of Saints* (U.K. Title *Sanctorum Communio*) |
| *DBW* | *Dietrich Bonhoeffer Werke*–German Edition |
| *DBWE* | *Dietrich Bonhoeffer Works*–English Edition |
| *E* | *Ethics* |
| *GS* | *Gesammelte Schriften* (Collected Works) |
| *ILTP* | *I Loved This People* |
| *LPP* | *Letters and Papers from Prison,* 4th ed. |
| *LT* | *Life Together* |
| *LW* | *[Martin] Luther's Works,* American Edition |
| *MW* | *Meditating on the Word* |
| *NL* | *Nachlaß Dietrich Bonhoeffer* |
| *NRS* | *No Rusty Swords* |
| *PB* | *The Prayerbook of the Bible* |
| *PP* | *Prayers from Prison* |
| *PTB* | *Preface to Bonhoeffer* |
| *SPC* | *Spiritual Care* |
| *TF* | *A Testament to Freedom* |
| *TP* | *True Patriotism* |
| *WA* | *Werke: Kritische Gesamtausgabe* (Martin Luther, Weimar Ausgabe) |
| *WF* | *The Way to Freedom* |
| *WP* | *Worldly Preaching* |

# DIETRICH BONHOEFFER

## *Life Together*

*Translated from the German Edition*
*Edited by*
GERHARD LUDWIG MÜLLER AND ALBRECHT SCHÖNHERR

*English Edition*
*Edited by*
GEFFREY B. KELLY

*Translated by*
DANIEL W. BLOESCH

FORTRESS PRESS                    MINNEAPOLIS

GEFFREY B. KELLY

# EDITOR'S INTRODUCTION TO THE ENGLISH EDITION

IN AN IRONICAL WAY we are indebted to the Gestapo[1] for this remarkable book. It was because they had shut down the preachers' seminary at Finkenwalde that Dietrich Bonhoeffer was finally persuaded to compose his thoughts on the nature and sustaining structures of Christian community, based on the "life together" that he and his seminarians had sustained both at the seminary and in the Brothers' House at Finkenwalde. Prior to this, except for a brief explanation of the practice of daily meditation, Bonhoeffer had been reluctant to publicize this experiment, feeling that the time was not ripe. With the closing of the seminary at Finkenwalde and the dispersal of the seminarians, however, Bonhoeffer felt compelled not only to record for posterity the daily regimen and its rationale, but also to voice his conviction that the worldwide church itself needed to promote a sense of community like this if it was to have new life breathed into it.

## Life Together and the Crises of 1938

With a new sense of urgency, therefore, Bonhoeffer, along with his close friend Eberhard Bethge, went to Göttingen in late September 1938, to the empty home belonging to his twin sister, Sabine, and her husband, Gerhard Leibholz. Though a popular professor of law at Göttingen University and a baptized Christian, Leibholz had been dismissed from his professorship because of his Jewish origins. On September 9,

---

1. The *Geheime Staatspolizei* or secret police in Nazi Germany.

1938, Bonhoeffer and Bethge had helped the Leibholz family escape Germany into Basel, Switzerland. Later they would emigrate to Oxford, England, where they would be safe during the war years. Working in the Leibholz home, Bonhoeffer completed *Life Together* [*Gemeinsames Leben*] in a single stretch of four weeks. Bethge recalls that, while he himself passed the time studying Karl Barth's *Church Dogmatics*, Bonhoeffer sat at Leibholz's desk and worked on the manuscript almost nonstop. Though they also took breaks for tennis and a music festival and had their work interrupted by the Sudetenland crisis, Bonhoeffer was able to block out these distractions and complete the book in the short time available.[2]

Those detours from the writing of *Life Together* were highlighted by the background drama of Hitler's bold move to gobble up the Sudetenland. The breather from this crisis came with the signing of the Munich agreement on September 30. Munich proved to be a mere deceptive prelude to Hitler's swallowing the whole of Czechoslovakia. Bonhoeffer was working, therefore, against the clock that seemed to be ticking away the time between a shaky peace and the impending conflict with France and England over the fate of Czechoslovakia. At the same time, the military draft was escalating with apparently only one purpose: war. Bonhoeffer and Bethge were plunged, too, into the turmoil of incertitude about the future of the Confessing Church. Throughout 1937 and 1938 Bonhoeffer had been irritated by the Confessing Church's accelerating weakness and its tendency to compromise in the face of Nazi threats. The oath of personal allegiance to Hitler that a majority of Confessing Church pastors had taken by the summer of 1938, absent any strong command to the contrary from church leaders, already filled him with bitterness and frustration. That latest failure in responsibility on the part of Bonhoeffer's church prompted his addressing a stinging rebuke to the synod that had passed responsibility for taking the oath onto the shoulders of individual pastors. His admonition of the leadership of the Confessing Church was characteristically blunt: "Will Confessing Synods ever learn that it is important to counsel and to decide in defiance of all dangers and difficulties . . . ? Will they ever learn that majority decision in matters of conscience kills the spirit?"[3]

---

2. Eberhard Bethge, "Afterword to the 1979 Edition of *Gemeinsames Leben*," 5.
3. Bonhoeffer, *TF*, 465 (GS 2:314).

By the time of the writing of *Life Together* in September 1938, the situation had worsened. Bethge described the "insane tension" of those days when, forced to interrupt their work, he and Bonhoeffer had driven to Berlin around long lines of cars and trucks in order to find out firsthand how far along the path to war Germany had marched. They also craved information about their own situation as pastors about to be inducted into the army. They wanted recognition from the Evangelical Church Council in order to be eligible for exemption from military service. It was not beyond imagining that the Nazis would dismantle the entire Confessing Church leadership. What then? In addition, both Bonhoeffer and Bethge were privy to the earliest conspiracy to overthrow the Hitler government in a coup d'etat in which Bonhoeffer's brother-in-law, Hans von Dohnanyi, was heavily involved. How advanced were plans for the conspirators' move against Hitler? The future of Jews in Nazi Germany was even more precarious. Harsher anti-Semitic measures, such as the stamping of "J" on Jewish citizens' passports to prevent their emigration, were already set in place. Within this political and ecclesiastical maelstrom, with its unusual distractions that ate into his available time, Bonhoeffer had to set aside time for work on his manuscript.

It is not surprising, then, that the political-religious situation and the unrest of those days worked their way into several of the comments that appear in the first section of the book. Bethge notes, for example, that the Nazi strangulation of the churches lay behind Bonhoeffer's remark that "the Christian cannot simply take for granted the privilege of living among other Christians," adding that Christians belong "in the midst of enemies. There they find their mission, their work."[4] That "mission" and "work," if we can extrapolate from *Life Together*, seemed to be the infusion of new life and a new sense of Christian community into a church grown cowardly and unchristlike.

The crises of 1938 made it even more imperative for Bonhoeffer to finish the book. The Finkenwalde community's "life together" had been rudely terminated by the Gestapo. But he was determined that not even Hitler's secret police would impede the message for the church that had taken shape during the Finkenwalde experiences of genuine Christian community. As Bonhoeffer stated in his own Preface, he wanted simply to tell others about this experiment in community and of how the life together in the Finkenwalde seminary could become a significant "con-

---

4. Bethge, "Afterword," 6; see 27 below.

tribution toward answering the extensive questions . . . raised" about Christian faith, Christian community, and the nature of the church in a world beset with forces destructive of them all.[5] Theirs was an experience that, with the help of responsible Christians and church leaders, might clarify what was involved in the formation of Christian community guided by the Word of God. The book itself was published in 1939 as volume 61 in the series of theological monographs, *Theologische Existenz heute* (Theological existence today). Beyond all expectations on Bonhoeffer's part, within one year it had been through a fourth printing.

## The Foundations of Bonhoeffer's Idea of Christian Community

The story of how *Life Together* came to be does not, however, begin in September 1938. Although the book grew out of his two years' experience as director of the Confessing Church's seminary in Finkenwalde and the establishment of a Brothers' House within the seminary, Bonhoeffer had a fascination with the formation of a Christian community from the earliest days of his lectures on the church at the University of Berlin. In fact, the interpretive key to so much of Bonhoeffer's ecclesiology and, therefore, of his understanding of the nature of community, was set in his doctoral dissertation on the church, *Sanctorum Communio*, and in his second dissertation, *Act and Being*, which grounded his interpretation of the church as a primary form of God's self-revelation. He was guided then, as he was later in the community of Finkenwalde, by the questions of how God in Christ becomes present in and among those who profess faith in the gospel—and how in turn faith, and communities of faith, must assume concrete form in the world. He claimed in that first foundational study that "God's will is ever directed to the concrete historical human being."[6] In short, the will of God is expressed in a tangible word spoken to specific human beings and their communities. God's "will" should never be allowed to die the death of abstraction through its institutional, dogmatic, or biblicist reductionism. *Life Together* was hardly a study in abstraction. The reality behind the book was the church in its most palpable, somatic form, the Christian community.

---

5. See below, 25.
6. Bonhoeffer, *CS,* 103.

In *Sanctorum Communio* we see, too, the guiding spirit of Martin Luther strongly influencing Bonhoeffer during those student days, in this case through the seminars at Berlin and the popular studies of Luther by the church historian, Karl Holl. It was Holl who had emphasized the genius of Luther's binding together a scripturally validated doctrine of justification with a reformed understanding of church. For Holl, the church can be conceptualized only as a community. If Luther's theology of church was to have any meaning in the light of God's Word, then confession of faith in the presence of Jesus Christ and the community's structuring of that confessed presence had to be integrated. This integration is behind Bonhoeffer's adroit refinement of the Hegelian definition of church into the expression for which *Sanctorum Communio* has been noted: "Christ existing as community" [Christus als Gemeinde existierend].[7]

For Bonhoeffer this was more than a theological device to explain the nature of church. The expression emanated from a deeply held conviction that Christian community had to integrate the gospel into its daily life and reflect this to the world. "Christ existing as community" challenges believers to behave as Christ to one another; this same Christ promises those who gather in his name to be present in, with, and for them. We see in both the Berlin dissertations and in *Life Together* the traces of Bonhoeffer's inner longing for a community life in which his call to the ministry and his love for God's Word would merge to bring a more meaningful sense of direction into his life. What Bonhoeffer wrote in *Life Together* on the nature of community, the dialectic of Christians' being together yet needing time to be alone, their service, their prayer life, and their practice of confession and the Lord's Supper, presupposes the Christo-ecclesiological groundwork of *Sanctorum Communio*. The faith-searching explorations that followed in *Act and Being* served to deepen Bonhoeffer's insights into the way that God's revelatory Word breaks through the impasse of human egotism and the manipulative desires of an emotionally grounded, self-centered "love," offering individuals and communities the chance to become hearers of that Word, as well as Christ one to another.

Though Bonhoeffer was later somewhat diffident about his Berlin dissertations, all his subsequent writings reveal an indebtedness to the insights he developed in these studies. His immersion in these projects

---

7. Cf. Bonhoeffer, *CS*, 85, 143, 197, 203 .

yielded for him the conceptual grist for setting in motion a new way of being the church. The community experience of Finkenwalde was memorable because it provided a unique occasion to test out in concrete experience his understanding of what a church could and should be. At the inner core of the Christology that emerges from the Berlin dissertations is God's Word present in the human being Jesus and in the community of those with whom Christ identifies. *Life Together* never strays from this form of Christocentrism.

One has only to notice coursing through *Sanctorum Communio* the dynamic reality of Jesus Christ, whose vicarious action [Stellvertretung] in the Christian Church is the life-giving principle of the visible communion of saints, to appreciate the connection with the way Bonhoeffer later depicts Jesus' presence inspiriting the Christian community in *Life Together*. Christ is depicted as the embodiment both of God and Christians, who are moved to do what, without Christ, they would be unable to accomplish: to live together, sharing faith, hope, and self-giving love in a prayerful, compassionate, caring community. Christ is present in the community as representative of God's graced outreach to God's children and the incarnate embodiment of all those who crave in their faith for community with God. The Christ of *Life Together* is the binding force of that community in its "togetherness," gracing Christians to go beyond the superficial, often self-centered, relationships of their everyday associations toward a more intimate sense of what it means to be Christ to others, to love others as Christ has loved them.

Jesus' vicarious action on behalf of his brothers and sisters, depicted so carefully by Bonhoeffer in *Sanctorum Communio*, likewise provides the Christocentric foundations for the ecclesiology of *Life Together*. Bonhoeffer's entire approach to the community life experienced at Finkenwalde depends on a strong faith in the vicarious action of Christ in Word, sacrament, intercessory prayer, and service that makes it possible for Christians to be both "*with* one another" [*mit*einander] and "*for* one another" [*für*einander]. The seminarians were to live *with* one another, but only in the spirit of being *for* one another. His community was a gathering of theological students whose "togetherness" was to be characterized by an unselfish love for one another expressed in the willingness to serve each other, even to be inconvenienced by one another, to intercede for one another in prayer, to extend forgiveness in the name of the Lord, and to share the bread of the Lord's Supper.

Bonhoeffer's experiment in Christian community was in many

respects an attempt to take the visible communion of saints depicted in *Sanctorum Communio* back to its roots in gospel praxis and the Reformation tradition. A church can be true to its commitment to *sola scriptura* and *sola fide* only in that sociality where the marks of oneness, holiness, universality, and apostolic sharing in suffering coalesce. This, by its very nature, demanded the structure of a Christian community whose daily regimen would reflect a practical commitment to Jesus Christ and the values embodied in the gospel. Bonhoeffer was unable to hide his aversion for attempts to etherialize the church into structures of empty ritual and perfunctory services that merely fronted for what purported to be an essentially "invisible heavenly reality."

As chaplain at the Technical University at Charlottenburg between 1931 and 1933, he once expressed his worry about such "invisibility" and the future of Christianity. He wondered, too, whether the great demise of the present form of Christianity had not already begun. "Is our time at an end," he asked in a letter to his friend and fellow student, Helmut Rössler, "and has the gospel been given to another people, to be preached perhaps with totally different words and deeds? How do you view the indestructibility of Christianity given the situation in the world and our own lifestyles today? . . . How is one to preach such things to these people here? Who still believes in these things? The invisibility is killing us. . . . To be continually cast backwards to the invisible God is insane; we can no longer accept it."[8] Having just returned from America in 1931, he was thinking about the possibility of finding a new concretion of Christianity and a new form of community in the India of the holy Hindu, Gandhi. In August of 1931, however, his quest for new forms of Christian community began to take shape in a different form through his teaching career at the University of Berlin.

## Beginnings: The Search for Christian Community in Berlin

Bonhoeffer's attempts to practice what was later to be structured into the community of Finkenwalde, from which *Life Together* would be derived, had their hesitant beginnings in the circle of his students at the University at Berlin. His seminars, open-ended evening discussions, and

---

8. Bonhoeffer, *GS* 1:61 [trans. GK].

excursions attracted a number of students, many of whom would become his closest colleagues in the nascent church struggle and some, his seminarians in Finkenwalde. In 1932 these young theological students would organize frequent weekend trips to a rented cottage in the country, there to "talk theology" and to work into the day some rudimentary spiritual exercises interspersed with long walks and hours of listening to Bonhoeffer's record collection of the African American spirituals that had so enthralled him during his stay in America. It was during these times apart that they thought seriously about how to form authentic Christian communities through a structured spiritual life into which would be integrated appropriate forms of service to people in need. Though these beginnings in community life were informal and spontaneous, they provided the earliest sparks for the creation of the kind of community life that Bonhoeffer felt might be able to reanimate the entire church.

The events of the church struggle that began in 1933 were to hinder Bonhoeffer from developing this first, more casual experience of community with his students into something more protracted and permanent. Yet, by the end of 1932, most of the conceptual underpinnings of the community life he would depict in *Life Together* were already in place. Aside from the strong convictions about the nature of Christian community and the insinuating power of God's revelatory Word that leap out of the Berlin dissertations, there is additional evidence in his lectures on the nature of the church and in the conferences he presented in 1932 that the idea of forming genuine Christian community continued to dominate him. Bonhoeffer was interested not merely in reflecting upon the church but in being part of a church-setting committed to God's Word, accepting the self-sacrifice embodied in the cross of Jesus Christ. Bonhoeffer apparently longed for a type of community that, with the courage of Christ born out of obedience to the Word, could live out the gospel more intensely, and thus courageously cope with the crises facing the German nation and, indeed, the world at large.

In his lectures on "The Nature of the Church" presented at Berlin during the summer semester of 1932, for example, Bonhoeffer was able to develop along more practical lines the finely tuned analyses of *Sanctorum Communio*. The language here is trimmed of the heaviness of his dissertation, though essentially he is speaking of the same reality. The church, he insists in these lectures, is not called to be a tiny, sacred haven from the world but, like Jesus, a presence in the midst of the world. The world of the present time, not some heavenly cloud, is the only locus of church life, even though this way of understanding its mission might lead the church into controversial areas in its struggle with evil. The church needed visibility in its sociality. But in its visibility this church was to be neither a church of privilege nor a church totally absorbed into the secularism of the day. It was destined to be, instead, the community of Jesus Christ that is within the world, yet free enough from the world to oppose secular idolatries and to do the courageous deeds required in serving others.

Here we see, even before the experiences at Finkenwalde, Bonhoeffer's affirmation of the need for a church to be thoroughly involved in and with the world. But, fortified with Christ's Word, this same church was never to succumb to the ideologies that parade themselves as wholly congruent with faith. "The church is no ideal church," Bonhoeffer told his students,

> but a reality in the world, a bit of the world reality. The worldliness of the church follows from the incarnation of Christ. The church, like Christ, has become world. It is a denial of the real humanity of Jesus and also heretical to take the concrete church as only a phantom church or an illusion. . . . This means that it is subjected to all the weakness and suffering of the world. The church can, at times, like Christ himself, be without a roof over its head. . . . Real worldliness consists in the church's being able to renounce all privileges and all its property but never Christ's Word and the forgiveness of sins. With Christ and the forgiveness of sins to fall back on, the church is free to give up everything else.[9]

The renunciation of privileges, the liberating Word of Christ, and the forgiveness of sins, would also be at the forefront of Bonhoeffer's concerns for his community of seminarians. His words here continued to reverberate in his lectures on following Christ. Indeed, they were the binding force that held the community together and were among the major themes of *Life Together*. By that time the world outside Finkenwalde had become a much more dangerous place.

## The Community of Finkenwalde

Bonhoeffer's students at Berlin in the years 1932–33, some of whom would join him later in the Finkenwalde seminary, had by then heard his

---

9. Bonhoeffer, "The Nature of the Church," in *TF,* 86–87, trans. altered.

words on Christ, community, and peace in many forms and on varying occasions. Bonhoeffer's biographer, Bethge, notes that because the ordinands from Berlin had maintained such close contact with Bonhoeffer they were already initiates by comparison with the other students.

The opportunity to direct one of the seminaries of the Confessing Church, located first at Zingst and later at Finkenwalde, was created out of a crisis moment in the church struggle. In March 1934, the National Bishop, in compliance with the anti-Jewish laws affecting church ministry, decreed the shutting down of the Old Prussian preachers' seminaries. Moreover, students for the ministry were forbidden to take the examinations unless they could present proof of their pure Aryan descent. This move, so clearly dictated by Nazi ideology, forced the opposition Confessing Church to take the matter of ordination under its own control and to organize seminaries under Confessing Church auspices.

Bonhoeffer had been approached in the early summer of 1934 to be part of this new undertaking. Although he had expressed his willingness to become involved, nevertheless he entertained hopes of traveling to India to learn from Gandhi about "community life as well as methods of training."[10] In India, perhaps somewhat idealized in his own imagination, he envisioned an as-yet-unexplored source of new ideas about community, as well as the possibility of counteracting Nazism by means of the Gandhian tactics that had proved so successful against imperial Britain. Hence, in forwarding his acceptance, he attached the proviso that his assumption of the leadership of one of the seminaries would have to wait until spring 1935. The trip to India never materialized. However, a letter to his Swiss friend, Erwin Sutz, reveals both the difficulty Bonhoeffer had in arriving at this decision and the way he intended to run the seminary. Writing from his pastorate in London on September 11, 1934, he confided to Sutz that he was "struggling over the decision on whether I should go back to Germany as director of the new Preachers' Seminary (still to be established) or whether I should remain here or whether I should go to India. I no longer believe in the university and never really have believed in it—a fact that used to rile you. The entire training of young seminarians belongs today in church-monastic schools in which the pure doctrine, the Sermon on the Mount, and wor-

---

10. George Bell, "Letter of October 22, 1934," quoted in Bethge, *Dietrich Bonhoeffer*, 331.

ship can be taken seriously—which is really not the case with all three things at the university and, in present-day circumstances, is impossible."[11] Another reason for his delay in accepting the position is seen in this letter. Bonhoeffer also wanted to study firsthand the "monastic" training in vogue in other traditions. This led him to ask George Bell, Anglican Bishop of Chichester, who had already intervened on his behalf regarding his proposed trip to India by writing a letter of recommendation to Gandhi, to write additional letters to the heads of several Anglican monasteries asking for hospitality in Bonhoeffer's endeavors "to have some acquaintance with our methods in England, both with regard to training for the ministry and with regard to community life."[12]

Bonhoeffer made the rounds of these communities and others as well, including the seminaries of Presbyterians and Congregationalists, plus the Methodist College in Richmond. The preparations for his move back to Germany and the setting up of the seminary seemed to help Bonhoeffer to consolidate a number of diverse aspirations that had preoccupied him since his return from the United States in 1931: to deepen the theology of the Sermon on the Mount; to form a Christian community based on commitment to the gospel; to live in a community committed to peace, given to prayer at regular intervals, and dedicated to service of those in need. He had observed diverse ways of attending to these concerns during his visits to the various monasteries and seminarian training centers in England. With that behind him, and with a vision before him of how he would structure seminary life for his church, Bonhoeffer took leave of his London parishioners on March 10, 1935. On April 26, Bonhoeffer and the first ordinands traveled to the site of the seminary, the empty Rhineland Bible School in Zingst. In June they moved to more permanent quarters in a rambling schoolhouse in the small country town of Finkenwalde.

Bonhoeffer called that summer the "fullest time" of his life. He was finally embarked on a mission he had always longed for: the formation of a genuine Christian community based on the Sermon on the Mount. Behind the scenes, numerous events of 1935 were influencing this venture, particularly legislation crafted with the express purpose of destroying the Confessing Church. The existence of the seminary would soon

---

11. Bonhoeffer, "Letter to Erwin Sutz, London, September 11, 1934," in *TF*, 412.

12. George Bell, quoted in Bethge, *Dietrich Bonhoeffer*, 335.

be in violation of the laws of the Nazi government relating to the regulation of church affairs. Maintaining the seminary now put Bonhoeffer
and the leaders of the Confessing Church not only squarely in opposition to the German Reich Church, but eventually in noncompliance with
the Nazi government as well. For the moment, though, that danger was
not paramount in their minds. Their immediate need was to furnish and
decorate the house, to convert the gymnasium into a chapel, and to
build up a library from nothing. In a move that impressed the seminarians, Bonhoeffer brought his own collection of books from Berlin and
placed them at the library's disposal. Their minds were kept focused on
the purpose of their seminary training by Bonhoeffer's imposition of a
daily schedule and by his intense method of working, always leaving
room for prayer and leisure time. We read in *Life Together* Bonhoeffer's
detailed account of how the day was to be spent in a balance of piety,
study, classes in theology and preaching, services of all sorts to one
another, meals together, worship, leisure, and play.

What we do not read in *Life Together* is the story of the tensions Bonhoeffer experienced in directing the seminary his way and in establishing the Brothers' House to provide continuity to the experiment in
community living within the seminary. At Finkenwalde, Bonhoeffer
finally had the time, through his lectures to the seminarians, to write
down his thoughts on what following Christ entailed for Christians.
These lectures subsequently would become his celebrated book *The Cost
of Discipleship*, published in the fall of 1937. For the seminarians, following Christ "Bonhoeffer's way" meant beginning each day with a period
of meditation for which they were ill prepared. Some read, some slept,
some smoked their pipes, some let their minds wander. Some voiced
their resentment over being the butt of jokes from other preachers' seminaries about their "unevangelical monasticism."

All of this became the center of one particular evening discussion,
which happened to come on the heels of a lengthy absence by Bonhoeffer from Finkenwalde. Instead of wavering about continuing the
practice, Bonhoeffer listened sympathetically to their complaints, then
suggested that once a week they have a communal meditation on given
texts of Scripture. This proved helpful. Gradually their opposition gave
way; most continued the practice after their seminary days. It brought
home to them that their faith was in God's Word as a word given to
them—not just something they doled out to others in their preaching.

Bonhoeffer also introduced them to the practice, more customary with the communities of the Church of the Brethren, of meditating on the *Losungen*, or brief daily texts drawn from the Scriptures. In circular letters, even during the war years, he called his seminarians' attention to the *Losungen* appropriate for the time. And, in prison, he wrote that meditation on these texts opened up to him a world of meaning.

Until the time of his arrest, through circular letters that contained the weekly texts for their reflection, Bonhoeffer continued to remind his seminarians of the importance of this practice of meditation. At the height of the war years, in response to requests for help in meditation from his "Finkenwaldians" now in harm's way at the front, he sent the following exhortation:

> So even today I will do no more than say a few words once again about the precious gift which is given us in meditation. . . . Daily, quiet attention to the Word of God which is meant for me, even if it is only for a few minutes, will become for me the focal point of everything which brings inward and outward order into my life. In the interruption and fragmentation of our previous ordered life which this time brings with it, in the danger of losing inner discipline . . . , meditation gives our life something like constancy. It maintains the link with our previous life, from baptism to confirmation, to ordination. It keeps us in the saving community of our congregation, of our brothers and sisters, of our spiritual home.[13]

That reminder from their seminary director brought back memories of Bonhoeffer's own approach to prayer. He had taught them how to pray as much by example as by instruction.

Bethge recalls the way Bonhoeffer often assumed responsibility for the extemporized prayers. These prayers included thanks for their faith, for their community life, for the gifts of nature; intercession for the Confessing Church, for those in captivity, and even for enemies; and confession of the failings typical of those in ministry and prayers for them. Bonhoeffer prepared carefully for these extemporaneous prayers during these shared periods of meditation. His own ability to concentrate exercised a great influence on the seminarians. "Such an indirect teacher of prayer we had never had before," Bethge remarked.[14] As much as possible, Bonhoeffer modeled his prayers on the Psalms and

---

13. Bonhoeffer, "Letter of March 1, 1942," in *TF,* 457, trans. altered.
14. Eberhard Bethge, *Bekennen und Widerstehen,* 163.

attempted to harmonize his petitions with that "prayerbook of the Bible." His enthusiasm for the community's reading the Psalms together, as a vital expression of their communal prayer, can be seen in large portions of the section "The Day Together." Bonhoeffer's word to the seminarians was direct: to pray the Psalms was to adopt as their own the prayer of Jesus Christ himself.

Even more problematic for many of the seminarians than the period of meditation was the practice of personal confession of sins. Just before he and the seminarians were to celebrate the Lord's Supper together on the sixth Sunday after Easter of 1935, while they were still at Zingst, Bonhoeffer announced that the celebration also required some form of reconciliation. He suggested that they might want to confess their sins privately to each other or else to him as the director of the community. This surprised them and, for some, even stirred up resentment, since it was not considered the "Protestant" thing to do. It cast a shade of gloom on their Saturday evening, though that evening was spent in reading aloud and in recreation. Gradually, however, the seminarians began to accustom themselves to the monthly celebration of the Lord's Supper. Some among them gradually began the practice of private confession during the summer. Bethge relates how the atmosphere changed, without in any way becoming inquisitorial. One day Bonhoeffer himself asked one of the brothers to hear his confession, thus setting an example for the others and helping the practice gain widespread acceptance.

Bonhoeffer writes at length about the private confession of sins both in the section "Confession and the Lord's Supper," and in his short treatise *Spiritual Care*.[15] In the latter work, echoing Luther's subsumption of confession under the graced exercise of the freedom of the Christian, Bonhoeffer situated confession squarely in the faith that recognizes God in the confessor. Bethge traces Bonhoeffer's enthusiasm for the practice of private confession of sins to several converging events, beginning with his first trip to Rome and his positive reaction to observing people of all ages going to confession in the church of Santa Maria Maggiore. Bonhoeffer's own appropriation of the private confession of sins was not, however, a mere carryover from that encounter with the widespread Catholic practice. And even in Rome, Bonhoeffer had reservations, similar to those of Martin Luther, about the Catholic "dogma of Confession." Yet Bethge points out that as early as 1932 Bonhoeffer would

---

15. See Bonhoeffer, *SPC*, 60–65. Cf. the references to this text on 110 below.

speak to his students of "oral confession," not as a mere theological issue, "but as an act to be carried out in practice." For those in the seminary unaware of Bonhoeffer's attitudes toward this practice, however, it came as a surprise that, in conjunction with their preparation for the communion service, he began to recommend the private confession of sins. Bethge reports that the procedure was conducted with neither vestments nor formal ceremony. And in his lectures Bonhoeffer strongly advised that future pastors preach at least annually on the blessings of private confession.[16]

The clearest example of his teaching on private confession and forgiveness of sins is seen in the way he incorporates the practice into his reflections in *Spiritual Care*. At the heart of the pastoral care a minister extends to parishioners, Bonhoeffer pinpoints the liberating effect of private confession of sins and insists that only in such a liberation can genuine community be formed. "In absolution God receives us once again in order to reign over our whole lives and to set us completely free. Confession is a conversion and a call to discipleship. We have nothing left, not even our sins; they are laid on Christ. He steps toward us and his joy and righteousness become our own. Genuine community is not established before confession takes place."[17] Bonhoeffer did set two conditions to the practice. First, only those who themselves practice confession of sins should act as confessors of another. Second, those engaged in the practice should not regard it as part of a pious act or routine. The essence of the confession of sins lay in the promise of forgiveness in Christ. Bonhoeffer conveyed to his seminarians his own conviction that those who are unreconciled to their sisters and brothers, or whose hearts are filled with anxiety about particular sins on their consciences, should not go to the altar. According to Bonhoeffer, it is the assurance of the forgiveness of sins that should make the day of the Lord's Supper a joyous occasion for the entire community.

## The Brothers' House

Bonhoeffer's book is, indeed, a study of Christian community and the practices, some devotional in their nature, some related to mutual service, that can help bond together people who share a common faith and

---

16. Bethge, *Dietrich Bonhoeffer*, 39–40, 154, 384.
17. Bonhoeffer, *SPC*, 63.

who desire to live in Christian community. It was his desire not only that the seminarians live a common life as the best possible preparation for their ministry, but also that there be a structured continuity in this "experiment." At the end of the first session at Finkenwalde and just before the August holiday, therefore, he began to discuss with some of the seminarians the possibility of some of them staying on in order to form a more tightly knit community, a Brothers' House, that could be a leaven for the incoming group of new students due to arrive in late autumn. Together they drew up a proposal to be sent to the Council of Brethren of the Old Prussian Union. This body would have to release the young ministers involved in this enterprise from their other duties. Eventually six of the "brothers" received permission to remain at Finkenwalde. Among the six were four who survived the war and became the core of the "Finkenwaldians" each of whom contributed in his own way to keeping alive the Bonhoeffer legacy: Eberhard Bethge, Joachim Kanitz, Winfried Maechler, and Albrecht Schönherr.

The proposal they submitted in September 1935 is informative for understanding the nature of the community life Bonhoeffer was trying to shape for the seminarians. In composing this proposal, Bonhoeffer argued, first, that a community, rather than an isolated individual, added strength and objectivity to preaching the Word. Second, Christian life, he claimed, can never be lived in the abstract. The expression of their faith itself called for community living and sensitivity to one another. Third, the very nature of the church, and in particular the present church struggle, demanded renunciation of clerical privileges and availability for service to people. Such was expected of a group of ministers whose solidarity in community would necessarily focus them on the service that they needed outside the community. Finally, Bonhoeffer pointed out that the provision for such a community would offer pastors a spiritual refuge where they could renew their strength for service in the church. Concerning the details of their daily routine, they envisaged a simple common life, a daily schedule of prayer, mutual encouragement, common theological studies, and worship together. In addition, and in full knowledge of how the members of this community might be needed elsewhere in given circumstances, Bonhoeffer pledged their readiness to answer any emergency call. Admission was to be by common consent. The freedom for anyone to leave the community was also stipulated. Monetary support for the enterprise was to come through pooling their resources but, as Bethge notes, Bonhoeffer invariably paid most of the expenses out of his own pocket.[18]

No description of the community life lived at this Brothers' House[19] or at the seminary itself can match the explanation Bonhoeffer gave to Wolfgang Staemmler, mentor of young candidates for the Saxony province, for permitting Bethge to be a member of this community.

> There are two things the brothers have to learn during their short time in the seminary—first, how to lead a community life in daily and strict obedience to the will of Christ Jesus, in the practice of the humblest and the noblest service one Christian brother can perform for another. They must learn to recognize the strength and liberation to be found in their brotherly service and their life together in a Christian community. For this is something they are going to need. Secondly, they have to learn to serve the truth alone in their study of the Bible and its interpretation in their sermons and teaching. I personally am responsible for this second duty, but the first I cannot attain by myself. For this, there must be a group of brothers who, without any fuss, will be able to involve the others through their life together. That is what the Brothers' House is all about.[20]

The Brothers' House within the seminary began in the autumn of 1935 and lasted until the Gestapo shut down the seminary two years later. As much as possible the brothers stuck to the seminary's own daily timetable. At noon, however, when the seminarians were at singing practice, the brothers would gather for a short discussion and common prayer in Bonhoeffer's room.

It came as a major disappointment to Bonhoeffer when the seminary had to close and the new, clandestine seminaries were unable to continue the idea of a community like that of Finkenwalde. In practice, however, Bonhoeffer would draw on the experience and solace of the prayer life of Finkenwalde to survive the difficult, lonely days of imprisonment.

---

18. Bethge, *Dietrich Bonhoeffer*, 385–86.

19. This Brothers' House was not a separate building at Finkenwalde. It was, rather, a name given to that community within the community, made up of those who had already trained at the seminary, and who would now be a source of continuity in the spirit of the seminary and who would provide supportive love, encouragement, and good example to the less experienced, sometimes wavering seminarians.

20. Bonhoeffer, "Letter of June 27, 1936," *GS* 6:376 [trans. GK].

As Bethge has put it, Bonhoeffer "dedicated himself and all that was his to the Brothers' House."[21]

Because much of the community life at Finkenwalde was oriented around a form of disciplined life not common to the Protestant background of the seminarians, as well as a daily schedule that seemed to come more out of Catholic monasticism than out of the Protestant tradition, the Christian community of Finkenwalde, and *Life Together*, have been for some interpreters problematic. Some have called it a detour from the heavy involvement in the church struggle and the evident worldliness of the prison correspondence. At the time of his tenure as director of the seminary, Bonhoeffer had to fend off accusations that he was catholicizing the seminarians, or inducing a hothouse atmosphere that was both esoteric and impractical. He was able to win over his critics and the seminarians who might have chafed at the daily schedule, however, by several counterbalancing aspects of their life together. First and foremost, the seminarians did experience, many for the first time, the sustaining power for their ministry of life in a faith-filled, caring community. Second, they were given a rigorous theological training that helped them distinguish between the task of theology and the mission of pastoral care, related but different aspects of their ministry. Third, their daily routine was also interrupted by periods of recreation, music, and other forms of entertainment, not the least of which was "the wit and imagination" of Bonhoeffer who, as Bethge relates, was adept at organizing these times of renewal.[22] Finally, Bonhoeffer was able to make it clear that their life together was not a withdrawal from the arena of combat against Nazism in the churches.[23] To the contrary, as Bonhoeffer states in his Preface, their life together was a unique way of preparing these young ministers to enter that combat and revitalize their church.

## The New Edition of *Life Together*

However controversial the community life at Finkenwalde, however limited the scope of Bonhoeffer's description of that experiment in Christian community, *Life Together* has enjoyed an immense popularity,

---

21. Bethge, *Dietrich Bonhoeffer*, 387, trans. altered.
22. Ibid., 382.
23. Ibid.

ranking it alongside *The Cost of Discipleship* and *Letters and Papers from Prison* in its appeal to the general public. In fact, when Eberhard Bethge attempted to complain to the head of a publishing company about the many mistranslations in an early English edition of the book—plus the failure again to include Bonhoeffer's Preface to the text, while employing a misleading cover photo—he was told not to worry. "The paperback has been out for only four months and we have already sold 40,000 copies."[24] Bethge was, of course, more concerned about the errors of translation and the missing Preface than about any sales figures. Yet, as he concludes: "After more than 40 years, this little book still displays an incomparable ability to attract readers."[25]

Despite its flaws, the success of *Life Together* has indeed been extraordinary. As has been mentioned above, following its initial publication by Christian Kaiser Verlag in the series *Theologische Existenz heute* (Theological existence today), it went through three additional printings in its first year. The publishing house of Albert Lempp supervised the fourth printing in early 1940 and corrected the original typographical errors that had lingered on through the earlier printings. Aside from these typos, the text remained essentially the same from its postwar printing in 1949 through periodic reprints during the next thirty years. The twentieth reprint of 1979 had the added attraction of an Afterword [Nachwort] by Eberhard Bethge that describes the original setting of the book and contributes valuable editorial comments looking back at its impact some forty years after its original publication. This Afterword was retained for the twenty-first reissuing of *Gemeinsames Leben* in 1986. Finally, the new, critical edition, volume 5 of the *Dietrich Bonhoeffer Werke*, was published by Kaiser Verlag in 1987. Since its first publication by Harper and Row in 1954, the prior translation of *Life Together* has gone through twenty-three reprintings.

In each of these reprintings, however, inconsistencies and errors of translation have remained. Both consistently rendering into English Bonhoeffer's German terminology and capturing as closely as possible his style of writing are of course of major importance to this new edition of *Life Together*. To give but two examples, the crucial words *Gemeinschaft* and *Gemeinde* have been subjected to several varying translations in previous English translations. *Gemeinschaft* had been rendered alternately

---

24. Bethge, "Afterword," 3.
25. Ibid., 4.

as "community," "fellowship," "communion," "association," or "relationship." In the current text, this word has been translated in every instance as "community." The word *Gemeinde* had translations as varied as "community," "congregation," "parish," and "church." Here, we have rendered the word for the most part either as "congregation" or "community of Christians," depending on the context. Where the words are compounded or do not easily lend themselves to a corresponding English translation, we have attempted to approximate the meaning of Bonhoeffer's German and then have indicated the difficulty by placing the original German word or phrase in brackets immediately following the corresponding English expression.

Among the thorniest of all the problems faced in this book, however, is the issue of gender-inclusive language. We have attempted to resolve this problem in a way that is faithful to Bonhoeffer's German yet conscious of the significant shifts in perspective that characterize the English-language reader today as contrasted with a German reader of *Life Together* in the 1940s. The issue of gender inclusivity has proved, as might well be expected, to be far easier in the case of references to human beings than in the case of references to God and Christ. In previous translations the term "man" was used to translate *Mensch*, although Bonhoeffer clearly differentiated his use of *Mensch*, which we have translated for the most part as "human being," and *Mann*, which he uses only to refer to someone of the male gender. Bonhoeffer's German was more limited, however, in references to God; for example, because all German nouns and pronouns have a gender, he could only use *er* ("he") in reference to *Gott* (God). In light of current English practice, however, we have in general avoided assigning any masculine gender to God, unless the reference is to a word that itself has a masculine gender in English, such as "Father" or "Son." And, given the deep historical connection that Bonhoeffer affirms between the man Jesus of Nazareth and the messianic title, Christ, we have retained the masculine pronoun "he" to refer to both.

What is more, Bonhoeffer frequently used the term *Bruder* ("brother") in *Life Together*. This has, in turn, led to an editorial dilemma. Should the expression be translated simply as "brother" with its corresponding pronoun, "he," particularly given the fact that the brothers at Finkenwalde were evidently all male? It is obvious that in a few instances Bonhoeffer was referring specifically to his community of seminarians or the men in the Brothers' House within the community of Finkenwalde. In these cases, we have occasionally retained the English usage of "brother." However, it is clear from Bonhoeffer's heretofore missing Preface, incorporated into *Life Together* for the first time in this edition, that Bonhoeffer was directing this work to the whole church. The experiment in community undertaken at Finkenwalde was "a mission entrusted to the church," "a responsibility to be undertaken by the church as a whole," something that necessitated both "a willingness of the church to assist in the work" and the "vigilant cooperation of every responsible party." It is clear that, for the most part, Bonhoeffer intended his study to be a description of one possibility in the formation of Christian community. Bonhoeffer uses the term "brother" to mean an attitude of looking on our fellow Christians as intimate kindred in Jesus Christ. Hence often *Bruder* has been translated with the inclusive equivalent, such as "other Christians" or "another Christian."

*Life Together* is still today a most popular book among those involved in Christian communities of all sorts and among parish study groups desirous of deepening their sense of community within the context of a larger congregation. Bethge's remark in the Afterword to the 1979 German edition is particularly apropos of this attractive volume: "This little book lives on as before and evidently still addresses an area in which there is hardly any practical advice or where practical advice has turned out poorly. Indeed, in terms of its availability around the whole world, it claims a place directly alongside *Letters and Papers from Prison*."[26]

That this new edition of *Life Together* should now be the first published volume of the *Dietrich Bonhoeffer Works* is due to the cooperative work of several people. I am first of all indebted to my translator, Daniel Bloesch, who contributed not only his skills in German, but also his patience in our seemingly endless discussions and in his reworking of so many of the problematic translations. John Godsey, himself a Bonhoeffer scholar, contributed a perceptive critical reading of the text in its manuscript form; and Beth Orling Farrera served as an additional consultant. Most of all, I acknowledge here the guiding hand of Wayne Whitson Floyd, Jr., general editor of the *Dietrich Bonhoeffer Works,* who worked closely with me in the final editing process and whose numerous suggestions regarding both theological substance and style have enhanced this volume immeasurably.

---

26. Ibid.

# PREFACE

THE SUBJECT MATTER I am presenting here is such that any further development can take place only through a common effort. We are not dealing with a concern of some private circles but with a mission entrusted to the church. Because of this, we are not searching for more or less haphazard individual solutions to a problem. This is, rather, a responsibility to be undertaken by the church as a whole. There is a hesitation evident in the way this task has been handled. Only recently has it been understood at all. But this hesitation must give way to the willingness of the church to assist in the work. The variety of new ecclesial forms of community makes it necessary to enlist the vigilant cooperation of every responsible party. The following remarks are intended to provide only one individual contribution toward answering the extensive questions that have been raised thereby. As much as possible, may these comments help to clarify this experience and put it into practice.

# COMMUNITY

"HOW VERY GOOD and pleasant it is when kindred live together in unity!" (Ps. 133:1).[1] In what follows we will take a look at several directions and principles that the Holy Scriptures give us for life together[2] [gemeinsame Leben] under the Word.

The Christian cannot simply take for granted the privilege of living among other Christians. Jesus Christ lived in the midst of his enemies. In the end all his disciples abandoned him. On the cross he was all alone, surrounded by criminals and the jeering crowds. He had come for the express purpose of bringing peace to the enemies of God. So Christians, too, belong not in the seclusion of a cloistered life but in the midst of enemies. There they find their mission, their work. "To rule is to be in the midst of your enemies. And whoever will not suffer this does not want to be part of the rule of Christ; such a person wants to be among friends and sit among the roses and lilies, not with the bad people but the religious people. O you blasphemers and betrayers of Christ! If

---

1. The biblical texts cited in *Life Together* are, for the most part, from the German translation of the Bible by Martin Luther, *Die Bibel oder die ganze Heilige Schrift des Alten und Neuen Testaments nach der deutschen Übersetzung D. Martin Luthers*, 1911. In the New Testament citations Bonhoeffer also depends on Eberhard Nestle's *Novum Testamentum Graece et Germanice,* 1929. Unless otherwise noted, the translation of the NRSV has been used here. [GK]

2. Where possible, the translation "life together" has been used for *gemeinsame Leben*. The phrase can also be translated as "common life," just as *gemeinsame Gebet* can mean "common prayer." Bonhoeffer often qualifies this phrase by referring to it as "life together under the Word." [GK]

Christ had done what you are doing, who would ever have been saved?"
(Luther).[3]

"Though I scattered them among the nations, yet in far countries they
shall remember me" (Zech. 10:9). According to God's will, the Christian
church is a scattered people, scattered like seed "to all the kingdoms of
the earth" (Deut. 28:25). That is the curse and its promise. God's people
must live in distant lands among the unbelievers, but they will be the
seed of the kingdom of God in all the world.

"I will . . . gather them in. For I have redeemed them, . . . and they shall
. . . return" (Zech. 10:8-9). When will that happen? It has happened in
Jesus Christ, who died "to gather into one the dispersed children of
God" (John 11:52), and ultimately it will take place visibly at the end of
time when the angels of God will gather God's elect from the four winds,
from one end of heaven to the other (Matt. 24:31). Until then, God's
people remain scattered, held together in Jesus Christ alone, having
become one because they remember *him* in the distant lands, spread out
among the unbelievers.

Thus in the period between the death of Christ and the day of judgment, when Christians are allowed to live here in visible community with
other Christians, we have merely a gracious anticipation of the end time.
It is by God's grace that a congregation is permitted to gather visibly
around God's word and sacrament in this world. Not all Christians partake of this grace. The imprisoned, the sick, the lonely who live in the
diaspora, the proclaimers of the gospel in heathen lands stand alone.
They know that visible community is grace. They pray with the psalmist:
"I went with the throng, and led them in procession to the house of God,
with glad shouts and songs of thanksgiving, a multitude keeping festival"
(Ps. 42:5).[4] But they remain alone in distant lands, a scattered seed
according to God's will. Yet what is denied them as a visible experience
they grasp more ardently in faith. Hence "in the Spirit on the Lord's
Day" (Rev. 1:10) the exiled disciple of the Lord, John the author of the
Apocalypse, celebrates the worship of heaven with its congregations in
the loneliness of the Island of Patmos. He sees the seven lampstands that

---

3. An abridged quotation from a longer passage by Martin Luther, *Auslegung
des 109. Psalms* (An interpretation of Psalm 109 [110]), 1518, in *WA*, 1:696–97.
The quotation is taken from Karl Witte, *Nun freut euch lieben Christen gmein*, 226.

4. The NRSV lists this verse as Ps. 42:4. [GK]

are the congregations, the seven stars that are the angels of the congregations, and in the midst and above it all, the Son of Man, Jesus Christ, in his great glory as the risen one. He strengthens and comforts John by his word. That is the heavenly community in which the exile participates on the day of his Lord's resurrection.

The physical presence of other Christians is a source of incomparable joy and strength to the believer. With great yearning the imprisoned apostle Paul calls his "beloved son in the faith,"[5] Timothy, to come to him in prison in the last days of his life. He wants to see him again and have him near. Paul has not forgotten the tears Timothy shed during their final parting (2 Tim. 1:4). Thinking of the congregation in Thessalonica, Paul prays "night and day . . . most earnestly that we may see you face to face" (1 Thess. 3:10). The aged John knows his joy in his own people will only be complete when he can come to them and speak to them face to face instead of using paper and ink (2 John 12). The believer need not feel any shame when yearning for the physical presence of other Christians, as if one were still living too much in the flesh. A human being is created as a body; the Son of God appeared on earth in the body for our sake and was raised in the body. In the sacrament the believer receives the Lord Christ in the body, and the resurrection of the dead will bring about the perfected community of God's spiritual-physical creatures. Therefore, the believer praises the Creator, the Reconciler and the Redeemer, God the Father, Son and Holy Spirit, for the bodily presence of the other Christian. The prisoner, the sick person, the Christian living in the diaspora recognizes in the nearness of a fellow Christian a physical sign of the gracious presence of the triune God. In their loneliness, both the visitor and the one visited recognize in each other the Christ who is present in the body. They receive and meet each other as one meets the Lord, in reverence, humility, and joy. They receive each other's blessings as the blessing of the Lord Jesus Christ. But if there is so much happiness and joy even in a single encounter of one Christian with another, what inexhaustible riches must invariably open up for those who by God's will are privileged to live in daily community life with other Christians! Of course, what is an inexpressible blessing from God for the lonely individual is easily disregarded and

17

---

5. 1 Tim. 1:2. Bonhoeffer alters slightly Luther's translation, which said "meinen rechtschaffenen Sohn im Glauben" ("My justified son in faith").

trampled under foot by those who receive the gift every day. It is easily forgotten that the community of Christians is a gift of grace from the kingdom of God, a gift that can be taken from us any day—that the time still separating us from the most profound loneliness may be brief indeed. Therefore, let those who until now have had the privilege of living a Christian life together with other Christians praise God's grace from the bottom of their hearts. Let them thank God on their knees and realize: it is grace, nothing but grace, that we are still permitted to live in the community of Christians today.[6]

18

The measure with which God gives the gift of visible community is varied. Christians who live dispersed from one another are comforted by a brief visit of another Christian, a prayer together, and another Christian's blessing. Indeed, they are strengthened by letters written by the hands of other Christians. Paul's greetings in his letters written in his own hand were no doubt tokens of such community.[7] Others are given the gift on Sundays of the community of the worship service. Still others have the privilege of living a Christian life in the community of their families. Before their ordination young seminarians receive the gift of a common life with their brothers for a certain length of time. Among serious Christians in congregations today there is a growing desire to meet together with other Christians during the midday break from work for life together under the Word.[8] Life together is again being under-

---

6. Literally "the community of Christian brothers today." Throughout *Life Together* Bonhoeffer uses the German term *Bruder*, or "brother," to speak of other Christians, particularly those with whom one comes in close contact in a worshiping community. This term had a clear double reference for Bonhoeffer. On the one hand, it indicated the male "brothers" or seminarians of the Finkenwalde community, indeed in any German seminary community with which he was familiar at that time. On the other hand, it referred to other Christians, other believers, more generally. This term has been variously translated in the present text with an eye toward gender inclusivity, whenever this is not in clear disagreement with Bonhoeffer's own meaning. Thus it has been rendered as "one another," "other Christians," "other believers," "brother" (when it clearly refers to male seminarians in the Finkenwalde community), and at times "brothers and sisters," when the term refers to all Christians (especially when Bonhoeffer supports his meaning by reference to biblical texts that have been rendered in the NRSV with the phrase "brothers and sisters"). [GK]

7. See 1 Cor. 16:21, Gal. 6:11, 2 Thess. 3:17.

8. It is a custom in several European cultures to break off work at midday for an extended lunch hour. Catholic churches, monasteries, and convents histori-

stood by Christians today as the grace that it is, as the extraordinary aspect, the "roses and lilies" of the Christian life (Luther).[9]

Christian community means community through Jesus Christ and in Jesus Christ. There is no Christian community that is more than this, and none that is less than this. Whether it be a brief, single encounter or the daily community of many years, Christian community is solely this. We belong to one another only through and in Jesus Christ.

What does that mean? It means, *first*, that a Christian needs others for the sake of Jesus Christ. It means, *second*, that a Christian comes to others only through Jesus Christ. It means, *third*, that from eternity we have been chosen in Jesus Christ, accepted in time, and united for eternity.

First, Christians are persons who no longer seek their salvation, their deliverance, their justification in themselves, but in Jesus Christ alone. They know that God's Word in Jesus Christ pronounces them guilty, even when they feel nothing of their own guilt, and that God's Word in Jesus Christ pronounces them free and righteous, even when they feel nothing of their own righteousness. Christians no longer live by their own resources, by accusing themselves and justifying themselves, but by God's accusation and God's justification. They live entirely by God's Word pronounced on them, in faithful submission to God's judgment, whether it declares them guilty or righteous. The death and life of Christians are not situated in a self-contained isolation. Rather, Christians encounter both death and life only in the Word that comes to them from the outside, in God's Word to them. The Reformers expressed it by calling our righteousness an "alien righteousness" ["fremde Gerechtigkeit"], a righteousness that comes from outside of us (*extra nos*).[10] They meant by this expression that Christians are dependent on the Word of God spoken to them. They are directed outward to the Word coming to

19

cally have rung out the Angelus at this hour to summon people to prayer. See below 77, editorial note 68. [GK]

9. See editorial note 3 above and Luther, *WA,* 1:697.

10. On this important aspect of Luther's doctrine of justification, see especially his *Disputatio de Homine* (Disputation on the human), January 14, 1536 (*WA,* 39/1:82–83): "It is now certain that Christ or the justice of Christ, since it is outside of us and alien to us [extra nos et aliena nobis], cannot be attained by our own works." Luther uses the expressions "alien justification" [fremde Gerechtigkeit] and "justification *extra nos*" to express his conviction that justification is given to people by God alone from without and beyond their own capacity for good. Its bestowal is purely gratuitous on God's part; it is grace. See also Luther's sermon of 1519, "Two Kinds of Righteousness," in *LW,* 31:297–306. [GK]

them. Christians live entirely by the truth of God's Word in Jesus Christ. If they are asked "where is your salvation, your blessedness, your righteousness?," they can never point to themselves. Instead, they point to the Word of God in Jesus Christ that grants them salvation, blessedness, and righteousness. They watch for this Word wherever they can. Because they daily hunger and thirst for righteousness, they long for the redeeming Word again and again.[11] It can only come from the outside. In themselves they are destitute and dead. Help must come from the outside; and it has come and comes daily and anew in the Word of Jesus Christ, bringing us redemption, righteousness, innocence, and blessedness. But God put this Word into the mouth of human beings so that it may be passed on to others. When people are deeply affected by the Word, they tell it to other people. God has willed that we should seek and find God's living Word in the testimony of other Christians, in the mouths of human beings. Therefore, Christians need other Christians who speak God's Word to them. They need them again and again when they become uncertain and disheartened because, living by their own resources, they cannot help themselves without cheating themselves out of the truth. They need other Christians as bearers and proclaimers of the divine word of salvation. They need them solely for the sake of Jesus Christ. The Christ in their own hearts is weaker than the Christ in the word of other Christians. Their own hearts are uncertain; those of their brothers and sisters are sure. At the same time, this also clarifies that the goal of all Christian community is to encounter one another as bringers of the message of salvation. As such, God allows Christians to come together and grants them community. Their community is based only on Jesus Christ and this "alien righteousness." Therefore, we may now say that the community of Christians springs solely from the biblical and reformation message of the justification of human beings through grace alone. The longing of Christians for one another is based solely on this message.

Second, a Christian comes to others only through Jesus Christ. Among human beings there is strife. "He is our peace" (Eph. 2:14), says Paul of Jesus Christ. In him, broken and divided humanity has become one. Without Christ there is discord between God and humanity and between one human being and another. Christ has become the mediator

---

11. See Matt. 5:6: "Blessed are those who hunger and thirst for righteousness, for they will be filled." [GK]

who has made peace with God and peace among human beings. Without Christ we would not know God; we could neither call on God nor come to God. Moreover, without Christ we would not know other Christians around us; nor could we approach them. The way to them is blocked by one's own ego [das eigene Ich]. Christ opened up the way to God and to one another. Now Christians can live with each other in peace; they can love and serve one another; they can become one. But they can continue to do so only through Jesus Christ. Only in Jesus Christ are we one; only through him are we bound together. He remains the one and only mediator throughout eternity.

Third, when God's Son took on flesh, he truly and bodily, out of pure grace, took on our being, our nature, ourselves. This was the eternal decree of the triune God. Now we are in him. Wherever he is, he bears our flesh, he bears us. And, where he is, there we are too—in the incarnation, on the cross, and in his resurrection. We belong to him because we are in him. That is why the Scriptures call us the body of Christ. But if we have been elected and accepted with the whole church in Jesus Christ before we could know it or want it, then we also belong to Christ 21 in eternity with one another. We who live here in community with Christ will one day be with Christ in eternal community. Those who look at other Christians should know that they will be eternally united with them in Jesus Christ. Christian community means community through and in Jesus Christ. Everything the Scriptures provide in the way of directions and rules for Christians' life together rests on this presupposition.

"Now concerning love of the brothers and sisters, you do not need to have anyone write to you, for you yourselves have been taught by God to love one another . . . . But we urge you, beloved, to do so more and more" (1 Thess. 4:9f.). It is God's own undertaking to teach such love. All that human beings can add is to remember this divine instruction and the exhortation to excel in it more and more. When God had mercy on us, when God revealed Jesus Christ to us as our brother, when God won our hearts by God's own love, our instruction in Christian love began at the same time. When God was merciful to us, we learned to be merciful with one another. When we received forgiveness instead of judgment, we too were made ready to forgive each other. What God did to us, we then owed to others. The more we received, the more we were able to give; and the more meager our love for one another, the less we were living by God's mercy and love. Thus God taught us to encounter one another as God has encountered us in Christ. "Welcome one another, therefore, just as Christ has welcomed you, for the glory of God" (Rom. 15:7).

In this way the one whom God has placed in common life with other Christians learns what it means to have brothers and sisters. "Brothers and sisters . . . in the Lord," Paul calls his congregation (Phil. 1:14). One is a brother or sister to another only through Jesus Christ. I am a brother or sister to another person through what Jesus Christ has done for me and to me; others have become brothers and sisters to me through what Jesus Christ has done for them and to them. The fact that we are brothers and sisters only through Jesus Christ is of immeasurable significance. Therefore, the other who comes face to face with me earnestly and **22** devoutly seeking community is not the brother or sister with whom I am to relate in the community. My brother or sister is instead that other person who has been redeemed by Christ, absolved from sin, and called to faith and eternal life. What persons are in themselves as Christians, in their inwardness and piety, cannot constitute the basis of our community, which is determined by what those persons are in terms of Christ. Our community consists solely in what Christ has done to both of us. That not only is true at the beginning, as if in the course of time something else were to be added to our community, but also remains so for all the future and into all eternity. I have community with others and will continue to have it only through Jesus Christ. The more genuine and the deeper our community becomes, the more everything else between us will recede, and the more clearly and purely will Jesus Christ and his work become the one and only thing that is alive between us. We have one another only through Christ, but through Christ we really do *have* one another. We have one another completely and for all eternity.

This dismisses at the outset every unhappy desire for something more. Those who want more than what Christ has established between us do not want Christian community. They are looking for some extraordinary experiences of community that were denied them elsewhere. Such people are bringing confused and tainted desires into the Christian community. Precisely at this point Christian community is most often threatened from the very outset by the greatest danger, the danger of internal poisoning, the danger of confusing Christian community with some wishful image of pious community, the danger of blending the devout heart's natural desire for community with the spiritual reality of Christian community. It is essential for Christian community that two things become clear right from the beginning. *First, Christian community is not an ideal, but a divine reality; second, Christian community is a spiritual [pneumatische] and not a psychic [psychische] reality.*[12] 23

On innumerable occasions a whole Christian community has been shattered because it has lived on the basis of a wishful image. Certainly serious Christians who are put in a community for the first time will often bring with them a very definite image of what Christian communal life [Zusammenleben] should be, and they will be anxious to realize it. But God's grace quickly frustrates all such dreams. A great disillusionment with others, with Christians in general, and, if we are fortunate, with ourselves, is bound to overwhelm us as surely as God desires to lead us to an understanding of genuine Christian community. By sheer grace God will not permit us to live in a dream world even for a few weeks and to abandon ourselves to those blissful experiences and exalted moods that sweep over us like a wave of rapture. For God is not a God of emotionalism, but the God of truth. Only that community which enters into the experience of this great disillusionment with all its unpleasant and evil appearances begins to be what it should be in God's sight, begins to grasp in faith the promise that is given to it. The sooner this moment of disillusionment comes over the individual and the community, the better for both. However, a community that cannot bear and

---

12. The contrast between "spiritual" [pneumatisch] and "psychic" [psychische] corresponds to the Pauline distinction between "spirit" [pneuma] and "flesh" [sarx]. Here Bonhoeffer is raising the issue of how an action stemming from God's grace and spirit is contrasted with self-centered human action and understanding opposed to God and God's order. The editors of the German critical edition of *Life Together* point out that Bonhoeffer's negative appraisal of *psyche/sarx* does not represent an attitude on his part opposed to psychology and psychotherapy insofar as these are construed as empirical sciences. As evidence, they cite the presence in Bonhoeffer's personal library of two books by C. G. Jung. It is equally evident that Bonhoeffer was antagonistic toward the practice of psychotherapy, often lumping it with existentialist philosophy as the secular counterparts of the worst qualities he criticizes in religion. Bonhoeffer seems, in retrospect, rather cavalier in his dismissal of psychotherapy as a path toward greater maturity; e.g., see *LPP*, 326, 341. On the question of Bonhoeffer's attitude toward psychology and psychotherapy, see especially Clifford J. Green, "Two Bonhoeffers on Psychoanalysis," in *A Bonhoeffer Legacy: Essays in Understanding*, ed. A. J. Klassen, 58–75. [GK]

cannot survive such disillusionment, clinging instead to its idealized image, when that should be done away with, loses at the same time the promise of a durable Christian community. Sooner or later it is bound to collapse. Every human idealized image that is brought into the Christian community is a hindrance to genuine community and must be broken up so that genuine community can survive. Those who love their dream of a Christian community more than the Christian community itself become destroyers of that Christian community even though their personal intentions may be ever so honest, earnest, and sacrificial.

God hates this wishful dreaming because it makes the dreamer proud and pretentious. Those who dream of this idealized community demand that it be fulfilled by God, by others, and by themselves. They enter the community of Christians with their demands, set up their own law, and judge one another and even God accordingly. They stand adamant, a living reproach to all others in the circle of the community. They act as if they have to create the Christian community, as if their visionary ideal binds the people together. Whatever does not go their way, they call a failure. When their idealized image is shattered, they see the community breaking into pieces. So they first become accusers of other Christians in the community, then accusers of God, and finally the desperate accusers of themselves. Because God already has laid the only foundation of our community, because God has united us in one body with other Christians in Jesus Christ long before we entered into common life with them, we enter into that life together with other Christians, not as those who make demands, but as those who thankfully receive. We thank God for what God has done for us. We thank God for giving us other Christians who live by God's call, forgiveness, and promise. We do not complain about what God does not give us; rather we are thankful for what God does give us daily. And is not what has been given us enough: other believers who will go on living with us through sin and need under the blessing of God's grace? Is the gift of God any less immeasureably great than this on any given day, even on the most difficult and distressing days of a Christian community? Even when sin and misunderstanding burden the common life, is not the one who sins still a person with whom I too stand under the word of Christ? Will not another Christian's sin be an occasion for me ever anew to give thanks that both of us may live in the forgiving love of God in Jesus Christ? Therefore, will not the very moment of great disillusionment with my brother or sister be incomparably wholesome for me because it so thoroughly teaches me that both of us can never live by our own words and deeds, but only by that one Word and deed that really binds us together, the forgiveness of sins in Jesus Christ? The bright day of Christian community dawns wherever the early morning mists of dreamy visions are lifting.

Thankfulness works in the Christian community as it usually does in the Christian life. Only those who give thanks for little things receive the great things as well. We prevent God from giving us the great spiritual gifts prepared for us because we do not give thanks for daily gifts. We think that we should not be satisfied with the small measure of spiritual knowledge, experience, and love that has been given to us, and that we must be constantly seeking the great gifts.[13] Then we complain that we lack the deep certainty, the strong faith, and the rich experiences that God has given to other Christians, and we consider these complaints to be pious. We pray for the big things and forget to give thanks for the small (and yet really not so small!) gifts we receive daily. How can God entrust great things to those who will not gratefully receive the little things from God's hand? If we do not give thanks daily for the Christian community in which we have been placed, even when there are no great experiences, no noticeable riches, but much weakness, difficulty, and little faith—and if, on the contrary, we only keep complaining to God that everything is so miserable and so insignificant and does not at all live up to our expectations—then we hinder God from letting our community grow according to the measure and riches that are there for us all in Jesus Christ. That also applies in a special way to the complaints often heard from pastors and zealous parishioners about their congregations. Pastors should not complain about their congregation, certainly    26 never to other people, but also not to God. Congregations have not been entrusted to them in order that they should become accusers of their congregations before God and their fellow human beings. When pastors lose faith in a Christian community in which they have been placed and begin to make accusations against it, they had better examine themselves

---

13. See Jer. 45:5. "And you, do you seek great things for yourself? Do not seek them; for I am going to bring disaster upon all flesh, says the Lord." This biblical verse was very significant to Bonhoeffer. In his own Bible he has underlined this passage several times. See also *LPP*, 279, where Bonhoeffer, in view of the "great decisions" then being taken to set "things moving on all fronts," expresses his feeling that, "God is about to accomplish something that, even if we take part in it either outwardly or inwardly, we can only receive with the greatest wonder and awe . . . and we shall have to repeat Jer. 45:5 to ourselves every day." [GK]

first to see whether the underlying problem is not their own idealized image, which should be shattered by God. And if they find that to be true, let them thank God for leading them into this predicament. But if they find that it is not true, let them nevertheless guard against ever becoming an accuser of those whom God has gathered together. Instead, let them accuse themselves of their unbelief, let them ask for an understanding of their own failure and their particular sin, and pray that they may not wrong other Christians. Let such pastors, recognizing their own guilt, make intercession for those charged to their care. Let them do what they have been instructed to do and thank God.

Like the Christian's sanctification, Christian community is a gift of God to which we have no claim. Only God knows the real condition of either our community or our sanctification. What may appear weak and insignificant to us may be great and glorious to God. Just as Christians should not be constantly feeling the pulse of their spiritual life, so too the Christian community has not been given to us by God for us to be continually taking its temperature. The more thankfully we daily receive what is given to us, the more assuredly and consistently will community increase and grow from day to day as God pleases.

Christian community is not an ideal we have to realize, but rather a reality created by God in Christ in which we may participate. The more clearly we learn to recognize that the ground and strength and promise of all our community is in Jesus Christ alone, the more calmly we will learn to think about our community and pray and hope for it.

Because Christian community is founded solely on Jesus Christ, it is a spiritual [pneumatische] and not a psychic [psychische] reality. In this respect it differs absolutely from all other communities. The Scriptures call pneumatic or "spiritual" [geistlich] what is created only by the Holy Spirit, who puts Jesus Christ into our hearts as lord and savior. The scriptures call psychic or emotional [seelisch] what comes from the natural urges, strengths, and abilities of the human soul.[14]

27

---

14. Bonhoeffer's use of *seelisch*, which we translate here either as "self-centered" or as "emotional," is idiosyncratic. Although the German word *psychisch* is not necessarily synonymous with either expression, nonetheless, in the context and in the parallel descriptions, these appear to be the senses that Bonhoeffer invests in the word. In this section he wishes to contrast the love mediated by Jesus Christ in a truly Christian community and that self-serving love in a community that will prove to be only a hollow imitation of authentic community. Hence he draws from Saint Paul the contrasts between *Pneuma—*

The basis of all pneumatic, or spiritual, reality is the clear, manifest Word of God in Jesus Christ. At the foundation of all psychic, or emotional, reality are the dark, impenetrable urges and desires of the human soul. The basis of spiritual community is truth; the basis of emotional community is desire. The essence of spiritual community is light. For "God is light and in [God] there is no darkness at all" (1 John 1:5); and "if we walk in the light as he himself is in the light, we have fellowship with one another" (1 John 1:7). The essence of emotional, self-centered community is darkness, "for it is from within, from the human heart, that evil intentions come" (Mark 7:21).[15] It is the deep night that spreads over the sources of all human activity, over even all noble and devout impulses. Spiritual community is the community of those who are called by Christ; emotional community is the community of pious [frommen] souls.[16] The bright love of Christian service, *agape*, lives in the spiritual

corresponding in his German text to *Geist, pneumatisch*, and *geistlich*, and translated in this section as "spiritual"—and *Psyche*, which he employs in its adjectival form in German, *psychische*, and which we have translated as "psychic." This contrast is paralleled further in the Pauline antithesis between *soma* (in German *Leib* or body) and *sarx* (in German *Fleisch* or flesh), the latter indicating that aspect which makes one's *soma* prone to corruption and death. In the New Testament *sarx* (*sarkisch* in German) means self-centered, as well as to be in confrontation with the Holy Spirit of God. Finally, these antitheses permit Bonhoeffer to contrast the kinds of love that are possible within the community: *Agape* or unselfish love, which he renders in the expression "spiritual love" [geistliche Liebe], and *Eros*, which he renders by "emotional, self-centered love" [seelische Liebe]. Bonhoeffer packs into *seelisch*, in contrast with *geistlich*, all the negative aspects of *psyche, sarx*, and *eros* that are the legacy of one's fallen nature. In this context, *seelisch* has the impact of "emotional," "self-centered," or even "self-gratifying," as opposed to "spiritual" [geistlich] or agapeic love, love mediated by one's faith in Jesus Christ. [GK]

15. The phrase "human heart" here points toward one's "fallen nature." This is another instance in *LT* where Bonhoeffer's German does not follow Luther's translation. Luther uses the plural *der Menschen* (of human beings) which corresponds to the Greek text. [GK]

16. *Fromm* can mean "pious," "devout," or "sanctimonious." In this instance, this word has been translated by "pious" despite the obvious negative connotation that Bonhoeffer wishes to convey. He was highly critical of some forms of pietism that appealed to various segments of the German church. However, Bonhoeffer also revered many pietist spiritual texts and hymns. His most obvious quarrel was with contemporary pietists who, it seemed to him, exhibited social irresponsibility by retreating behind their devotions as a pretext for avoiding concrete action to achieve justice in the society of Nazi Germany. See 58, editorial note 31. [GK]

community; the dark love of pious-impious urges, *eros*, burns in the self-centered community. In the former, there is ordered, Christian service; in the latter, disordered desire for pleasure. In the former, there is humble submission of Christians one to another; in the latter, humble yet haughty subjection of other Christians to one's own desires.[17] In the spiritual community the Word of God alone rules; in the emotional, self-centered community the individual who is equipped with exceptional powers, experience, and magical, suggestive abilities rules along with the Word. In the one, God's Word alone is binding; in the other, besides the Word, human beings bind others to themselves. In the one, all power, honor, and rule are surrendered to the Holy Spirit; in the other, power and personal spheres of influence are sought and cultivated. So far as these are devout people, they certainly seek this power with the intention of serving the highest and the best. But in reality they end up dethroning the Holy Spirit and banishing it to the realm of unreal remoteness; only what is self-centered remains real here. Thus, in the spiritual community the Spirit rules; in the emotional community, psychological techniques and methods. In the former, unsophisticated, nonpsychological, unmethodical, helping love is offered to one another; in the latter, psychological analysis and design. In the former, service to one another is simple and humble; in the latter, it is to strangers treated in a searching, calculating fashion.

Perhaps the contrast between spiritual and emotional, self-centered reality can be made most clear in the following observation. Within the

---

17. See *CS*, 120–21, 226–27, for Bonhoeffer's earlier development of the contrast of *agape* with *eros* in order to clarify his concept of Christian community and to avoid confusing these two kinds of love. To make his point, he draws on the insights of Karl Barth, who, with reference to Søren Kierkegaard, had declared of Christian love that "it is not *eros*, which always only desires something; it is *agape*, which never ceases to love" (Barth, *The Epistle to the Romans*, 496). In the prison letters, he applauds Barth for invoking the God of Jesus Christ to oppose the pretensions of religion, calling this "*pneuma* against *sarx*" (*LPP*, 328). This distinction of *pneuma* and *sarx* is, as we have seen above in editorial notes 12 and 14, a parallel to the antithesis, *agape–eros*. It is uncertain to what extent Bonhoeffer may have been influenced by Anders Nygren's massive study of the distinction between *agape* and *eros*, in which one finds several points of agreement with Bonhoeffer in his analysis of Christian love. According to the editors of the German edition of the present text, Bonhoeffer's remarks here should be compared with Nygren's *Agape and Eros*, the first volume of the German translation having appeared in 1930 and the second in 1937. [GK]

spiritual community there is never, in any way whatsoever, an "immediate" relationship of one to another.[18] However, in the self-centered community there exists a profound, elemental emotional desire for community, for immediate contact with other human souls, just as in the flesh there is a yearning for immediate union with other flesh. This desire of the human soul seeks the complete intimate fusion of I and You,[19] whether this occurs in the union of love or—what from this self-centered perspective is after all the same thing—in forcing the other into one's own sphere of power and influence. Here is where self-centered, strong persons enjoy life to the full, securing for themselves the admiration, the love, or the fear of the weak. Here human bonds, suggestive influences, and dependencies are everything. Moreover, everything that is originally and solely characteristic of the community mediated through Christ reappears in the nonmediated community of souls in a distorted form.

There is, likewise, such a thing as "emotional" conversion. It has all

---

18. One here is reminded strongly of Kierkegaard's maxim that "the direct relationship with God is simply paganism, and only when the break has taken place, . . . can there be a true God-relationship" (*Concluding Unscientific Postscript,* 243). In rejecting the notion of "immediacy" Bonhoeffer relies on two key concepts. First, the sinful condition of one's human nature is seen as an alienation from God, from others, and from oneself. From this derives the Christian's need to be drawn into Christ's body, the Christian community, in order for righteous relationships to be made possible. Second, the New Testament insists that Jesus Christ is our mediator who transforms our relationships by his presence in the "other." This presence permits Christians to affirm the other as truly brother and sister in Christ. Christ then becomes the foundation for the love and peace that must characterize the Christian community. See *CS,* 115–36, and *AB,* 124–25. [GK]

19. Bonhoeffer's term, translated here as "You," is *Du,* the intimate-familiar form of the German word for "you." Bonhoeffer's description of the kind of communion that should exist among believers who profess spiritual love for one another within the Christian community is in some respects an echo of *Sanctorum Communio,* where he opposes the obliteration of the other's uniqueness in "self-centered love." The expression *Ich-Du,* literally "I-You," has been used to describe a relationship in which a certain quality of intimacy has been reached. When it refers to the relationship God has with us and we with God and to a relationship people have with one another, "You" connotes the other as personal limit, boundary, or challenge to the self-centered ego. It has often been translated as "I-Thou" (e.g., see earlier English translations of *CS* and *LT*) in order to bring out the distinction between the various degrees of friendship and intimacy signaled by the different words for "you" in German. See 76, editorial note 64, for further explanation of the translation of the German *Du.* [GK]

the appearances of genuine conversion and occurs wherever the superior power of one person is consciously or unconsciously misused to shake to the roots and draw into its spell an individual or a whole community. Here one soul has had an immediate effect on another. The result is that the weak individual has been overcome by the strong; the resistance of the weaker individual has broken down under the influence of the other person. One has been overpowered by something, but not won over. This becomes apparent the moment a commitment is demanded, a commitment that must be made independently of the person to whom one is bound or possibly in opposition to this person. Here is where those emotional converts fail. They thus show that their conversion was brought about not by the Holy Spirit, but by a human being. It is, therefore, not enduring.

There is, likewise, a "merely emotional" love of neighbor. Such love is capable of making the most unheard-of sacrifices. Often it far surpasses the genuine love of Christ in fervent devotion and visible results. It speaks the Christian language with overwhelming and stirring eloquence. But it is what the apostle Paul is speaking of when he says: "If I give all I possess to the poor, and surrender my body to the flames" (1 Cor. 13:3)—in other words, if I combine the utmost deeds of love with the utmost of devotion—"but do not have love (that is, the love of Christ), I would be nothing" (1 Cor. 13:2).[20] Self-centered love loves the other for the sake of itself; spiritual love loves the other for the sake of Christ. That is why self-centered love seeks direct contact with other persons. It loves them, not as free persons, but as those whom it binds to itself. It wants to do everything it can to win and conquer; it puts pressure on the other person. It desires to be irresistible, to dominate. Self-centered love does not think much of truth. It makes the truth relative, since nothing, not even the truth, must come between it and the person loved. Emotional, self-centered love desires other persons, their company. It wants them to return its love, but it does not serve them. On the contrary, it continues to desire even when it seems to be serving.

---

20. Bonhoeffer reverses the order of these two passages from 1 Cor. 13; his version of this text is translated here, rather than the text of the NRSV. During his ministry as pastor of two German-speaking parishes in and around London in 1934, Bonhoeffer preached four sermons on 1 Cor. 13 (*GS* 5:534–60). Lengthy excerpts from these London sermons can be found in *TF*, 239–52. For example, see Bonhoeffer's sermon of October 21, 1934, based on the text of 1 Cor. 13:4-8 in *TF*, 245–48. [GK]

29

Two factors, which are really one and the same thing, reveal the difference between spiritual and self-centered love. Emotional, self-centered love cannot tolerate the dissolution of a community that has   30 become false, even for the sake of genuine community. And such self-centered love cannot love an enemy, that is to say, one who seriously and stubbornly resists it. Both spring from the same source: emotional love is by its very nature desire, desire for self-centered community. As long as it can possibly satisfy this desire, it will not give it up, even for the sake of truth, even for the sake of genuine love for others. But emotional, self-centered love is at an end when it can no longer expect its desire to be fulfilled, namely, in the face of an enemy. There it turns into hatred, contempt, and slander.

Spiritual love, however, begins right at this point. This is why emotional, self-centered love turns into personal hatred when it encounters genuine spiritual love that does not desire but serves. Self-centered love makes itself an end in itself. It turns itself into an achievement, an idol it worships, to which it must subject everything. It cares for, cultivates, and loves itself and nothing else in the world. Spiritual love, however, comes from Jesus Christ; it serves him alone. It knows that it has no direct access to other persons. Christ stands between me and others. I do not know in advance what love of others means on the basis of the general idea of love that grows out of my emotional desires. All this may instead be hatred and the worst kind of selfishness in the eyes of Christ. Only Christ in his Word tells me what love is. Contrary to all my own opinions and convictions, Jesus Christ will tell me what love for my brothers and sisters really looks like. Therefore, spiritual love is bound to the word of Jesus Christ alone. Where Christ tells me to maintain community for the sake of love, I desire to maintain it. Where the truth of Christ orders me to dissolve a community for the sake of love, I will dissolve it, despite all the protests of my self-centered love. Because spiritual love does not desire but rather serves, it loves an enemy as a brother or sister. It originates neither in the brother or sister nor in the enemy, but in Christ and his word. Self-centered, emotional love can never comprehend spiritual love, for spiritual love is from above. It is something completely strange, new, and incomprehensible to all earthly love.   31

Because Christ stands between me and an other, I must not long for unmediated community with that person. As only Christ was able to speak to me in such a way that I was helped, so others too can only be helped by Christ alone. However, this means that I must release others from all my attempts to control, coerce, and dominate them with my love. In their freedom from me, other persons want to be loved for who they are, as those for whom Christ became a human being, died, and rose again, as those for whom Christ won the forgiveness of sins and prepared eternal life. Because Christ has long since acted decisively for other Christians, before I could begin to act, I must allow them the freedom to be Christ's. They should encounter me only as the persons that they already are for Christ. This is the meaning of the claim that we can encounter others only through the mediation of Christ. Self-centered love constructs its own image of other persons, about what they are and what they should become. It takes the life of the other person into its own hands. Spiritual love recognizes the true image of the other person as seen from the perspective of Jesus Christ. It is the image Jesus Christ has formed and wants to form in all people.

Therefore, spiritual love will prove successful insofar as it commends Christ to the other in all that it says and does. It will not seek to agitate another by exerting all too personal, direct influence or by crudely interfering in one's life. It will not take pleasure in pious, emotional fervor and excitement. Rather, it will encounter the other with the clear word of God and be prepared to leave the other alone with this word for a long time. It will be willing to release others again so that Christ may deal with them. It will respect the other as the boundary that Christ establishes between us; and it will find full community with the other in the Christ who alone binds us together. This spiritual love will thus speak to Christ about the other Christian more than to the other Christian about Christ. It knows that the most direct way to others is always through prayer to Christ and that love of the other is completely tied to the truth found in Christ. It is out of this love that John the disciple 32 speaks: "I have no greater joy than this, to hear that my children are walking in the truth" (3 John 4).

Emotional love lives by uncontrolled and uncontrollable dark desires; spiritual love lives in the clear light of service ordered by the *truth*. Self-centered love results in human enslavement, bondage, rigidity; spiritual love creates the *freedom* of Christians under the Word. Emotional love breeds artificial hothouse flowers; spiritual love creates the *fruits* that grow healthily under God's open sky, according to God's good pleasure in the rain and storm and sunshine.

The existence of any Christian communal life essentially depends on whether or not it succeeds at the right time in promoting the ability to distinguish between a human ideal and God's reality, between spiritual and emotional community. The life and death of a Christian community is decided by its ability to reach sober clarity on these points as soon as possible. In other words, a life together under the Word will stay healthy only when it does not form itself into a movement, an order, a society, a *collegium pietatis*,[21] but instead understands itself as being part of the one, holy, universal, Christian church,[22] sharing through its deeds and suffering in the hardships and struggles and promise of the whole church. Every principle of selection, and every division connected with it that is not necessitated quite objectively by common work, local conditions, or family connections is of the greatest danger to a Christian community. Self-centeredness always insinuates itself in any process of intellectual or spiritual selectivity, destroying the spiritual power of the community and robbing the community of its effectiveness for the church, thus driving it into sectarianism. The exclusion of the weak and insignificant, the seemingly useless people, from everyday Christian life in community [Lebensgemeinschaft] may actually mean the exclusion of

33

---

21. An "association of piety." As examples of these "associations of piety," one can cite the private circles for mutual edification that Philipp Jakob Spener (1635-1705), a prominent theologian of Lutheran Pietism, began to establish when he was senior clergyman in Frankfurt in 1666. Despite Bonhoeffer's use of the hymns of Count Nicholas Ludwig von Zinzendorf and Zinzendorf's commentary on Jeremiah, and Bonhoeffer's later enthusiasm for the "Daily Texts" [*Losungen*] pioneered by Zinzendorf, Bonhoeffer's antagonism against Pietism is well documented. See, for example, his letter to Bethge, July 31, 1936, *WF*, 72 (*GS* 2:278); Bethge, *Dietrich Bonhoeffer*, 378, 389, 447, 521, 778-79; and *LPP*, 157, 286, 327, 381. Also see editorial note 16 above and 58-59, editorial note 31. [GK]

22. The four classical marks of the church (one, holy, catholic, and apostolic) were incorporated into the Nicean-Constantinopolitan Symbol of Faith at the Council of Constantinople in 381. The German translation of the Old Church confessions, preserved in the Reformation confessional writings, replaces "catholic" (literally, "universal," though actually meaning, "correctness of belief" or "orthodox") with the then more palatable word, "Christian." Bonhoeffer's manner of naming these four marks was undoubtedly drawn from vol. 2 of *Die Bekenntnisschriften der evangelisch-lutherischen Kirche* published in Göttingen in conjunction with the 1930 anniversary of the Augsburg Confession. See *The Book of Concord: The Confessions of the Evangelical Lutheran Church*, ed. Theodore G. Tappert, 171-72.

Christ; for in the poor sister or brother, Christ is knocking at the door.[23] We must, therefore, be very careful on this point.

The undiscerning observer may think that this mixture of ideal and real, self-centered and spiritual, would be most obvious where there are a number of layers in the structure of a community, as in marriage, the family, friendship—where the element of self-centeredness as such already assumes a central importance in the community's coming into being at all, and where the spiritual is only something added to humanity's physical-emotional [leiblich-seelischen] nature. According to this view, it is only in these multifaceted communities that there is a danger of confusing and mixing the two spheres, whereas such a danger could hardly arise in a community of a purely spiritual nature. Such ideas, however, are a grand delusion. On the basis of all our experience—and as can be easily seen from the very nature of things—the truth is just the opposite. A marriage, a family, a friendship knows exactly the limitations of its community-building power. Such relationships know very well, if they are sound, where the self-centered element ends and the spiritual begins. They are aware of the difference between physical-emotional and spiritual community. On the other hand, whenever a community of a purely spiritual nature comes together, the danger is uncannily near that everything pertaining to self-centeredness will be brought into and intermixed with this community. Purely spiritual life in community [Lebensgemeinschaft] is not only dangerous but also not normal. Whenever physical-familial community, the community formed among those engaged in serious work, or everyday life with all its demands on work-

---

23. Bonhoeffer's statement here should be seen in the context of Nazism's deliberate attempt to exclude, even exterminate, the weak, insignificant, "seemingly useless people." Christ's identification with the "least" of people is at the heart of Bonhoeffer's Christology. See, for example, a little known sermon he gave during Advent in Barcelona in which he declared that the congregation was "faced with the shocking reality: Jesus stands at the door and knocks, in complete reality. He asks you for help in the form of a beggar, in the form of a ruined human being in torn clothing. He confronts you in every person that you meet" ("Sermon for the First Sunday in Advent," Barcelona, December 2, 1928, in *TF*, 186). This exhortation was echoed in that section of the Christology lectures in which Bonhoeffer reminded his students that Jesus hides himself in human weakness, going about "incognito, as a beggar among beggars, as an outcast among outcasts, as despairing among the despairing, as dying among the dying" (*CC*, 107). [GK]

ing people is not introduced into the spiritual community, extraordinary vigilance and clear thinking are called for. That is why it is precisely on short retreats that, as experience has shown, self-centeredness develops most easily. Nothing is easier than to stimulate the euphoria of community in a few days of life together [gemeinsame Leben]; and nothing is more fatal to the healthy, sober, everyday life in community of Christians. 34

There is probably no Christian to whom God has not given the uplifting and blissful *experience* of genuine Christian community at least once in her or his life. But in this world such experiences remain nothing but a gracious extra beyond the daily bread of Christian community life. We have no claim to such experiences, and we do not live with other Christians for the sake of gaining such experiences. It is not the experience of Christian community, but firm and certain faith within Christian community that holds us together. We hold fast in faith to God's greatest gift, that God has acted for us all and wants to act for us all. This makes us joyful and happy, but it also makes us ready to forgo all such experiences if at times God does not grant them. We are bound together by faith, not by experience.

"How very good and pleasant it is when kindred live together in unity." This is the Scripture's praise of life together under the Word. But now we can correctly interpret the words "in unity" and say "when kindred live together through Christ." For Jesus Christ alone is our unity. "He is our peace." We have access to one another, joy in one another, community with one another through Christ alone.

# THE DAY TOGETHER

35

> To you our morning song of praise,
> To you our evening prayer we raise;
> In lowly song your glory we adore
> O God, now, forever and forevermore.
> (Luther, following Ambrose)[1]

"LET THE WORD of Christ dwell in you richly" (Col. 3:16). The Old Testament day begins on one evening and ends with the sundown of the next evening. That is the time of expectation. The day of the New Testament church begins at sunrise in the early morning and ends with the dawning light of the next morning. That is the time of fulfillment, the resurrection of the Lord. At night Christ was born, a light in the darkness; noonday turned to night when Christ suffered and died on the cross. But early on Easter morning Christ emerged victorious from the grave. "Ere yet the dawn has filled the skies / Behold my Savior Christ arise, / He chases from us sin and night, / And brings us joy and life and light. Halleluia"[2] So sang the church of the Reformation. Christ is the "Sun of

---

1. These lines are taken from Martin Luther's translation of Ambrose's hymn, "O Lux Beata" (O blessed light), *WA,* 35:473. The English translation here is a slightly altered version of John Mason Neale's text in *The Service Book and Hymnal*, no. 133, v. 2. [GK]

2. Translation by Catherine Winkworth of the Easter hymn, "Frühmorgens da die Sonn' aufgeht" (Ere yet the dawn has filled the skies), by Johann Heermann (1585–1647), which appears in *The American Lutheran Hymnal*, no. 437. Bonhoeffer cites, with slight alterations, the text from the *Evangelisches Gesangbuch*

righteousness,"[3] who has risen upon the expectant congregation (Mal. 4:2),[4] and they who love him will be like the sun when it rises in its strength (Judg. 5:31). The early morning belongs to the church of the risen Christ. At the break of light it remembers the morning on which death, the devil, and sin were brought low in defeat, and new life and salvation were given to human beings.

What do we, who today no longer have any fear or awe of the darkness or night, know about the great joy that our forebears and the early Christians felt every morning at the return of the light? If we were to learn again something of the praise and adoration that is due the triune God early in the morning, then we would also begin to sense something of the joy that comes when night is past and those who dwell with one another come together early in the morning to praise their God and hear the Word and pray together. We would learn again of God the Father and Creator who has preserved our life through the dark night and awakened us to a new day; God the Son and Savior of the World, who vanquished death and hell for us, and dwells in our midst as Victor; God the Holy Spirit who pours the bright light of God's Word into our hearts early in the morning, driving away all darkness and sin and teaching us to pray the right way. Morning does not belong to the individual; it belongs to all the church of the triune God, to the community of Christians living together [Hausgemeinschaft], to the community of brothers [Bruderschaft].[5] The ancient hymns that call the community of

36

---

*für Brandenburg und Pommern*, no. 61, v. 1. Heermann's hymn, which Hymn 85 of the *Evangelisches Kirchengesangbuch* dates to the year 1630, is based on Mark 16:1–6. [GK]

3. Bonhoeffer cites these words from "Sonne der Gerechtigkeit" (Sun of righteousness) of the *Evangelisches Kirchengesangbuch*, no. 218. The lyrics of this hymn were written by Christian David (1690–1751), cofounder of the Herrnhuter community of the Brethren in the year 1741; in the *Evangelisches Kirchengesangbuch* the words were set to a melody of the Bohemian Brethren dating from the year 1566.

4. Contrary to many Bible translations widely used in Germany, and based on the Hebrew Bible that lists the verse cited here as 3:20, Bonhoeffer refers to Luther's text that follows the Septuagint and the Vulgate in listing the verse as 4:2, as does the NRSV: "But for you who revere my name the sun of righteousness shall rise, with healing in its wings." [GK]

5. The literal translation of the German term *Hausgemeinschaft*, as "house community," cannot adequately convey the wider application of the German

faith to praise God together in the early morning are inexhaustible.[6]
That is why the Bohemian Brethren sing in this manner at the break of
day: "The day does now dark night dispel; / Dear Christians, wake and
rouse you well. / Your praises to the Lord sing true; / And pondering
the image of God in you, / Proclaim the Lord's wonders ever anew.[7] /
Once more the daylight shines abroad, / O brethren, let us praise the
Lord, / Whose grace and mercy thus have kept / The nightly watch
while we have slept. / We beg your care this new born day, / For us,
poor pilgrims on our way, / O by us stand to help and guide, / That evil
on us ne'er betide.[8] / For this there comes the light of day, / O
brethren, let us thanksgiving say, / To gentle God who guarded us this
darkened night, / Whose grace stood watch o'er us in every plight. / We
offer up ourselves to you, / may our wants, words, and deeds be true. /
In union with your heart will you us lead. / In you will our work be
37   graced indeed."[9]

---

meaning. *Hausgemeinschaft* refers to those who live together in varying structures
and in varying degrees of association and intimacy. In that sense a *Hausgemeinschaft* can consist of many households, e.g., the *Hausgemeinschaft* of an apartment
building or that of a seminary. Here, however, Bonhoeffer uses the term specifically to indicate the community that can emerge when varying clusters of Christians share a life together through their faith. *Bruderschaft*, on the other hand,
has a directly religious connotation. [GK]

6. "Community of faith" translates *Gemeinde*, which also can be translated
"congregation," especially when it refers to the community specifically at worship. We have usually translated *Gemeinde* as "community of faith" in order to
distinguish this term from the phrase *Gemeinschaft der Christen*, which has been
translated "community of Christians." The reader should be aware, however, of
the danger of too subjective an interpretation of the phrase "community of
faith"; the emphasis should be placed on the "community," not on the qualifier
"faith." *Gemeinde* is primarily a sociological, not a psychological, term. [GK]

7. [Trans. GK] This verse is cited by Bonhoeffer from the collection of hymns
edited by Otto Riethmüller, *Ein neues Lied*, no. 276, expanded for the Evangelical Youth Movement.

8. Trans. by Catherine Winkworth. Bonhoeffer is citing *Ein neues Lied*, no.
277, vs. 1–2. The hymn is attributed to Melchior Vulpius and is generally
believed to have been written in 1609. It appears as "Am Morgen" (In the morning) in *Evangelisches Kirchengesangbuch*, no. 333.

9. [Trans. GK] Again Bonhoeffer quotes a hymn from the Bohemian Brethren
hymnal, *Ein neues Lied*. These lines are the first and sixth verses of "Es geht
daher des Tages Schein" (For this there comes the light of day), a hymn attrib-

Life together under the Word begins at an early hour of the day with a worship service together. A community living together gathers for praise and thanks, Scripture reading, and prayer. The profound silence of morning is first broken by the prayer and song of the community of faith. After the silence of the night and early morning, hymns and the Word of God will be heard all the more clearly. Along these lines the Holy Scriptures tell us that the first thought and the first word of the day belong to God: "O Lord, in the morning you hear my voice; in the morning I plead my case to you, and watch" (Ps. 5:4 [3]).[10] "In the morning my prayer comes before you" (Ps. 88:14 [13]). "My heart is steadfast, O God, my heart is steadfast; I will sing and make melody. Awake, my soul! Awake, O harp and lyre! I will awake the dawn" (Ps. 57:8f. [7f.]). At the break of dawn the believer thirsts and yearns for God: "I rise before dawn and cry for help. I put my hope in your words" (Ps. 119:147). "O God, you are my God, I seek you, my soul thirsts for you; my flesh faints for you, as in a dry and weary land where there is no water" (Ps. 63:2 [1]). The Wisdom of Solomon would have it "known that one must rise before the sun to give you thanks, and must pray to you at the dawning of the light" (16:28), and Jesus Ben Sirach says especially of the teacher of the law that "he sets his heart to rise early to seek the Lord who made him, and to petition the Most High" (39:6 [5]).[11] The Holy Scriptures also speak of the morning hours as the time of God's special help. It is said of the city of God: "God will help it when the morning dawns" (Ps. 46:6 [5]), and again, that God's blessings "are new every morning" (Lam. 3:23).[12]

For Christians the beginning of the day should not be burdened and haunted by the various kinds of concerns they face during the working day. The Lord stands above the new day, for God has made it. All the darkness and confusion of the night with its dreams gives way to the

---

uted to Michael Weisse from the year 1531, which also can be found in the *Evangelisches Kirchengesangbuch*, no. 334.

10. Bonhoeffer's text, following the enumeration of Luther and the Hebrew Bible, lists this as Ps. 5:4. We follow here the NRSV versification. Bonhoeffer's numbering is given in notes 11–15. [GK]

11. Jesus Sirach is called Ecclesiasticus or Sirach in the NRSV. See editorial note 61. [GK]

12. Bonhoeffer's Bible has: "Seine Güte ist alle Morgen neu." [GK]

clear light of Jesus Christ and his awakening Word. All restlessness, all impurity, all worry and anxiety flee before him. Therefore, in the early morning hours of the day may our many thoughts and our many idle words be silent, and may the first thought and the first word belong to the one to whom our whole life belongs. "Sleeper, awake! Rise from the dead, and Christ will shine on you" (Eph. 5:14).

38

With remarkable frequency the Holy Scriptures remind us of various men of God[13] who got up early to seek God and carry out God's commands, as for example, Abraham, Jacob, Moses, and Joshua (cf. Gen. 19:27, 22:3; Exod. 8:16 [20], 9:13, 24:4; Josh. 3:1, 6:12, etc.). The Gospel, which never speaks a superfluous word, reports about Jesus himself: "In the morning, while it was still very dark, he got up and went out to a deserted place, and there he prayed" (Mark 1:35). Some people get up early because of uneasiness and worry; the Scriptures call that pointless, saying, "It is in vain that you rise up early . . . eating your bread with tears" (Ps. 127:2).[14] But there is such a thing as rising early for the love of God. That was the practice of the men of the Holy Scriptures.

Scripture reading, song, and prayer should be part of daily morning *worship together* [gemeinsame Andacht]. Daily morning worship will take as many different forms as there are communities. That is the way it is bound to be. When a community living together includes children, it needs a different sort of daily worship than a community of seminarians.[15] It is by no means healthy when one becomes like the other, when, for example, a brotherhood of seminarians is content with a form of family daily worship for children. However, the *word of Scripture, the*

---

13. *Männer Gottes.* Bonhoeffer infrequently used the gender specific term *Männer* (men) rather than the gender-inclusive term *Menschen* (human beings). Where he has used the former, we have retained the masculine English forms "man" or "men"; whenever he has used the latter, we have employed gender inclusive forms such as "human beings," "people," or "persons." [GK]

14. The NRSV translation has been slightly altered to reflect more accurately Bonhoeffer's text. Bonhoeffer's own German rendering of this passage, translated here as "It is in vain that you rise up early . . . eating your bread with tears," departs from Luther's version, which reads: ". . . früh aufsteht und hernach lange sitzet und esset euer Brot mit sorgen." ([In vain] you rise early and sit thereafter for a long time and eat your bread with anxiety.) [GK]

15. This is clearly a reference to the difference between the practice of the seminarians at Finkenwalde and that of other Christian communities to whom Bonhoeffer also addresses this book. [GK]

*hymns of the church, and the prayer of the community* should form a part of every daily worship that they share together. I will now speak here of the individual parts of such daily worship together.

"Speak to one another with psalms" (Eph. 5:19).[16] "Teach and admonish one another . . . and . . . sing psalms" (Col. 3:16).[17] From ancient times in the church a special significance has been attached to the *praying of Psalms* together. In many churches to this day the Psalter is used at the beginning of every service of daily worship together. The practice has been lost to a large extent, and we must now recover the meaning of praying the Psalms. The Psalter occupies a unique place in all the Holy Scriptures. It is God's Word, and with few exceptions it is at the same time the prayer of human beings. How are we to understand this? How can God's Word be at the same time prayer to God?[18] This question is followed by an observation made by all who begin to pray the Psalms. First, they try to repeat the Psalms personally as their own prayer. But soon they come across passages that they feel they cannot pray as their own personal prayers. We remember, for example, the psalms of innocence, the psalms of vengeance, and also, in part, the psalms of suffering. Nevertheless, these prayers are words of the Holy Scriptures that believing Christians cannot simply dismiss as obsolete and antiquated, as a "preliminary stage of religion" ["religiöse Vorstufe"].[19] Thus they do

39

---

16. This is a literal translation of the text Bonhoeffer quotes from Luther's Bible: "Redet untereinander mit Psalmen." The NRSV has: "Be filled with the Spirit, as you sing psalms and hymns and spiritual songs among yourselves, singing and making melody to the Lord in your hearts" (Eph. 5:18b-19). [GK]

17. This is a literal translation of Bonhoeffer's text: "Lehret und vermahnet euch selbst mit Psalmen." The NRSV has: "Teach and admonish one another in all wisdom; and with gratitude in your hearts sing psalms, hymns, and spiritual songs to God." [GK]

18. This is a question that Bonhoeffer addresses in two significant works, *The Prayerbook of the Bible: An Introduction to the Psalms*, found below in this volume, and his Finkenwalde lecture of July 31, 1935, "Christus in den Psalmen" (Christ in the Psalms) (*GS* 3:294–300). [GK]

19. See Bonhoeffer's treatment of the troubling aspects of the psalms of vengeance in *The Prayerbook of the Bible*, below, 174–76. It is important to note that in arguing for the need to integrate even these seemingly atypically Christian passages into the Christian gospel, Bonhoeffer was combating not only the tradition of Marcion, who rejected the Old Testament, but also the views of Bonhoeffer's contemporary Emanuel Hirsch, whose exegesis of portions of the Old Testament seemed tainted with Nazism's regnant anti-Jewish ideology. Bonhoeffer's consistency on this point can be seen by examining his "Predigt über

not desire to gain control over the word of Scripture, and yet they realize that they cannot pray these words. They can read and hear them as the prayer of another person, wonder about them, be offended by them, but they can neither pray them themselves nor expunge them from the Holy Scriptures. The practical thing to say here would be that people in this situation should first stick to the psalms they can understand and pray, and that in reading the other psalms they should quite simply learn to overlook what is incomprehensible and difficult in the Holy Scriptures, returning again and again to what is simple and understandable. However, this difficulty actually indicates the point at which we may get our first glimpse of the secret of the Psalter. The psalms that will not cross our lips as prayers, those that make us falter and offend us, make us suspect that here someone else is praying, not we—that the one who is here affirming his innocence, who is calling for God's judgment, who has come to such infinite depths of suffering, is none other than Jesus Christ himself. It is he who is praying here, and not only here, but in the whole Psalter. The New Testament and the church have always recognized and testified to this truth. The *human* Jesus Christ to whom no affliction, no illness, no suffering is unknown, and who yet was the wholly innocent and righteous one, is praying in the Psalter through the mouth of his congregation. The Psalter is the prayer book of Jesus Christ in the truest

---

einen Rachepsalm: Psalm 58" (Sermon on a psalm of vengeance: Psalm 58), July 11, 1937, where he notes that the pleas of the innocent and the avenging wrath of God converge in the cross of the innocent Jesus who suffers for the just and unjust alike. Bonhoeffer declares toward the end of this sermon: "In the midst of this distress, Christ prays this psalm vicariously as our representative. He accuses the godless, he calls down upon them God's vengeance and justice, and he gives himself for all the godless with his innocent suffering on the cross. And now we too pray this psalm with him, in humble thanks that we have been granted deliverance from wrath through the cross of Christ, in our fervent prayer that God will bring all our enemies under the cross of Christ and grant them grace . . ." (*TF,* 282–83 [*GS* 4:422]). In context, "our enemies" are to be understood as those who collaborate with National Socialism, and clearly do *not* include the Jews, as had often been the case in Christian anti-Semitic rhetoric. Earlier in the sermon Bonhoeffer had interpreted the psalm in the context of Christ's prayer from the cross for forgiveness of his enemies (*TF,* 282 [*GS* 4:420]). Not all exegetes would agree from a historical point of view with Bonhoeffer's attempt to interpret the psalms of wrath in terms of the Christian gospel's insistence on forgiving one's enemies. On this point and on Bonhoeffer's entire approach to Old Testament exegesis, see especially Martin Kuske, *The Old Testament as the Book of Christ: An Appraisal of Bonhoeffer's Interpretation,* 60–124. [GK]

sense of the word. He prayed the Psalter, and now it has become his prayer for all time. Can we now comprehend how the Psalter is capable of being simultaneously prayer to God and yet God's own Word, precisely because the praying Christ encounters us here? Jesus Christ prays the Psalter in his congregation. His congregation prays too, and even   40 the individual prays. But they pray only insofar as Christ prays within them; they pray here not in their own name, but in the name of Jesus Christ. They pray not from the natural desires of their own hearts, but rather out of the humanity assumed by Christ. They pray on the basis of the prayer of the human Jesus Christ. Their prayer will be met with the promise of being heard only when they pray on this basis. Because Christ prays the prayer of the Psalms with the individual and with the church before the heavenly throne of God, or rather, because those who pray the Psalms are joining in the prayer of Jesus Christ, their prayer reaches the ears of God. Christ has become their intercessor.

The Psalter is the vicarious prayer of Christ for his congregation.[20] Now that Christ is with the Father, the new humanity of Christ—the body of Christ—on earth continues to pray his prayer to the end of time. This prayer belongs not to the individual member, but to the whole body of Christ. All the things of which the Psalter speaks, which individuals can never fully comprehend and call their own, live only in the whole Christ. That is why the prayer of the Psalms belongs in the community in a special way. Even if a verse or a psalm is not my own prayer, it is nevertheless the prayer of another member of the community; and it is quite certainly the prayer of the truly human Jesus Christ and his body on earth.

In the Psalter we learn to pray on the basis of Christ's prayer. The Psalter is the great school of prayer. *First*, we learn here what prayer means: it means praying on the basis of the Word of God, on the basis of promises. Christian prayer takes its stand on the solid ground of the revealed Word and has nothing to do with vague, self-seeking desires. We pray on the basis of the prayer of the truly human Jesus Christ. This is what the Scripture means when it says that the Holy Spirit prays in us and for us, that Christ prays for us, that we can pray to God in the right way only in the name of Jesus Christ.

---

20. Bonhoeffer's usage here dates to his doctoral dissertation, where he speaks of Jesus as *Stellvertreter* (a term that can mean "vicarious representative," "substitute," or "deputy"), one who acts on behalf of and for others, especially representing humanity before God. See *CS*, 107, 113–14, 136. [GK]

*Second*, we learn from the prayer of the Psalms what we should pray. As certain as it is that the prayer of the Psalms ranges far beyond the experiences of the individual, nevertheless, the individual prays in faith the whole prayer of Christ, the prayer of one who was truly human and who alone possesses the full range of experiences expressed in these 41 prayers. Can we, then, pray the psalms of vengeance? Insofar as we are sinners and associate evil thoughts with the prayer of vengeance, we must not do so. But insofar as Christ is in us, we, too, as members of Jesus Christ, can pray these psalms through and from the heart of Jesus Christ, who took all the vengeance of God on himself, who was afflicted in place of us by the vengeance of God, who was in this way stricken by the wrath of God and in no other way could forgive his enemies, and who himself suffered this wrath so that his enemies might go free.[21] Can we, with the psalmist, call ourselves innocent, devout, and righteous? We cannot do so insofar as we are ourselves. We cannot do it as the prayer of our own perverse heart. But we can and should do it as a prayer from the heart of Jesus Christ that was sinless and pure, from the innocence of Christ in which he has given us a share by faith. Insofar as "Christ's blood and righteousness" have become "our robe of honor and adornment,"[22] we can and we should pray the psalms of innocence as Christ's prayer for us and gift to us. These psalms, too, belong to us through Christ. And how should we pray those prayers of unspeakable misery and suffering, since we have hardly begun to sense even remotely something of what is meant here? We can and we should pray the psalms of suffering, not to become completely caught up in something our heart does not know from its own experience, nor to make our own complaints, but because all this suffering was genuine and real in Jesus Christ, because the human being Jesus Christ suffered sickness, pain,

---

21. See Bonhoeffer's "Sermon on a Psalm of Vengeance: Psalm 58" (*TF*, 277–83 [*GS* 4:413–22]). See also Kuske's commentary on this psalm in *The Old Testament as the Book of Christ*, 85–86. [GK]

22. In *The Service Book and Hymnal*, no. 376, the words cited by Bonhoeffer are translated as "Jesus, thy blood and righteousness, my beauty are, my glorious dress." Also see the *Evangelisches Gesangbuch*, used by Bonhoeffer, no. 154. The verse suggests Rev. 7:14, which says "These are they who have come out of the great ordeal; they have washed their robes and made them white in the blood of the lamb." The *Evangelisches Kirchengesangbuch*, no. 273, traces the first verse to Leipzig in the year 1638, verses 2 and 3 to Christian Gregor, 1778, and verses 4 and 5 to Count Zinzendorf, 1739. [GK]

shame, and death, and because in his suffering and dying all flesh suffered and died. What happened to us on the cross of Christ, the death of our old self, and what actually does happen and should happen to us since our baptism in the dying of our flesh, is what gives us the right to pray these prayers. Through the cross of Jesus these psalms have been granted to his body on earth as prayers that issue from his heart. We cannot elaborate on this theme here. Our concern has been only to suggest the depth and breadth of the Psalter as the prayer of Christ. In this regard, we can only grow into the Psalter gradually.　42

*Third*, the prayer of the Psalms teaches us to pray as a community. The body of Christ is praying, and I as an individual recognize that my prayer is only a tiny fraction of the whole prayer of the church. I learn to join the body of Christ in its prayer. That lifts me above my personal concerns and allows me to pray selflessly. Many of the Psalms were very probably prayed antiphonally by the Old Testament congregation. The so-called parallelism of the verses (*parallelismus membrorum*),[23] that remarkable repetition of the same idea in different words in the second line of the verse, is not merely a literary form. It also has meaning for the church and theology. It would be worthwhile sometime to pursue this question very thoroughly. One might read, as a particularly clear example, Psalm 5. Repeatedly there are two voices, bringing the same prayer request to God in different words. Is that not meant to be an indication that the one who prays never prays alone? There must always be a second person, another, a member of the church, the body of Christ, indeed Jesus Christ himself, praying with the Christian in order that the prayer of the individual may be true prayer. In the repetition of the same subject, which is heightened in Psalm 119 to such a degree that it seems it does not want to end and becomes so simple that it is virtually impervious to our exegetical analysis, is there not the suggestion that every word of prayer must penetrate to a depth of the heart which can be reached only by unceasing repetition? And in the end not even in that way! Is that not an indication that prayer is not a matter of a unique pouring out of the human heart in need or joy, but an unbroken, indeed

---

23. In his *The Prayerbook of the Bible* Bonhoeffer observes, "The Psalms were probably most often sung antiphonally. They were also specifically suited for this through their verse form, according to which the two parts of each verse are so bound to one another that they express essentially the same thought in different words. This is the so-called structural parallelism" (161 below). [GK]

continuous, process of learning, appropriating and impressing God's will in Jesus Christ on the mind?[24] Ötinger, in his exegesis of the Psalms, brought out a profound truth when he arranged the whole Psalter according to the seven petitions of the Lord's Prayer.[25] What he meant was that the long and extensive book of Psalms was concerned with nothing more or less than the brief petitions of the Lord's Prayer. In all our praying there remains only the prayer of Jesus Christ, which has the promise of fulfillment and frees us from the vain repetitions of the heathen. The more deeply we grow into the Psalms and the more often we ourselves have prayed them, the more simple and rewarding will our praying become.

The prayer of the Psalms, concluded with a hymn by the house church [Hausgemeinde],[26] is followed by a *Scripture reading*. "Give attention to the public reading of scripture" (1 Tim. 4:13). Here, too, we will have to overcome some harmful prejudices before we achieve the right way of reading the Scripture together. Almost all of us have grown up with the idea that the Scripture reading is solely a matter of hearing the Word of God for today. That is why for many the Scripture reading consists only of a few brief selected verses that are to form the central idea of the day. There can be no doubt that the daily Bible passages published by the Moravian Brethren, for example, are a real blessing to all who have ever used them.[27] Many people have realized that to their great amazement

43

---

24. On the connection between the deliberate repetitiveness of the verses of the Psalms and the manner in which prayer is an impression on our hearts of God's word and will, see especially Bonhoeffer's "Meditation on Psalm 119," presented to the candidates for ordination of the collective pastorates of the Confessing Church during the winter semester, 1939–40, in *MW*, 101–45 (*GS* 4:505–43). [GK]

25. Bonhoeffer refers here to Friedrich Christoph Ötinger's *Die Psalmen Davids nach den sieben Bitten des Gebets des Herrn in sieben Klassen dargebracht. Ein Wort zur Erbauung,* found in Ötinger's *Sämtliche Schriften* 2/3.

26. *Hausgemeinde* is translated by the phrase "house church" because of its clear emphasis on being an ecclesiastical community in the manner of the first-century Christian house churches. [GK]

27. The "Daily Texts of the Church of the Brethren" (*Losungen der Brüdergemeine*) are small meditation books with a short Bible text from the Old Testament (*Losung*) and a selected passage from the New Testament (*Lehrtext*) for every day of the year, as well as a verse from a hymn or a short prayer text. It was in the Herrnhut settlement of Saxony founded in 1722 by Moravian emigrants that, in 1728, Count Nicholas Ludwig von Zinzendorf permitted, for the first

and have been grateful for the daily Bible readings particularly during the time of the church struggle [Kirchenkampf].[28] But equally there can be little doubt that brief passages cannot and must not take the place of reading the Scripture as a whole. The verse for the day is not yet the Holy Scriptures that will remain throughout all time until the Day of Judgment. The Holy Scriptures are more than selected Bible passages. It is also more than "Bread for Today."[29] It is God's revealed Word for all

---

time, a Bible text to be proclaimed in their homes as the maxim (*Parole*) for the day. The "Daily Texts" were, from their first publication in 1731, printed up for one year at a time. They have appeared each year since then without interruption. Considered the most widely read daily worship guide in the world next to the Bible, every year approximately 1.25 million copies are published in 34 languages and dialects. On Bonhoeffer's appreciation and use of the "Daily Texts," see especially his letter of December 20, 1937, to the ordinands of the collective pastorates that had been organized after the forced closing of the seminary at Finkenwalde, in which he transcribed all the "Daily Texts" from Christmas Eve until New Year's Eve (*GS* 2:524–30). See Bonhoeffer's meditations on the "Herrnhuter Daily Texts" for Pentecost, May 28–29, 1944, Pentecost Tuesday, May 30, 1944, and for June 7 and June 8, 1944, included in the letters sent to Bethge, dated May 24 and June 2, 1944 (*GS* 4:588–96). See also the many references to the "Daily Texts" in *LPP*. On Bonhoeffer's relationship with the Church of the Brethren, with particular reference to the "Daily Texts," see especially Walther Günther, "Dietrich Bonhoeffer und die Brüdergemeinde" (Dietrich Bonhoeffer and the Church of the Brethren), 62–70, and F. Burton Nelson, "Bonhoeffer and the Spiritual Life: Some Reflections." Copies of the English version of the *Losungen, The Text Book of the Moravian Church: Being the Scripture "Watchwords" and Doctrinal Texts*, which Bonhoeffer used between 1936 and 1944, are available through the Moravian Church of America, Bethlehem, Pa. [GK]

28. The "church struggle" refers to the conflicts within the German churches and the collective resistance of churches, and of individuals, to the policies of the National Socialist Party under Hitler. During the 1930s the Nazis attempted to dominate and control the church by integrating it into the Nazi bureaucratic structure. At stake in the struggle were the authenticity and integrity of the churches to be what they were called to be according to biblical and confessional criteria. Within the Protestant Church of Germany this led to the split between those that supported the policies of Adolf Hitler—the German Reich Church whose members called themselves the "German Christians"—and the Confessing Church of which Bonhoeffer was an outspoken leader. See *TF,* 544–46. [GK]

29. This is an allusion to the title of a well-known tear-off calendar of that period, "Brot für den Tag" (Bread for the day).

44   peoples, for all times. The Holy Scriptures do not consist of individual sayings, but are a whole and can be used most effectively as such. The Scriptures are God's revealed Word as a whole. The full witness to Jesus Christ the Lord can be clearly heard only in its immeasurable inner relationships, in the connection of Old and New Testaments, of promise and fulfillment, sacrifice and law, Law and Gospel, cross and resurrection, faith and obedience, having and hoping. That is why daily worship together must include a longer Old and New Testament lesson besides the prayer of the Psalms. A community of Christians living together surely should be able to read and listen to a chapter of the Old Testament and at least half a chapter of the New Testament every morning and evening.[30] When the practice is first tried, however, such a community will discover that even this modest measure represents a maximum demand for most people and will meet with resistance. It will be objected that it is impossible really to take in and retain such an abundance of ideas and interconnections, that it even shows disrespect for God's Word to read more than one can seriously digest. In the face of these objections, we will easily content ourselves again with reading only verses. In truth, however, a serious failing lies hidden beneath this attitude. If it is really true that it is hard for us, as adult Christians, to comprehend a chapter of the Old Testament in its context, then that can only fill us with profound shame. What kind of testimony is that to our knowledge of the Scriptures and all our previous reading of them? If we were familiar with the substance of what we read, we could follow the reading of a chapter without difficulty, especially if we have an open Bible in our hands and are reading it at the same time. However, since that is not the case, we must admit that the Holy Scriptures are still largely unknown to

45   us. Can this sin of our own ignorance of God's Word have any other consequence than that we should earnestly and faithfully recover lost ground and catch up on what we have missed? And should not the seminarians[31] be the very first to get to work here? Let us not argue that it is not the purpose of daily worship together to get to know the contents of Scripture, that this is too profane a purpose, something that must be achieved apart from daily worship. This argument is based on a completely wrong understanding of what a daily worship service is. God's

---

30. This appears to be an indication of the actual expectations Bonhoeffer had for the Finkenwalde community. [GK]

31. This again refers to the students at Finkenwalde. [GK]

Word is to be heard by all in their own way and according to the measure of their understanding. A child hears and learns the biblical story for the first time during daily worship. Mature Christians keep on learning it and learn it better and better; and as they read and hear it on their own, they will never finish this learning.

Not only immature Christians, but also mature Christians will complain that the Scripture reading is often too long for them and that there is much they do not grasp. In response to this complaint it must be said that indeed for the mature Christian every Scripture reading will be "too long," even the shortest one. What does that mean? The Scripture is a complex unity, and every word, every sentence, contains such a diversity of relationships to the whole that it is impossible always to keep track of the whole when listening to an individual portion of it. Therefore, it appears that the whole of Scripture as well as every passage in it far surpasses our understanding. It can only be a good thing when we are daily reminded of this fact, which again refers us to Jesus Christ himself "in whom are *hidden* all the treasures of wisdom and knowledge" (Col. 2:3).[36] So one may perhaps say that every Scripture reading always has to be somewhat "too long" if it is not to be aphoristic worldly wisdom, but God's Word of revelation in Jesus Christ.

Because the Scripture is a corpus, a living whole, the so-called *lectio continua*,[37] or consecutive reading, will above all be worth considering for the Scripture reading of the house church. Historical books, the Prophets, Gospels, Epistles, and Revelation are read and heard as God's    46 Word in their context. They put the listening congregation in the midst of the wonderful revelatory world of the people of Israel with their prophets, judges, kings, and priests, with their wars, festivals, sacrifices, and sufferings. The community of believers is drawn into the Christmas story, the baptism, the miracles and discourses, the suffering, dying, and rising of Jesus Christ. It participates in the events that once occurred on this earth for the salvation of the whole world. In so doing, it receives sal-

---

32. The emphasis has been added by Bonhoeffer.

33. For a long time in the ancient church the biblical books were read consecutively in the sequence of their canonical ordering, especially in the monasteries. In contemporary times, with the new Roman Catholic lectionary of 1969, the ideal of a *lectio continua*, with its three-year cycle of readings, was again restored in the Catholic liturgy. In Germany today, despite the ecumenical movement, Lutheran churches do not as yet follow a cycle of consecutive readings from a liturgical lectionary. [GK]

vation in Jesus Christ here and in all these events. For those who want to hear, reading the biblical books in a sequential order forces them to go, and to allow themselves to be found, where God has acted once and for all for the salvation of human beings. The historical books of the Holy Scriptures come alive for us in a whole new way precisely when they are read during worship services. We receive a part of that which once took place for our salvation. Forgetting and losing ourselves, we too pass through the Red Sea, through the desert, across the Jordan into the promised land. With Israel we fall into doubt and unbelief and through punishment and repentance experience again God's help and faithfulness. All this is not mere reverie, but holy, divine reality. We are uprooted from our own existence and are taken back to the holy history of God on earth. There God has dealt with us, and there God still deals with us today, with our needs and our sins, by means of the divine wrath and grace. What is important is not that God is a spectator and participant in our life today, but that we are attentive listeners and participants in God's action in the sacred story, the story of Christ on earth. God is with us today only as long as we are there. A complete reversal occurs here. It is not that God's help and presence must still be proved in our life; rather God's presence and help have been demonstrated for us in the life of Jesus Christ. It is in fact more important for us to know what God did to Israel, in God's son Jesus Christ, than to discover what God intends for us today. The fact that Jesus Christ died is more important than the fact that I will die. And the fact that Jesus Christ was raised from the dead is the sole ground of my hope that I, too, will be raised on the day

47   of judgment. Our salvation is "from outside ourselves" (*extra nos*).[34] I find salvation not in my life story, but only in the story of Jesus Christ. Only those who allow themselves to be found in Jesus Christ—in the incarnation, cross, and resurrection—are with God and God with them.

From this perspective the whole reading of the Holy Scriptures in worship services becomes every day more meaningful and more beneficial. What we call our life, our troubles, and our guilt is by no means the whole of reality; our life, our need, our guilt, and our deliverance are there in the Scriptures. Because it pleased God to act for us there, it is only there that we will be helped. Only in the Holy Scriptures do we get to know our own story. The God of Abraham, Isaac, and Jacob is the God and Father of Jesus Christ and our God.

---

34. See 31, editorial note 10.

We must once again get to know the Scriptures as the reformers and our forebears knew them. We must not shy away from the work and the time required for this task. We must become acquainted with the Scriptures first and foremost for the sake of our salvation. But, besides this, there are enough weighty reasons to make this challenge absolutely urgent for us. For example, how are we ever to gain certainty and confidence in our personal deeds and church activity if we do not stand on solid biblical ground? It is not our heart that determines our course, but God's Word. But who in this day has any proper awareness of the need for evidence from Scripture? How often do we hear innumerable arguments "from life" and "from experience" to justify the most crucial decisions? Yet the evidence of Scripture is excluded even though it would perhaps point in exactly the opposite direction. It is not surprising, of course, that those who attempt to discredit the evidence of Scripture are the people who themselves do not seriously read, know, or make a thorough study of the Scriptures. But those who are not willing to learn how to deal with the Scriptures for themselves are not Protestant Christians [evangelischer Christ].[35]

Perhaps we should ask a further question: How are we supposed to help rightly other Christians who are experiencing troubles and temptation [Anfechtung] if not with God's own Word? All our own words quickly fail. However, those who "like the master of a household who brings out of his treasure what is new and what is old" (Matt. 13:52)—who can speak out of the abundance of God's Word the wealth of instructions, admonitions, and comforting words from the Scriptures—will be able to drive out demons and help one another through God's Word. We will stop here. "From childhood you have known the sacred writings that are able to instruct you for salvation" (2 Tim. 3:15).[36]

How should we read the Holy Scriptures? In a community living together it is best that its various members assume the task of consecutive reading by taking turns. When this is done, the community will see

35. The translation of the German term *evangelisch* by means of the English word "Protestant" is called for by common usage in German where, for example, *Die Evangelische Kirche Deutchlands* means "The Protestant Church of Germany." The term "evangelical" in English has widely disparate meanings depending on its use in the various religious denominations and thus has not been used here to translate the German word for "Protestant." [GK]

36. The NRSV adds: "through faith in Christ Jesus." [GK]

that it is not easy to read the Scriptures aloud for others. The reading will better suit the subject matter the more plain and simple it is, the more focused it is on the subject matter, the more humble one's attitude. Often the difference between an experienced Christian and a beginner comes out clearly when Scripture is read aloud. It may be taken as a rule for the correct reading of Scripture that the readers should never identify themselves with the person who is speaking in the Bible. It is not I who am angry, but God; it is not I giving comfort, but God; it is not I admonishing, but God admonishing in the Scriptures. Of course, I will be able to express the fact that it is God who is angry, God who is giving comfort and admonishing, by speaking not in a detached, monotonous voice, but only with heartfelt involvement, as one who knows that I myself am being addressed. However, it will make all the difference between a right and a wrong way of reading Scripture if I do not confuse myself with, but rather quite simply serve, God. Otherwise I become rhetorical, over-emotional, sentimental, or coercive; that is to say, I divert the reader's attention to myself instead of the Word—this is the sin of Scripture reading. If we could illustrate this with an example from everyday life, the situation of the one who is reading the Scripture would probably come closest to that in which I read to another person a letter from a friend.[37] I would not read the letter as though I had written it myself. The distance between us would be clearly noticeable as it was read. And yet I would

49  also not be able to read my friend's letter as if it were of no concern to me. On the contrary, because of our close relationship, I would read it with personal interest. Proper reading of Scripture is not a technical exercise that can be learned; it is something that grows or diminishes according to my own spiritual condition. The ponderous, laborious reading of the Bible by many a Christian who has become seasoned through experience often far surpasses a minister's reading, no matter how perfect the latter in form. In a community of Christians living together, one person may also give counsel and help to another in this matter.

The short devotional Bible texts do not need to be lost but can supplement the continuous reading of the Scriptures. They may find their

---

37. Bonhoeffer uses a similar analogy in his lectures on preaching from Finkenwalde. For example, see the student lecture notes edited by Eberhard Bethge from the spring semester of 1935 and 1936, "The Causality and Finality of Preaching," in *WP*, 111–15 (*GS* 4:250–54). [GK]

place as weekly or as daily Bible verses at the beginning of daily worship or at some other time.

*Singing together* [das gemeinsame Lied] joins the praying of the Psalms and the reading of the Scriptures. In this, the voice of the church is heard in praise, thanksgiving, and intercession.

"O sing to the Lord a new song,"[38] the Psalter calls out to us again and again. It is the Christ hymn, new every morning, that a community living together begins to sing in the early morning, the new song that is sung by the whole community of faith in God on earth and in heaven. We are called to join in the singing of it. It is God who has prepared one great song of praise throughout eternity, and those who enter God's community join in this song. It is the song that "the morning stars sang together and all the children of God shouted for joy" (Job 38:7).[39] It is the victory song of the children of Israel after passing through the Red Sea,[40] the Magnificat of Mary after the Annunciation,[41] the song of Paul and Silas when they praised God in the darkness of prison,[42] the song of the singers on the sea of glass after their deliverance, the "song of Moses, the servant of God, and the song of the Lamb" (Rev. 15:3). It is the new song of the heavenly community. Every day in the morning the community of faith on earth joins in this song and in the evening it closes the day with this hymn. The triune God and the works of God are being extolled here. This song has a different sound on earth than it does in heaven. On earth, it is the song of those who believe; in heaven, the song of those who see. On earth, it is a song expressed in inadequate human words; in heaven they are the "things that are not to be told, that no mortal is permitted to repeat" (2 Cor. 12:4), the "new song that no one could learn, except the 144,000" (Rev. 14:3),[43] the song to which the "harps of *God*" are played (Rev. 15:2).[44] What do we know of that new song and the

50

---

38. Pss. 96:1, 98:1.

39. In the NRSV, Job 38:7b reads, "and all the heavenly beings shouted for joy." [GK]

40. See Exod. 15:1-21.

41. See Luke 1:46-55.

42. See Acts 16:25.

43. In the NRSV translation, Rev. 14:3 says "No one could learn that song except the one hundred forty-four thousand who have been redeemed from the earth." [GK]

44. The full passage to which Bonhoeffer refers reads in the NRSV: "And I saw

harps of God? Our new song is an earthly song, a song of pilgrims and sojourners on whom the Word of God has dawned to light their way. Our earthly song is bound to God's Word of revelation in Jesus Christ. It is the simple song of the children of this earth who have been called to be God's children, not ecstatic, not enraptured, but soberly, gratefully, devoutly focused on God's revealed Word.

"Sing and make music in your heart to the Lord" (Eph. 5:19).[45] The new song is sung first in the heart. It cannot be sung at all in any other way. The heart sings because it is filled with Christ. That is why all singing in the congregation is a spiritual thing. Devotion to the Word, incorporation into the community, great humility, and much discipline—these are the prerequisites of all singing together. Wherever the heart does not join in the singing, there is only the dreadful muddle of human self-praise. Wherever the singing is not to the Lord, it is singing to the honor of the self or the music, and the new song becomes a song to idols.

"Speak to one another with psalms, hymns and spiritual songs" (Eph. 5:19).[46] Our song on earth is speech. It is the sung Word. Why do Christians sing when they are together? The reason is, quite simply, that in singing together it is possible for them to speak and pray the same Word at the same time—in other words, for the sake of uniting in the Word. All daily worship, all human concentration should be focused on the Word in the hymn. The fact that we do not speak it in unison, but sing it, only expresses the fact that our spoken words are inadequate to express what we want to say, that the object of our singing reaches far beyond all human words. Nevertheless, we do not mumble unintelligible words; rather we sing words of praise to God, words of thanksgiving, confes-
51   sion, and prayer. Thus the music is completely the servant of the Word. It elucidates the Word in its incomprehensibility.

Because it is completely bound to the Word, the singing of the con-

---

what appeared to be a sea of glass mixed with fire, and those who had conquered the beast and its image and the number of its name, standing beside the sea of glass with harps of God in their hands." Bonhoeffer's allusion to the "beast" of Nazism is subtle. The emphasis in the text is added by Bonhoeffer. [GK]

45. The NRSV varies slightly from Bonhoeffer's text in its translation of Eph. 5:19, which it connects to 5:18b: ". . . but be filled with the Spirit, as you sing psalms and hymns and spiritual songs among yourselves, singing and making melody to the Lord in your hearts." [GK]

46. See note 45 above.

gregation in its worship service, especially the singing of the house church, is essentially singing in unison. Here words and music combine in a unique way. The freely soaring tone of unison singing finds its sole and essential inner support in the words that are sung. It does not need, therefore, the musical support of other parts. The Bohemian Brethren sang: "With one voice let us sing today, in unison and from the bottom of our heart."[47] "So that together you may with one voice glorify the God and Father of our Lord Jesus Christ" (Rom. 15:6). The essence of all congregational singing on this earth is the purity of unison singing—untouched by the unrelated motives of musical excess—the clarity unclouded by the dark desire to lend musicality an autonomy of its own apart from the words; it is the simplicity and unpretentiousness, the humanness and warmth, of this style of singing. Of course, this truth is only gradually and by patient practice disclosed to our oversophisticated ears. Whether or not a community achieves proper unison singing is a question of its spiritual discernment. This is singing from the heart, singing to the Lord, singing the Word; this is singing in unity.

There are several elements hostile to unison singing, which in the community ought to be very rigorously weeded out. There is no place in the worship service where vanity and bad taste can so assert themselves as in the singing. First, there is the improvised second part that one encounters almost everywhere people are supposed to sing together. It attempts to give the necessary background, the missing richness to the free-floating unison sound and in the process kills both the words and the sound. There are the bass or the alto voices that must call everybody's attention to their astonishing range and therefore sing every hymn an octave lower. There is the solo voice that drowns out everything else, bellowing and quavering at the top of its lungs, reveling in the glory of its own fine organ. There are the less dangerous foes of congregational singing, the "unmusical" who cannot sing, of whom there are far fewer than we are led to believe. Finally, there are often those who will not join in the singing because they are particularly moody or nursing hurt feelings; and thus they disturb the community. 52

As difficult as it is, unison singing is much less a musical than a spiritual matter. Only where everybody in the community is prepared to assume an attitude of devotion and discipline can unison singing give us the joy that is its alone, even if it exhibits many musical shortcomings.

---

47. *Ein neues Lied*, no. 74. See editorial note 7 above.

Primarily the Reformation chorales, as well as the hymns of the Bohemian Brethren and pieces from the historic church, are worth considering for practice in unison singing. Starting here, the community will form an opinion on its own as to which hymns in our hymnbook lend themselves to unison singing and which do not. Any doctrinaire attitude, which we encounter so often in this area, is a bad thing. The decision on this issue can only be made on the merits of each case, and here too we should not become iconoclastic. A community of Christians living together will therefore try hard to master as rich a store of hymns as possible that can be sung without music and from memory. It will achieve this goal if in addition to a freely chosen hymn it inserts in every daily worship service several set verses that can be sung between the readings.

Singing, however, should be practiced not just in the daily worship services, but at regular times during the day or week. The more we sing, the more joy we will derive from it. But, above all, the more concentration and discipline and joy we put into our singing, the richer will be the blessing that will come to the whole life of the community from singing together.

It is the voice of the church that is heard in singing together. It is not I who sing, but the church. However, as a member of the church, I may share in its song. Thus all true singing together must serve to widen our spiritual horizon. It must enable us to recognize our small community as a member of the great Christian church [Christenheit] on earth and 53 must help us willingly and joyfully to take our place in the song of the church with our singing, be it feeble or good.

God's Word, the voice of the church, and our prayer belong together. So we must now speak of prayer together. "If two of you agree about anything you ask for, it will be done for you by my Father in heaven" (Matt. 18:19).[48] There is no part of daily worship together that causes us such serious difficulties and trouble as does common prayer, for here we ourselves are supposed to speak. We have heard God's Word and we have had the privilege of joining in the song of the church, but now we are to pray to God as a community, and this prayer must really be *our* word, *our* prayer—for this day, for our work, for our community, for the particular needs and sins that commonly oppress us, for the persons who are com-

---

48. In both Luther's translation and in the NRSV the words "on earth" are included in this quotation. [GK]

mitted to our care. Or should we really not pray for ourselves at all?
Should the desire for prayer together with our own lips and in our own
words be a forbidden thing? No matter what objections there may be to
prayer together, it simply could not be any other way. Christians may and
should pray together to God in their own words when they desire to live
together under the Word of God. They have requests, gratitude, and
intercessions to bring in common to God, and they should do so joyfully
and confidently. All our fear of one another, all our inhibitions about
praying freely in our own words in the presence of others, can diminish
where the common prayer of the community is brought before God by
one of its members with dignity and simplicity. Likewise, however, all
our observations and criticisms should cease whenever weak words of
prayer are offered in the name of Jesus Christ. It is in fact the most normal thing in our common Christian life to pray together. As good and
useful as our scruples may be about keeping our prayer pure and biblical, they must nevertheless not stifle the free prayer itself that is so necessary, for it has been endowed with great promise by Jesus Christ.      54

The extemporaneous prayer at the close of daily worship normally
will be said by the head of the house [Hausvater]. But in any case it is
best that it always be said by the same person. That places an unexpected responsibility on this person, but in order to safeguard the prayer
from the wrong kind of scrutiny and from false subjectivity, one person
should pray for all the community for an extended period of time.

The first condition that makes it possible for individuals to pray for
the community is the intercession of all the others for such persons and
for their praying. How could one person pray the prayer of the community without being held up and supported in prayer by the community
itself? At precisely this point every word of criticism must be transformed into more faithful intercession and mutual help. How easily a
community can split apart if this is not done!

Extemporaneous prayer in daily worship together should be the
prayer of the community and not that of the individual who is praying.
It is this individual's task to pray for the community. Thus such a person
will have to share the daily life of the community and must know the
cares and needs, the joys and thanksgivings, the requests and hopes of
the others. The community's work and everything that it involves must
not be unknown to the individual who prays for the community. One
prays as a believer among other Christians. It will require self-examina-

tion and watchfulness if individuals are not to confuse their own hearts with the heart of the community, if a person really is to be guided solely by the task of praying for the community. For this reason it will be good if the persons who have been assigned this task are constantly given the benefit of counsel and help from others in the community, if they receive suggestions and requests to remember this or that need, work, or even a particular person in the prayer. Thus the prayer will become more and more the common prayer of all.

Even extemporaneous prayer will be determined by a certain internal order. It is not the chaotic outburst of a human heart, but the prayer of an internally ordered community. Thus certain prayer requests will recur daily, even if they may perhaps recur in different ways. At first there may be some monotony in the daily repetition of the same petitions that are entrusted to us as a community, but later freedom from an all too individualistic form of prayer will surely be found. If it is possible to add to the number of daily recurring petitions, a weekly order might be tried, as has been proposed on occasion. If that is not possible in the common prayers, it is certainly a help in one's personal times of prayer. Relating the prayer to one of the Scripture readings also will prove helpful for liberating spontaneous prayer from the arbitrariness of subjectivity. This gives support and substance to the prayer.

From time to time a problem will arise where the person given the job of offering prayer for the community feels inwardly unable to offer prayer and would prefer to turn over the task to someone else for the day. However, that is not advisable. Otherwise, the community's prayers will be too easily controlled by moods that have nothing to do with life in the spirit. The persons assigned to pray for the community should learn what it means to have a duty to perform in the congregation even at a time when they would like to avoid this task because they are weighed down by inner emptiness and weariness or by personal guilt. The other members of the community should support them in their weakness, in their inability to pray. Perhaps then the words of Paul will come true: "We do not know how to pray as we ought, but that very Spirit intercedes with sighs too deep for words" (Rom. 8:26).[49] It is of great importance that the community understands, supports, and prays the prayer of these individuals as its own.

---

49. Bonhoeffer's biblical text states "*what* we ought to pray for" ["*was wir beten sollen*"] and adds the word "holy" to designate the Spirit [*Heilige Geist*]. [GK]

The use of set prayers can be a help even for a small community living together under certain circumstances, but often it becomes only an evasion of real prayer. By using ecclesial forms and the church's wealth of thought, we can easily deceive ourselves about our own prayer life. The prayers then become beautiful and profound, but not genuine. As helpful as the church's tradition of prayer is for learning how to pray, nevertheless it cannot take the place of the prayer that I owe to my God today. Here the poorest stammering can be better than the best-phrased prayer. It goes without saying that the state of affairs in public worship services is different from the daily worship of the community living together.

Often in Christian everyday-life communities [Lebensgemeinschaft] there will be a desire for special communities of prayer over and above the prayers in the daily worship together. Here there can probably be no set rule except one—the meetings of such groups should be held only where there is a common desire for them and where it is certain that there will be common participation in a particular prayer service [Gebetstunde]. Any individual undertakings of this kind can easily plant the seed of corruption in the community. It is precisely in this area that it must prove true that the strong support the weak, and the weak not rule over the strong.[50] The New Testament teaches us that a free community of prayer is the most obvious and natural thing and may be viewed without suspicion. But where mistrust and anxiety exist, one must bear with the other in patience. Let nothing be done by force, but everything be done in freedom and love.

We have considered thus far the daily morning worship of Christian everyday-life communities. God's Word, the hymns of the church, and the prayers of the community of faith stand at the beginning of the day. Only when the community has been provided and strengthened with the bread of eternal life does it gather together to receive from God earthly bread for this bodily life. Giving thanks and asking God's bless-

---

50. This is an allusion to Rom. 14:1-15 and 1 Cor. 8:1-13. In the background lurk the arguments over the Aryan Clause and the continued resistance of the Confessing Church to the proposed laws that appeared to legalize discrimination against baptized members of Jewish ancestry. Eberhard Bethge reports that Bonhoeffer used Romans 14 in his stinging rejection of proposals that the churches effect a compromise on the issue of expelling the Jewish Christians from their ranks, perhaps even to the extent of setting up separate congregations based on racial conformity or nonconformity. See Bethge, *Dietrich Bonhoeffer*, 219–20. [GK]

56

ing, the Christian house church takes its daily bread from the hand of
the Lord. Ever since Jesus Christ sat at table with his disciples, the community at the table [*Tischgemeinschaft*] of Christ's congregation has been
blessed by his presence. "When he was at the table with them, he took
bread, blessed and broke it, and gave it to them. Then their eyes were
opened, and they recognized him" (Luke 24:30-31a). The Scriptures
speak of three kinds of community at the table that Jesus keeps with his
own: the daily breaking of bread together at meals, the breaking of
bread together at the Lord's Supper, and the final breaking of bread
together in the reign of God. But in all three, the one thing that counts
is that "their eyes were opened and they recognized him." What does it
mean to recognize Jesus Christ by way of these gifts? It means, *first*, to
recognize Christ as the giver of all gifts, as the Lord and Creator—with
57    the Father and the Holy Spirit—of this our world. Therefore, the community at the table prays "and let *your* gifts to us be blessed,"[51] and thus
declares its faith in the eternal deity of Jesus Christ. *Second*, the congregation recognizes that all earthly gifts are given to it only for the sake of
Christ, as this whole world is preserved only for the sake of Jesus Christ—
for the sake of Christ's Word and its proclamation. Christ is the true
bread of life, not only the giver but the gift itself, for whose sake all
earthly gifts exist. God patiently preserves us with God's own good gifts
only because the Word of Jesus Christ is still to go forth and encounter
faith, because our faith is not yet perfected. That is why the Christian
congregation breaking bread together at the table prays in Luther's
words, "O Lord God, dear heavenly Father, bless us and these your gifts
which we receive from your bountiful goodness, through *Jesus Christ our
Lord*. Amen"[52]—and thus declares its faith in Jesus Christ as the divine
mediator and savior. *Third*, the community of Jesus believes that its Lord

---

51. Bonhoeffer's text reads: "Und segne, was du uns bescheret hast." These
words were taken by Bonhoeffer from the "Prayer before Meals" attached to
"Lieder Anhang" of the *Evangelisches Gesangbuch*, 72, no. 5. Cf. *Evangelisches
Kirchengesangbuch*, 662. See the following editorial note. [GK]

52. This full "Prayer Before Meals" is cited from the text attached to the
"Lieder Anhang" of the *Evangelisches Gesangbuch*, 72, no. 3. Luther's "Grace
Before Meals" can be found in his *Enchiridion: Der kleine Katechismus für die
gemeine Pfarrherrn und Prediger*, WA, 30/1:378, and *The Book of Concord: The Confessions of the Evangelical Lutheran Church*, 353. The translation here is by courtesy
of Timothy Wengert.

desires to be present wherever it asks him to be present. That is why it prays: "Come, Lord Jesus, be our guest,"[53] thus confessing the gracious omnipresence of Jesus Christ. Every breaking of bread together fills Christians with gratitude for the present Lord and God, Jesus Christ. It is not as if they were seeking any unhealthy spiritualization of material gifts; rather, in their wholehearted joy in the good gifts of this physical life, Christians recognize their Lord as the true giver of all good gifts. And beyond this, they recognize their Lord as the true gift, the true bread of life itself, and finally as the one who calls them to the joyful banquet in the reign of God. So in a special way, the daily breaking of bread together binds Christians to their Lord and to one another. At the table they recognize their Lord as the one who breaks bread for them. The eyes of their faith are opened.

The breaking of bread together has a festive quality. In the midst of the working day given to us again and again, it is a reminder that God rested after God's work, and that the Sabbath is the meaning and the goal of the week with its toil. Our life is not only a great deal of trouble and hard work; it is also refreshment and joy in God's goodness. We labor, but God nourishes and sustains us. That is a reason to celebrate. People should not eat the bread of anxious toil (Ps. 127:2). Rather "eat your bread with enjoyment" (Eccles. 9:7), "so I commend enjoyment, for there is nothing better for people under the sun than to eat, and drink, and enjoy themselves" (Eccles. 8:15). But of course, "apart from him, who can eat or who can have enjoyment?" (Eccles. 2:25). It is said of the seventy elders of Israel who climbed Mount Sinai with Moses and Aaron that "they beheld God, and they ate and drank" (Exod. 24:11). God will not tolerate the unfestive, joyless manner in which we eat our bread with sighs of groaning, with pompous, self-important busyness, or even with shame. Through the daily meal God is calling us to rejoice, to celebrate in the midst of our working day.

Christian community at the table also signifies obligation. It is *our* daily bread that we eat, not my own.[54] We share our bread. Thus we are firmly bound to one another not only in the Spirit, but with our whole physical being. The *one* bread that is given to our community unites us in

58

---

53. "Komm, Herr Jesu, sei unser Gast." This the first line of the prayer cited by Bonhoeffer from *Evangelisches Gesangbuch*, 72, no. 5. See note 51 above.

54. Matt. 6:11 says "Give us this day *our* daily bread"; in Luke 11:3 we read "Give us each day *our* daily bread." [GK]

a firm covenant.[55] Now no one must hunger as long as the other has bread, and whoever shatters this community of our bodily life also shatters the community of the Spirit. Both are inextricably linked together. "Share your bread with the hungry" (Isa. 58:7).[56] "Do not despise the hungry" (Sirach 4:2),[57] for the Lord meets us in the hungry (Matt. 25:37). "If a brother or sister is naked and lacks daily food, and one of you says to them, 'Go in peace; keep warm and eat your fill,' and yet you do not supply their bodily needs, what is the good of that?" (James 2:15f.). As long as we eat our bread together, we will have enough even with the smallest amount. Hunger begins only when people desire to keep their own bread for themselves. That is a strange divine law. Could not the story of the miraculous feeding of the 5,000 with two fish and five loaves of bread also have this meaning, along with many others?[58]

The breaking of bread together teaches Christians that here they still eat the perishable bread of the earthly pilgrimage. But if they share this bread with one another, they will also one day receive together imperishable bread in the Father's house. "Blessed is the one who will eat bread in the reign of God" (Luke 14:15).

After the first morning hour, the Christian's day until evening belongs to *work*. "People go out to their work and to their labor until the evening" (Ps. 104:23). In most cases a community of Christians living together will separate for the duration of the working hours. Praying and working are two different things. Prayer should not be hindered by work, but neither should work be hindered by prayer. Just as it was God's will that human beings should work six days and rest and celebrate before the face of God on the seventh, so it is also God's will that every day should

---

55. Bonhoeffer bases this statement on 1 Cor. 10:17, which reads, "Because there is one bread, we who are many are one body, for we all partake of the one bread." This passage is underlined in Bonhoeffer's Greek New Testament.

56. The context of this passage from Isaiah is the prophet's demand that the people not fool themselves into thinking God is pleased with the mere external observance of the fast days. Instead, the prophet challenges the people to do something really pleasing to the Lord God of Israel, namely, to practice justice and the works of mercy. Bonhoeffer's German text varies slightly from the NRSV. [GK]

57. Bonhoeffer refers to Ecclesiasticus, or The Wisdom of Jesus Son of Sirach. His German text differs slightly from the NRSV, which has "Do not grieve the hungry." [GK]

58. See Matt. 14:13-21.

be marked for the Christian both by prayer and work. Prayer also requires its own time. But the longest part of the day belongs to work. The inseparable unity of both will only become clear when work and prayer each receives its own undivided due. Without the burden and labor of the day, prayer is not prayer; and without prayer, work is not work. Only the Christian knows that. Thus it is precisely in the clear distinction between them that their oneness becomes apparent.

Work puts human beings in the world of things. It requires achievement from them. Christians step out of the world of personal encounter into the world of impersonal things, the "It"; and this new encounter frees them for objectivity, for the world of the It is only an instrument in the hand of God for the purification of Christians from all self-absorption and selfishness. The work of the world can only be accomplished    60 where people forget themselves, where they lose themselves in a cause, reality, the task, the It. Christians learn at work to allow the task to set the bounds for them. Thus, for them, work becomes a remedy for the lethargy and laziness of the flesh. The demands of the flesh die in the world of things. But that can only happen where Christians break through the It to the "You" ["Du"] of God,[59] who commands the work and the deed and makes them serve to liberate Christians from themselves. In this process work does not cease to be work; but the severity and rigor of labor is sought all the more by those who know what good it does them. The continuing conflict with the It remains. But at the same time the breakthrough has been made. The unity of prayer and work, the unity of the day, is found because finding the You of God[60] behind

59. On the question of the distinction Bonhoeffer makes between a material-reified and a personalized-social understanding of being, see *AB* 111f., 115, 123f., where he insists that one can understand the mode of being of divine revelation only with reference to the personal. In appreciating this distinction, it is likewise helpful to read Bonhoeffer's letter of February 21, 1944, in which he reflects on the difference between fate and God's providence, between resistance and submission (*LPP*, 217–18).

60. The pronoun *Du* in German represents the familiar, intimate form of "you." It is used to address members of one's family, children, and close friends. Otherwise, one must use the "polite," more formal pronoun *Sie*, along with the third-person form of the verb. In theological discourse, the *Ich-Du* relationship often has been translated into English by "I-Thou." See 41, editorial note 19 above. Cf. Martin Buber's oft-quoted distinction between "I-Thou (You)" (*Ich-Du*) relationships and "I-It" (*Ich-Es*) relationships to indicate the various levels of one's being human; see Buber, *I and Thou*, 54, 62, 66. Walter Kaufmann, the

the It of the day's work is what Paul means by his admonition to "pray without ceasing" (1 Thess. 5:17). The prayer of the Christian reaches, therefore, beyond the time allocated to it and extends into the midst of the work. It surrounds the whole day, and in so doing, it does not hinder the work; it promotes work, affirms work, gives work great significance and joyfulness. Thus every word, every deed, every piece of work of the Christian becomes a prayer, not in the unreal sense of being constantly distracted from the task that must be done, but in a real breakthrough from the hard It to the gracious You [Du]. "And whatever you do, in word or deed, do everything in the name of the Lord Jesus" (Col. 3:17).[61]

The whole day now acquires an order and a discipline gained by winning this unity of the day. This order and discipline must be sought and found in the morning prayer. It will stand the test at work. Prayer offered in early morning is decisive for the day. The wasted time we are ashamed of, the temptations we succumb to, the weakness and discouragement in our work, the disorder and lack of discipline in our thinking and in our dealings with other people—all these very frequently have their cause in our neglect of morning prayer. The ordering and scheduling of our time will become more secure when it comes from prayer. The temptations of the working day will be overcome by this breakthrough to God. The decisions that are demanded by our work will become simpler and easier when they are made not in fear of other people, but solely before the face of God. "Whatever you do, do it from your hearts, as done for the Lord and not done for human beings" (Col. 3:23).[62] Even routine mechanical work will be performed more patiently when it comes from the knowledge of God and God's command. Our strength and energy for work increase when we have asked God to give us the strength we need for our daily work.

61

---

English translator of this edition, uses the more customary form "you" instead of "thou" and makes a case for this in his Prologue. Here, we translate *Du* as "you" in order to avoid the archaic "Thou." [GK]

61. In using the singular, "word or deed" (*Wort oder Werk*) Bonhoeffer, following the Greek text, is correcting Martin Luther's translation. Luther's Bible has the plural, "with words or with deeds" (*mit Worten oder mit Werken*).

62. [Trans. GK] The NRSV has: "Whatever your task, put yourselves into it, as done for the Lord and not for your masters." In a footnote, the NRSV concedes that the Greek text has, "not for men," but notes also that the same word is used in Greek for "master" and "lord." Here Bonhoeffer's word is "Menschen" or human beings. [GK]

Where it is possible, the midday hour becomes for a community of Christians living together a brief rest on their journey through the day. Half of the day is past. The congregation thanks God and asks for protection until evening. It receives its daily bread and prays in the words of a Reformation hymn: "Feed your children, God most holy, / Comfort sinners poor and lowly."[63] It is God who must feed us. We cannot and dare not take it for ourselves because we poor sinners have not merited it. Thus the meal God serves us becomes a consolation for the afflicted, for it is proof of the grace and faithfulness with which God preserves and guides God's children. It is true that the Scripture says that "anyone unwilling to work should not eat" (2 Thess. 3:10) and thus makes the receiving of bread strictly dependent on working for it. But the Scriptures do not say anything about any claim that working persons have on God for their bread. It is true that work is commanded, but the bread is God's free and gracious gift. We cannot simply take it for granted that our own work provides us with bread; rather this is God's order of grace. The day belongs to God alone. Hence in the middle of the day, the Christian community of faith gathers and lets God invite them to the table. The midday hour is one of the seven prayer hours of the church and of the singer of the Psalms.[64] At the height of the day the church

---

63. This prayer is cited by Bonhoeffer from *Evangelisches Gesangbuch*, 275. The same prayer is included in the *Evangelisches Kirchengesangbuch*, 662. It is part of a hymn by Johann Heermann (1585–1647), based on Psalm 145:15-16. The translation here is a slight variant of the translation prepared for *The Lutheran Hymnal*, based in turn on the English version in the *Australian Lutheran Hymn-Book* of 1925. [GK]

64. The "Hour of Sext" is what is meant here. In the Jewish system of counting, the day begins at six o'clock, according to contemporary ways of telling time. Bonhoeffer was clearly familiar with the structure of prayer at the prescribed hours in the "Divine Office" and Breviary of the Roman Catholic Church's liturgical practice: Matins, Lauds, Terce, Sext, None, Vespers, and Compline. In fact, Bonhoeffer had in his possession two liturgical texts then in use in Roman Catholic monasteries and seminaries: *Liber usualis Missae et Officii pro Dominicis et Festis cum cantu Gregoriano* and *Die Komplet–nach dem Benediktinischen und Römischen Brevier*. The idea of sanctifying the day and the night is of long standing in both Judaism and Christianity. Early Christian communities began to link the stipulated hours of prayer with the various phases of Christ's passion, death, and resurrection. That practice did not last. Quite soon other moments of Christ's life, beginning with the incarnation, were incorporated into the hours of prayer. See Josef Jungmann, *The Early Liturgy to the Time of Gregory the Great*, 100–107. [GK]

62   invokes the triune God in praise of God's wonders and in prayer for help
     and speedy redemption. At midday the heavens were darkened above
     the cross of Jesus.[65] The work of atonement was approaching its comple-
     tion.[66] Where a community of Christians living together is able to be
     together at this hour for a brief daily worship time of song and prayer, it
     will not do so in vain.

     The day's work comes to an end. When the day has been hard and toil-
     some, the Christian will understand what Paul Gerhardt meant when he
     sang: "Head, hands and feet so tired, / Are glad the day's expired, /
     That work comes to an end; / My heart is fill'd with gladness / That
     God from all earth's sadness, / And from sin's toil relief will send."[67]
     One day is long enough to keep one's faith; the next day will have its own
     worries.

     The community of Christians living together gathers together again.
     The evening breaking of bread together and the final daily worship ser-
     vice bring them together. With the disciples in Emmaus they ask: "Lord,
     stay with us, because it is almost evening and the day is now nearly
     over."[68] It is a good thing if the daily evening worship can really be held
     at the end of the day, thus becoming the last word before the night's rest.
     When night falls, the true light of God's Word shines brighter for the
     community of faith. The prayer of the Psalms, a Scripture reading, a
     hymn, and a prayer together close the day as they opened it. We still
     need to say a few words on the subject of evening prayer. This is the
     special place for intercession together. After the day's work has been
     completed, we ask for God's blessing, peace, and preservation for the
     whole of Christianity, for our congregation, for pastors in their min-

     ----

     65. Bonhoeffer is alluding to Mark 15:33. See editorial note 64 above on the
     early Christian practice of having the hours of prayer correspond to the phases
     of Christ's passion, death, and resurrection. [GK]

     66. The allusion here is to John 19:28.

     67. This is v. 5 of Paul Gerhardt's hymn, "Nun ruhen alle Wälder" (Now all the
     woods are sleeping), from *Evangelisches Gesangbuch*, no. 280, which is also in-
     cluded in the *Evangelisches Kirchengesangbuch*, no. 361, Gerhardt (1607–76) based
     this hymn on Ps. 63:5-9. The translation is by John Kelly in *Paul Gerhardt's Spiri-
     tual Songs*, 285. An alternate translation, often used where the hymn is sung in
     English, can be found in Catherine Winkworth, *Lyra Germanica*, 227. [GK]

     68. Luke 24:29. The NRSV omits the word "Lord."

istries, for the poor, the wretched and lonely, for the sick and dying, for our neighbors, for our family at home, and for our community. When could we ever have a deeper awareness of God's power and working than in the hour when we lay aside our own work and entrust ourselves to God's faithful hands? When are we more prepared to pray for blessing, peace, and preservation than the time when our activity is at an end? When we grow tired, God works. "The Guardian of Israel neither slumbers nor sleeps."[69] Our request for the forgiveness of every wrong we have done to God and to one another, for God's forgiveness and that of our brothers, and for the willingness gladly to forgive any wrong done to us, belongs then, too, especially in the evening prayers of a community of Christians living together. It is an old custom of the monasteries that by set practice in the daily evening worship the abbot asks his brothers to forgive him for all the sins of omission and wrongdoings committed against them. After the brothers assure him of their forgiveness, they likewise ask the abbot to forgive them for their sins of omission and wrongdoings and receive his forgiveness. "Do not let the sun go down on your anger" (Eph. 4:26). It is a decisive rule of every Christian community that every division that the day has caused must be healed in the evening. It is perilous for the Christian to go to bed with an unreconciled heart. Therefore, it is a good idea especially to include the request for mutual forgiveness in every evening's prayers, so that reconciliation can be achieved and renewal of the community established. Finally, in all the old evening prayers, it is striking how frequently we encounter their plea for preservation during the night from the devil, from terror and from an evil, sudden death. The ancients were keenly aware of human helplessness while sleeping, the kinship of sleep with death, and the devil's cunning in causing our downfall when we are defenseless. That is why they prayed for the assistance of the holy angels and their golden weapons, for the presence of the heavenly hosts at the time when Satan would gain power over us. Most remarkable and profound is the ancient church's request that, when our eyes are closed in sleep, God may nevertheless keep our hearts alert to God. It is a prayer that God may dwell with us and in us, even when we feel and know nothing, that God may keep our hearts pure and holy in spite of all the worries and temptations

63

---

69. Ps. 121:4. The NRSV has: "He who keeps Israel will neither slumber nor sleep." [GK]

of the night, that God may prepare our hearts to hear the call at any time and, like the boy Samuel, answer even in the night, "Speak, Lord, for your servant is listening" (1 Sam. 3:10).[70] Even while sleeping we are in the hands of God or in the power of the evil one. Even while we sleep, God can perform miracles upon us or the evil one can cause devastation in us. So we pray in the evening: "Though our eyes in sleep will close, / May our hearts in you repose, / Protect us, God, with your right arm, / And shield our souls from sin's cruel harm" (Luther).[71] But the word of the Psalter stands over the morning and the evening: "Yours is the day, yours also the night" (Ps. 74:16).

---

70. The NRSV omits the word "Lord." [GK]

71. [Trans. GK] Bonhoeffer's German text is taken from *Ein neues Lied*, no. 303. These lines, with slight variations, are from *Evangelisches Gesangbuch*, no. 481, v. 3, and *Evangelisches Kirchengesangbuch*, no. 353, v. 4. The hymn, based on Ps. 121:7, is derived from a translation into German by Erasmus Alber (1500–53) of the early church hymn, "Christe, qui Splendor et Dies" (O Christ who are splendid light and day). The *Evangelisches Kirchengesangbuch* traces the melody of the "Low German translation" of this hymn to Martin Luther in the year 1529. [GK]

# THE DAY ALONE

"THE PRAISE OF SILENCE befits you, O God, in Zion" (Ps. 65:2 [1]).[1] Many persons seek community because they are afraid of loneliness [der Einsamkeit]. Because they can no longer endure being alone, such people are driven to seek the company of others. Christians, too, who cannot cope on their own, and who in their own lives have had some bad experiences, hope to experience help with this in the company of other people. More often than not, they are disappointed. They then blame

---

1. It is not certain which Bible translation, if not his own, Bonhoeffer is using here. Bonhoeffer's text is a wide departure from Luther's Bible, which reads: "God, you are praised by silence in Zion [and vows will be rendered to you]." Bonhoeffer's German rendering of the text follows closely the Hebrew of this verse, which translated literally is "To you the praise of silence (is given) in Zion." Certainly, this Hebrew version fits into the theme of this chapter of *Life Together*. The NRSV lists this as v. 1 and renders the text: "Praise is due to you, O God, in Zion." Bonhoeffer's positive attitude toward silence and solitude also comes across in his Christology lectures in his opening statement: "Teaching about Christ begins in silence. 'Be still, for that is the absolute,' writes Kierkegaard. That has nothing to do with the mystagogical silence that in its dumbness is nothing more than secret chattering of the soul with itself. The silence of the church is silence before the Word" (*CC*, 27; trans. altered). This section of *Life Together* also has strong connections with several passages from *The Imitation of Christ*, where Thomas à Kempis writes: "In silence and quietness of heart a devout soul profits much and learns the hidden meaning of Scripture, and finds there many sweet tears of devotion as well, with which every night the soul washes itself mightily from all sin, that it may be the more familiar with God, to the degree that it is separated from the clamorous noise of worldly business" (1:20, 57). See editorial note 10 below on Bonhoeffer's fondness for this religious classic. [GK]

the community for what is really their own fault. The Christian community is not a spiritual sanatorium. Those who take refuge in community while fleeing from themselves are misusing it to indulge in empty talk and distraction, no matter how spiritual this idle talk and distraction may appear. In reality they are not seeking community at all, but only a thrill that will allow them to forget their isolation [Vereinsamung] for a short time. It is precisely such misuse of community that creates the deadly isolation of human beings. Such attempts to find healing result in the undermining of speech and all genuine experience and, finally, resignation and spiritual death.

*Whoever cannot be alone [allein] should beware of community.*[2] Such people will only do harm to themselves and to the community. Alone you stood before God when God called you. Alone you had to obey God's voice. Alone you had to take up your cross, struggle, and pray and alone you will die and give an account to God. You cannot avoid yourself, for it is precisely God who has singled you out. If you do not want to be alone, you are rejecting Christ's call to you, and you can have no part in the community of those who are called. "The confrontation with death and its demands comes to us all; no one can die for another. All must fight their own battle with death by themselves, alone. I will not be with you then, nor you with me" (Luther).[3]

But the reverse is also true. *Whoever cannot stand being in community should beware of being alone.* You are called into the community of faith; the call was not meant for you alone. You carry your cross, you struggle, and you pray in the community of faith, the community of those who are

66

---

2. Bonhoeffer uses a number of terms in this section to express the shades of meaning between being alone [allein] and being lonely [einsam], between social isolation [Einsamkeit] that one does not choose—which we have translated as "loneliness"—and intentionally chosen times alone with one's self [Alleinsein or Einsamkeit]— which we have rendered as either "being alone" (which in English has a more neutral connotation) or "solitude" (which in English has a more positive connotation). Because Bonhoeffer's own usage is not entirely consistent in this regard, where it might otherwise be unclear which term Bonhoeffer is using, we have included the German term. [GK]

3. Luther, "Erste der Invocavitpredigten," 1522, *WA*, 10/3: 1–2. Bonhoeffer quotes this same passage in *CS*, 128, but there Bonhoeffer reverses the order of the dialectic, and insists that while one dies alone, one dies in communion with Jesus Christ and the communion of saints, which are made concrete in the Christian congregation. See editorial note 4 below. [GK]

called. You are not alone even when you die, and on the day of judgment you will be only one member of the great community of faith of Jesus Christ. If you neglect the community of other Christians, you reject the call of Jesus Christ, and thus your being alone [Alleinsein] can only become harmful for you. "If I die, then I am not alone in death; if I suffer, they (the community of faith) suffer with me" (Luther).[4]

We recognize, then, that only as we stand within the community can we be alone, and only those who are alone can live in the community.[5] Both belong together. Only in the community do we learn to be properly alone [allein]; and only in being alone [Alleinsein] do we learn to live properly in the community. It is not as if the one preceded the other; rather both begin at the same time, namely, with the call of Jesus Christ.

Each taken by itself has profound pitfalls and perils. Those who want community without solitude [Alleinsein] plunge into the void of words and feelings, and those who seek solitude without community perish in the bottomless pit of vanity, self-infatuation, and despair.

Whoever cannot be alone should beware of community. Whoever cannot stand being in community should beware of being alone.

The day together of Christians who live in community is accompanied by each individual's day alone. That is the way it must be. The day together will be unfruitful without the day alone, both for the community and for the individual.

The mark of solitude [Einsamkeit] is silence, just as speech is the mark of community. Silence and speech have the same inner connection and distinction as do being alone [Alleinsein] and community. One does not exist without the other. Genuine speech comes out of silence, and genuine silence comes out of speech.

67

---

4. Bonhoeffer quotes from Luther's sermon, "A Treatise Concerning the Blessed Sacrament of the Holy and True Body of Christ and Concerning the Brotherhood," 1519, in *LW*, 35/1: 54 (*WA*, 2:745). Bonhoeffer omits the remaining portion of the sentence: "with all the holy angels and the blessed in heaven, and pious people on earth." Bonhoeffer refers to this sermon in *CS* 127 and 229, notes 60, 61; *AB* 131, note 1 and 134, note 1; and in "Das Wesen der Kirche" (The nature of the church), Lectures in the Summer Semester, 1932, *GS* 5:263–64. [GK]

5. The reader should note the similar dialectical relationship between belief [*Glaube*] and obedience [*Gehorsamkeit*] as stated in *CD* (61–86), which also is from the Finkenwalde period. [GK]

Silence does not mean being incapable of speech, just as speech[6] does not mean idle talk. Being incapable of speech does not create solitude, and idle talk does not create community. "Silence is the excess, the inebriation, the sacrifice of speech. But being incapable of speech is not holy; it is like a thing that has only been mutilated, not sacrificed. Zachary was incapable of speech, rather than being silent. If he had accepted the revelation, he may perhaps have come out of the temple not incapable of speaking, but silent" (Ernest Hello).[7] That speaking which reestablishes and binds the community together is accompanied by silence. "There is a time . . . to keep silence and a time to speak" (Eccles. 3:7).[8] Just as there are certain times in a Christian's day for speaking the Word, particularly the time of daily worship and prayer together, so the day also needs certain times of silence under the Word and silence that comes out of the Word. These will mainly be the times before and after hearing the Word. The Word comes not to the noise-makers but to those who are silent. The stillness of the temple is the sign of God's holy presence in the Word.

There is an indifferent or even negative attitude toward silence which sees in it a disparagement of God's revelation in the Word. Silence is misunderstood as a solemn gesture, as a mystical desire to get beyond the Word. Silence is no longer seen in its essential relationship to the Word, as the simple act of the individual who falls silent under the Word of God. We are silent before hearing the Word because our thoughts are already focused on the Word, as children are quiet when they enter their father's room.[9] We are silent after hearing the Word because the Word is

68

6. "Speech" here translates the German *Wort,* which also can be translated as "speaking," "words," or "the Word (of God)." Because as a noun *Wort* is always capitalized, it is impossible in the German to tell which is meant, other than from context. [GK]

7. Ernest Hello, *Worte Gottes* (Word of God), 91. Bonhoeffer's quotation from Hello omits several words after the initial word, "silence," hence, for greater accuracy the quotation should read "Silence . . . is," etc. Ernest Hello (1828–85) was a distinguished religious writer and advocate of renewal in the Catholic church.

8. Bonhoeffer, following the Luther Bible, gives as reference for this text *Pred. Sal.,* the abbreviation for *Prediger Salomo* (Preacher Solomon). The NRSV calls this the book of Ecclesiastes, from the Greek translation of the Hebrew title Qoheleth, the "Teacher," who assumes the name of Solomon. [GK]

9. Bonhoeffer's biographer, Eberhard Bethge, has observed that "Seventy years ago this is the way the children stepped into the room of Karl Bonhoeffer

still speaking and living and dwelling within us. We are silent early in the morning because God should have the first word, and we are silent before going to bed because the last word also belongs to God. We remain silent solely for the sake of the Word, not thereby to dishonor the Word but rather to honor and receive it properly. In the end, silence means nothing other than waiting for God's Word and coming from God's Word with a blessing. But everybody knows this is something that needs to be learned in these days when idle talk has gained the upper hand. Real silence, real stillness, really holding one's tongue, comes only as the sober consequence of spiritual silence.

This silence before the Word, however, will have an impact on the whole day. If we have learned to be silent before the Word, we will also learn to manage our silence and our speech during the day. Silence can be forbidden, self-satisfied, haughty, or insulting. From this it follows that silence in itself can never be the issue. The silence of the Christian is listening silence, humble stillness that may be broken at any time for the sake of humility. It is silence in conjunction with the Word. This is what Thomas à Kempis meant when he said: "No one speaks more confidently than the one who gladly remains silent."[10] There is a wonderful power in being silent—the power of clarification, purification, and focus on what is essential. This is true even when considered from a purely profane point of view. But silence before the Word leads to proper hearing and thus also to proper speaking of God's Word at the right time. Much that is unnecessary remains unsaid. But what is essential and helpful can be said in a few words.

When a community lives close together in a confined space and outwardly cannot give the individual the necessary quiet, then regular times of silence are absolutely essential. After a period of silence, we            69

---

(Dietrich's father) when they lived in the Wangenheimstrasse." Bethge, "Afterword," 4.

10. [Trans. GK] Cf. *The Imitation of Christ*, 1:20, 56. *The Imitation of Christ* was one of Bonhoeffer's favorite texts and sources of spiritual inspiration both in his work as director of the Finkenwalde Seminary and during his imprisonment. He cites it under the literature recommended in *SPC,* 78. The personal copy he read from in his cell in Tegel Prison was later given to the Anglican Bishop George Bell of Chichester, when Bell visited Bonhoeffer's parents in their Berlin home toward the end of October 1945. After Bishop Bell's death in 1958, Mrs. Bell donated this book to the Dietrich Bonhoeffer Church in the Sydenham section of London, where it is located today. [GK]

encounter others in a different and fresh way. Many a community living together will only be able to ensure the individual's right to be alone by adopting a set daily discipline, and thereby will keep the community itself from harm.

We will not discuss here all the wonderful fruits that can come to Christians in solitude [Alleinsein] and silence. It is all too easy to go dangerously astray in this matter. We could also probably cite many a dubious experience that can grow out of silence. Silence can be a dreadful wasteland with all its isolated stretches and terrors. It can also be a paradise of self-deception. One is not better than the other. Be that as it may, let none expect from silence anything but a simple encounter with the Word of God for the sake of which Christians have entered into silence. This encounter, however, is given to them as a gift. Their silence will be richly rewarded if they do not set any conditions on how they expect this encounter to take place or what they hope to get from it, but simply accept it as it comes.

There are three things for which the Christian needs a regular time alone during the day: *meditation on the Scripture, prayer,* and *intercession.* All three should find a place in the *daily period of meditation.*[11] There is no reason to be concerned about the use of this word "meditation." In this case we are making our own an old word of the church and the Reformation.

One might ask why a special time is needed for this, since we already have everything we need in daily worship together. In the following we will arrive at the answer to this question.

The period of meditation is useful for personal consideration of Scripture, personal prayer, and personal intercession. It serves no other purpose. Spiritual experiments have no place here. But there must be time for these three things, because it is precisely God who requires them of us. Even if for a long time meditation were to mean nothing but that we are performing a service we owe to God, this would be reason enough to do it.

70

This time for meditation does not allow us to sink into the void and bottomless pit of aloneness [Alleinsein], rather it allows us to be alone

---

11. See Bonhoeffer's "Introduction to Daily Meditation" in *WF,* 56–61; the original was edited by Bethge and sent along with the eighth circular letter from Finkenwalde, May 22, 1936 (*GS* 2:478–82). See also the letter of March 1, 1942, in *TP,* 164–67. [GK]

[allein] with the Word. In so doing it gives us solid ground on which to stand and clear guidance for the steps we have to take.

Whereas in our daily worship together we read long, continuous texts, in our personal meditation on Scripture we stick to a brief selected text that will possibly remain unchanged for an entire week. If in our communal reading of the Scriptures we are led more into the whole length and breadth of the Holy Scriptures, here we are guided into the unfathomable depths of a particular sentence and word. Both are equally necessary, "that you may have the power to comprehend, with all the saints, what is the breadth and length and height and depth" (Eph. 3:18).[12]

In our meditation we read the text given to us on the strength of the promise that it has something quite personal to say to us for this day and for our standing as Christians—it is not only God's Word for the community of faith, but also God's Word for me personally. We expose ourselves to the particular sentence and word until we personally are affected by it. When we do that, we are doing nothing but what the simplest, most unlearned Christian does every day. We are reading the Word of God as God's Word for us. Therefore, we do not ask what this text has to say to other people. For those of us who are preachers that means we will not ask how we would preach or teach on this text, but what it has to say to us personally. It is true that to do this we must first have understood the content of the text. But in this situation we are neither doing an exegesis of the text, nor preparing a sermon or conducting a Bible study of any kind; we are rather waiting for God's Word to us. We are not waiting in vain; on the contrary, we are waiting on the basis of a clear promise. Often we are so burdened and overwhelmed with other thoughts, images, and concerns that it may take a long time before God's Word has cleared all that away and gets through to us. But it will surely come, just as surely as none other than God has come to human beings and wants to come again. For that very reason we will begin our meditation with the prayer that God may send the Holy Spirit to us through the Word, and reveal God's Word to us, and enlighten our minds.    71

It is not necessary for us to get through the entire text in one period of meditation. Often we will have to stick to a single sentence or even to one word because we have been gripped and challenged by it and can no longer evade it. Are not the words "father," "love," "mercy," "cross,"

---

12. See 51, editorial note 13, and 59, editorial note 33. [GK]

"sanctification," or "resurrection" often enough to fill amply the brief time set aside for our meditation?

It is not necessary for us to be anxious about putting our thoughts and prayers into words as we meditate. Silent thinking and praying, which comes only from our listening, can often be more beneficial.

It is not necessary for us to find new ideas in our meditation. Often that only distracts us and satisfies our vanity. It is perfectly sufficient if the Word enters in and dwells within us as we read and understand it. As Mary "pondered . . . in her heart" what the shepherds told her,[13] as a person's words often stick in our mind for a long time—as they dwell and work within us, preoccupy us, disturb us, or make us happy without our being able to do anything about it—so as we meditate, God's Word desires to enter in and stay with us. It desires to move us, to work in us, and to make such an impression on us that the whole day long we will not get away from it. Then it will do its work in us, often without our being aware of it.

Above all, it is not necessary for us to have any unexpected, extraordinary experiences while meditating. That can happen, but if it does not, this is not a sign that the period of meditation has been unprofitable. Not only at the beginning, but time and again a great inner dryness and lack of concern will make itself felt in us, a listlessness, even an inability to meditate. We must not get stuck in such experiences. Above all, we must not allow them to dissuade us from observing our period of meditation with great patience and fidelity. That is why it is not good for us to take too seriously the many bad experiences we have with ourselves during the time of meditation. It is here that our old vanity and the wrongful demands we make on God could sneak into our lives in a pious, roundabout way, as if it were our right to have nothing but edifying and blissful experiences, and as if the discovery of our inner poverty were beneath our dignity. But we will not make any headway with such an attitude. Impatience and self-reproach only foster our complacency and entangle us ever more deeply in the net of self-centered introspection. But there is no more time to observe ourselves in meditation than there is in the Christian life as a whole. We should pay attention to the Word alone and leave it to the Word to deal effectively with everything. For may it not be the case that it is none other than God who sends us these hours of emptiness and dryness, so that we might once again expect

---

13. Luke 2:19.

everything from God's Word? "Seek God, not happiness"[14]— that is the fundamental rule of all meditation. If you seek God alone, you will gain happiness—that is the promise of all meditation.

The consideration of Scripture leads into prayer. We have already said that the most promising way to pray is to allow oneself to be guided by the words of the Bible, to pray on the basis of the words of Scripture. In this way we will not fall prey to our own emptiness. Prayer means nothing else but the readiness to appropriate the Word, and what is more, to let it speak to me in my personal situation, in my particular tasks, decisions, sins, and temptations. What can never enter the prayer of the community may here silently be made known to God. On the basis of the words of Scripture we pray that God may throw light on our day, preserve us from sin, and enable us to grow in holiness, and that we may be faithful in our work and have the strength to do it. And we may be certain that our prayer will be heard because it issues from God's Word and promise. Because God's Word has found its fulfillment in Jesus Christ, all the prayers we pray on the basis of this Word are certainly fulfilled and answered in Jesus Christ.

A special difficulty in the time of meditation is that it is so easy for our thoughts to wander and go their own way, toward other persons or to some events in our life. As much as this may sadden and shame us, we must not become despondent and anxious, or even conclude that meditation is really not something for us. If we find ourselves in this situation, it is often a help not frantically to restrain our thoughts, but quite calmly to draw into our prayer those people and events toward which our thoughts keep turning, and thus patiently to return to the starting point of the meditation.[15]

73

---

14. This phrase is a succinct amalgamation of several related thoughts expressed by Thomas à Kempis in chapters 9 and 11–36 of *The Imitation of Christ* (2:118–19, 121–58). Here à Kempis says that one ought not to seek God for the sake of some personal advantage but, whether we experience consolation or desolation, or even if we are going through a period of spiritual aridity, we ought nonetheless to seek God alone who is always lovingly near to us as our Lord and Savior. [GK]

15. Bonhoeffer counseled his seminarians to integrate the duty of intercession into prayerful meditation as a way of overcoming personal distractions that can creep into the time set aside for such silent prayer. "If, while we are meditating, our thoughts wander toward those who are close to us or to those with whom we are concerned, then let them linger there. This is the right place for our intercession" (*GS* 2:480; trans. GK). [GK]

Just as we tie our personal prayers to the words of the Bible, we do the same with our intercessions. It is not possible to remember in the intercessory prayers of daily worship together all the persons who are entrusted to our care, or at any rate to do it in the way that is required of us. All Christians have their own circle of those who have requested them to intercede on their behalf, or people for whom for various reasons they know they have been called upon to pray. First of all, this circle will include those with whom they must live every day. With this we have advanced to the point at which we hear the heartbeat of all Christian life together. A Christian community either lives by the intercessory prayers of its members for one another, or the community will be destroyed. I can no longer condemn or hate other Christians for whom I pray, no matter how much trouble they cause me. In intercessory prayer the face that may have been strange and intolerable to me is transformed into the face of one for whom Christ died, the face of a pardoned sinner. That is a blessed discovery for the Christian who is beginning to offer intercessory prayer for others. As far as we are concerned, there is no dislike, no personal tension, no disunity or strife, that cannot be overcome by intercessory prayer. Intercessory prayer is the purifying bath into which the individual and the community must enter every day. We may struggle hard with one another in intercessory prayer, but that struggle has the promise of achieving its goal.[16]

How does that happen? Offering intercessory prayer means nothing other than Christians bringing one another into the presence of God, seeing each other under the cross of Jesus as poor human beings and sinners in need of grace. Then, everything about other people that repels me falls away. Then I see them in all their need, hardship, and distress. Their need and their sin become so heavy and oppressive to me that I feel as if they were my own, and I can do nothing else but bid: Lord, you yourself, you alone, deal with them according to your firmness and your goodness.[17] Offering intercessory prayer means granting other Chris-

74

---

16. See Rom. 12:14-21. This section of *Life Together* has obvious ramifications for a Christian community's attitude toward the enemies of that community. Eberhard Bethge reports in his biography that the seminarians of Finkenwalde prayed for their enemies (*Dietrich Bonhoeffer*, 382). See also Bonhoeffer's sermon on Rom. 12:17-21, the third Sunday after Epiphany, January 23, 1938, in *TF*, 284–88. [GK]

17. See Rom. 11:29-36, where Paul speaks of God's inscrutable mercy to all God's children. [GK]

tians the same right we have received, namely, the right to stand before Christ and to share in Christ's mercy.

Thus it is clear that intercessory prayer is also a daily service Christians owe to God and one another.[18] Those who deny their neighbors prayers of intercession deny them a service Christians are called to perform. Furthermore, it is clear that intercessory prayer is not something general and vague, but something very concrete. It is interested in specific persons and specific difficulties and therefore specific requests. The more concrete my intercessory prayer becomes, the more promising it is.

Finally, we can no longer close our eyes to the realization that the ministry of intercession demands time of every Christian, but most of all of the pastor on whom the needs of the whole community of faith rest. Intercessory prayer alone would occupy the entire time of daily meditation if it were done properly. All this proves that intercessory prayer is a gift of God's grace for every Christian community and for every Christian. Because God has made us such an immeasurably great offer here, we should accept it joyfully. The very time we give to intercession will turn out to be a daily source of new joy in God and in the Christian congregation.

Because consideration of the Scriptures, prayer, and intercession involve a service that is our duty, and because the grace of God can be found in this service, we should train ourselves to set a regular time during the day for them, just as we do for every other service we perform. That is not "legalism," but discipline and faithfulness.[19] For most people, the early morning will prove to be the best time. We have a right to this time, even prior to the claims of other people, and we may demand it as a completely undisturbed quiet time despite all external pressures. For the pastor, it is an indispensable duty on which the whole practice of ministry will depend. Who can really be faithful in great things, if they have not learned to be faithful in the things of daily life?

75

Every day brings the Christian many hours of being alone in an unchristian environment. These are times of *testing*. This is the proving ground of a genuine time of meditation and genuine Christian community. Has the community served to make individuals free, strong, and

---

18. On Bonhoeffer's "theology of intercession," see especially *CS*, 132–34, and the section on intercession from his lectures,"Das Wesen der Kirche," during the summer semester 1932, in *GS* 5:266.

19. See editorial note 11 above. [GK]

mature, or has it made them insecure and dependent? Has it taken them by the hand for a while so that they would learn again to walk by themselves, or has it made them anxious and unsure? This is one of the toughest and most serious questions that can be put to any form of everyday Christian life in community [Lebensgemeinschaft]. Moreover, we will see at this point whether Christians' time of meditation has led them into an unreal world from which they awaken with a fright when they step out into the workaday world, or whether it has led them into the real world of God from which they enter into the day's activities strengthened and purified. Has it transported them for a few short moments into a spiritual ecstasy that vanishes when everyday life returns, or has it planted the Word of God so soberly and so deeply in their heart that it holds and strengthens them all day long, leading them to active love, to obedience, to good works? Only the day can decide. Is the invisible presence of the Christian community a reality and a help to the individual? Do the intercessory prayers of the others carry me through the day? Is the Word of God close to me as a comfort and a strength? Or do I misuse my solitude [Alleinsein] against the community, against the Word and prayer? Individuals must be aware that even their hours of being alone [Alleinsein] reverberate through the community. In their solitude they can shatter and tarnish the community or they can strengthen and sanctify it. Every act of self-discipline by a Christian is also a service to the community. Conversely, there is no sin in thought, word, or deed, no matter how personal or secret, that does not harm the whole community. When the cause of an illness gets into one's body, whether or not anyone knows where it comes from, or in what member it has lodged, the body is made

76   ill. This is the appropriate metaphor for the Christian community. Every member serves the whole body, contributing either to its health or to its ruin, for we *are* members of one body not only when we want to be, but in our whole existence. This is not a theory, but a spiritual reality that is often experienced in the Christian community with shocking clarity, sometimes destructively and sometimes beneficially.

Those who return to the community of Christians who live together, after a successful day, bring with them the blessing of their solitude, but they themselves receive anew the blessing of the community. Blessed are those who are alone in the strength of the community. Blessed are those who preserve community in the strength of solitude. But the strength of solitude and the strength of community is the strength of the Word of God alone, which is meant for the individual in the community.

# SERVICE

"AN ARGUMENT STARTED among the disciples as to which of them would 77 be the greatest" (Luke 9:46).[1] We know who sows this dissension in the Christian community. But perhaps we do not think enough about the fact that no Christian community ever comes together without this argument appearing as a seed of discord. No sooner are people together than they begin to observe, judge, and classify each other. Thus, even as Christian community is in the process of being formed, an invisible, often unknown, yet terrible life-and-death struggle commences. "An argument started among them"—this is enough to destroy a community. It is vitally necessary, therefore, that every Christian community keep an eye on this dangerous enemy from the very outset and eradicate it. There is no time to lose here, because from the first moment two people meet, one begins looking for a competitive position to assume and hold against the other. There are strong people and weak ones. If people are not strong, they immediately claim the right of the weak as their own and use it against the strong.[2] People are talented and untalented, simple and difficult, devout and less devout, sociable and loners. Does not the untalented person have a position to assume just as well as the talented person, the difficult person just as well as the simple one? And if I am not talented, then perhaps I am, nonetheless, devout, or if I am not devout, it is only because I do not want to be. May not the sociable individuals win everyone over to their side and compromise the loner? And

---

1. Bonhoeffer's German text has "would be [*wäre*] the greatest," whereas the NRSV has the argument over "which one of them *was* the greatest." [GK]

2. See 71, editorial note 54.

yet, may not the loner become the invincible enemy and ultimate conqueror of the sociable individual? Are there any people who do not with instinctive assurance find the place where they can stand and defend themselves, but which they will never give up to another, for which they will fight with all the natural drive to self-assertion? All this can occur in the most respectable or even the most pious forms. But it is really important for a Christian community to know that somewhere in it there will certainly be an "argument among the disciples as to which of them would be the greatest." It is the struggle of natural human beings for self-justification. They find it only by comparing themselves with others, by condemning and judging others. Self-justification and judging belong together in the same way that justification by grace and serving belong together.

Often we combat our evil thoughts most effectively if we absolutely refuse to allow them to be verbalized. It is certain that the spirit of self-justification can only be overcome by the spirit of grace; and it is just as certain that the individual judgmental thought can be limited and suppressed by never allowing it to be spoken except as a confession of sin, which we will talk about later. Those who keep their tongue in check control both spirit and body (James 3:3ff.). Thus it must be a decisive rule of all Christian community life that each individual is prohibited from talking about another Christian in secret.[3] It is clear and will be shown in what follows that this prohibition does not include the word of admonition that is spoken personally to another. However, talking about others in secret is not allowed even under the pretense of help and goodwill. For it is precisely in this guise that the spirit of hatred between believers always creeps in, seeking to cause trouble. This is not the place to specify the limitations placed on such a rule in particular cases. They are subject to decisions made in each instance. However, the point is clear and biblical. "You sit and speak against your kin; you slander your own mother's child. . . . But now I rebuke you, and lay the charge before

---

3. According to Eberhard Bethge, Bonhoeffer was aware of the dangers to their community that could arise from the tensions of living in such close proximity to one another over a protracted period of time. Hence "he asked the ordinands to observe only one rule—never to speak about a fellow ordinand in his absence or, if this should happen, to tell him about it afterwards." Bethge comments on this rule that "almost as much was learned from the failure to observe this simple rule and from the renewed resolution to keep it as from sermons and exegeses" (*Dietrich Bonhoeffer*, 349–50). [GK]

you" (Ps. 50:20f.). "Do not speak evil against one another, brothers and sisters. Whoever speaks evil against another or judges another, speaks evil against the law and judges the law; but if you judge the law, you are not a doer of the law but a judge. There is one lawgiver and judge who is able to save and to destroy. So who, then, are you to judge your neighbor?" (James 4:11-12). "Let no evil talk come out of your mouths, but only what is useful for building up, as there is need, so that your words may give grace to those who hear" (Eph. 4:29).

Where this discipline of the tongue is practiced right from the start, individuals will make an amazing discovery. They will be able to stop constantly keeping an eye on others, judging them, condemning them, and putting them in their places and thus doing violence to them. They can now allow other Christians to live freely, just as God has brought them face to face with each other. The view of such persons expands and, to their amazement, they recognize for the first time the richness of God's creative glory shining over their brothers and sisters. God did not make others as I would have made them. God did not give them to me so that I could dominate and control them, but so that I might find the Creator by means of them. Now other people, in the freedom with which they were created, become an occasion for me to rejoice, whereas before they were only a nuisance and trouble for me. God does not want me to mold others into the image that seems good to me, that is, into my own image. Instead, in their freedom from me God made other people in God's own image. I can never know in advance how God's image should appear in others. That image always takes on a completely new and unique form whose origin is found solely in God's free and sovereign act of creation. To me that form may seem strange, even ungodly. But God creates every person in the image of God's Son, the Crucified, and this image, likewise, certainly looked strange and ungodly to me before I grasped it.

Strong and weak, wise or foolish, talented or untalented, pious or less pious, the complete diversity of individuals in the community is no longer a reason to talk and judge and condemn, and therefore no longer a pretext for self-justification. Rather this diversity is a reason for rejoicing in one another and serving one another. Even in this new situation all the members of the community are given their special place; this is no longer the place, however, in which they can most successfully promote themselves, but the place where they can best carry out their service. In a Christian community, everything depends on whether each individual is an indispensable link in a chain. The chain is unbreakable only when even the smallest link holds tightly with the others. A community, which permits within itself members who do nothing, will be destroyed by them. Thus it is a good idea that all members receive a definite task to perform for the community, so that they may know in times of doubt that they too are not useless and incapable of doing anything. Every Christian community must know that not only do the weak need the strong, but also that the strong cannot exist without the weak. The elimination of the weak is the death of the community.[4]

The Christian community should not be governed by self-justification, which violates others, but by justification by grace, which serves others. Once individuals have experienced the mercy of God in their lives, from then on they desire only to serve. The proud throne of the judge no longer lures them; instead they want to be down among the wretched and lowly, because God found them down there themselves. "Do not be haughty, but associate with the lowly" (Rom. 12:16).

Those who would learn to serve must first learn to think little of themselves. "[You should] not . . . think of yourself more highly than you ought to think" (Rom. 12:3). "The highest and most useful lesson is to truly know yourself and to think humbly of yourself. Making nothing of yourself and always having a good opinion of others is great wisdom and perfection" (Thomas à Kempis).[5] "Do not claim to be wiser than you are" (Rom. 12:17).[6] Only those who live by the forgiveness of their sin in Jesus Christ will think little of themselves in the right way. They will know that their own wisdom completely came to an end when Christ forgave them. They remember the cleverness of the first human beings, who wanted to know what is good and evil and died in this cleverness. The first person, however, who was born on this earth was Cain, the murderer of his brother. His crime is the fruit of humanity's wisdom. Because they can no longer consider themselves wise, Christians will also have a modest opinion of their own plans and intentions. They will know that it is good for their own will to be broken in their encounter with their neighbor. They will be ready to consider their neighbor's will more important and urgent than their own. What does it matter if our own plans are thwarted? Is it not better to serve our neighbor than to get our own way?

81

---

4. See 53–54, editorial note 23, and 71, editorial note 54. [GK]

5. Thomas à Kempis, *The Imitation of Christ*, 1,2: 33–34, trans. altered.

6. The NRSV lists this text as Rom. 12:16b. [GK]

Not only the will, but also the honor of the other is more important than my own. "How can you believe when you accept glory from one another and do not seek the glory that comes from the one who alone is God?" (John 5:44). The desire for one's own honor hinders faith. Those who seek their own honor are no longer seeking God and their neighbor. What does it matter if I suffer injustice? Would I not have deserved even more severe punishment from God if God had not treated me with mercy? Is not justice done to me a thousand times over even in injustice? Must it not be beneficial and conducive to humility for me to learn to bear such petty ills silently and patiently? "Patience is better than pride" (Eccles. 7:8).[7] Those who live by justification by grace are prepared to accept even insults and slights without protest, taking them as from God's chastising and gracious hand. It is not a good sign when we can no longer stand to hear such things without immediately recalling that even Paul insisted on his rights as a Roman citizen[8] and that Jesus replied to the man who struck him, "Why do you strike me?"[9] In any case, none of us will really act as Jesus and Paul did if we have not first learned like them to keep silent amidst insults and humiliations. The sin of irritability that blossoms so quickly in the community shows again and again how much inordinate ambition, and thus how much unbelief, still exists in the community.

Finally, one extreme statement must still be made, without any platitudes, and in all soberness. Not considering oneself wise, but associating with the lowly, means considering oneself the worst of sinners. This arouses total opposition not only from those who live at the level of nature, but also from Christians who are self-aware. It sounds like an exaggeration, an untruth. Yet even Paul said of himself that he was the foremost, i.e., the worst of sinners (1 Tim. 1:15). He said this at the very place in scripture where he was speaking of his ministry as an apostle. There can be no genuine knowledge of sin that does not lead me down to this depth. If my sin appears to me to be in any way smaller or less reprehensible in comparison with the sins of others, then I am not yet recognizing my sin at all. My sin is of necessity the worst, the most serious, the most objectionable. Christian love will find any number of excuses

82

---

7. The NRSV says "the patient in spirit are better than the proud in spirit." [GK]

8. Acts 22:25-29.

9. John 18:23.

for the sins of others; only for my sin is there no excuse whatsoever. That is why my sin is the worst. Those who would serve others in the community must descend all the way down to this depth of humility. How could I possibly serve other persons in unfeigned humility if their sins appear to me to be seriously worse than my own? If I am to have any hope for them, then I must not raise myself above them. Such service would be a sham. "Do not believe that you have made any progress in the work of sanctification, if you do not feel deeply that you are less than all others" (Thomas à Kempis).[10]

How, then, is true Christian service performed in the Christian community? We are inclined these days to reply too quickly that the one real service to our neighbor is to serve them with the Word of God. It is true that there is no service that can equal this one, and even more, that every other service is oriented to the service of the Word. Yet a Christian community does not consist solely of preachers of the Word. The improper use of this could become oppressive if several other things were overlooked at this point.

The *first* service one owes to others in the community involves listening to them. Just as our love for God begins with listening to God's Word, the beginning of love for other Christians is learning to listen to them. God's love for us is shown by the fact that God not only gives us God's Word, but also lends us God's ear. We do God's work for our brothers and sisters when we learn to listen to them. So often Christians, especially preachers, think that their only service is always to have to "offer" something when they are together with other people. They forget that listening can be a greater service than speaking. Many people seek a sympathetic ear and do not find it among Christians, because these Christians are talking even when they should be listening. But Christians who can no longer listen to one another will soon no longer be listening to God either; they will always be talking even in the presence of God. The death of the spiritual life starts here, and in the end there is nothing left but empty spiritual chatter and clerical condescension which chokes on pious words. Those who cannot listen long and patiently will always be talking past others, and finally no longer will even notice it. Those who think their time is too precious to spend listening will never really have time for God and others, but only for themselves and for their own words and plans.

---

10. Thomas à Kempis, *The Imitation of Christ*, 2,2: 78, trans. altered.

For Christians, pastoral care differs essentially from preaching in that here the task of listening is joined to the task of speaking the Word. There is also a kind of listening with half an ear that presumes already to know what the other person has to say. This impatient, inattentive listening really despises the other Christian and finally is only waiting to get a chance to speak and thus to get rid of the other. This sort of listening is no fulfillment of our task. And it is certain that here, too, in our attitude toward other Christians we simply see reflected our own relationship to God. It should be no surprise that we are no longer able to perform the greatest service of listening that God has entrusted to us—hearing the confession of another Christian—if we refuse to lend our ear to another person on lesser subjects. The pagan world [heidnische Welt] today knows something about persons who often can be helped only by having someone who will seriously listen to them. On this insight it has built its own secular form of pastoral care [säkularisierte Seelsorge],[11] which has become popular with many people, including Christians. But Christians have forgotten that the ministry of listening has been entrusted to them ‎84 by the one who is indeed the great listener and in whose work they are to participate. We should listen with the ears of God, so that we can speak the Word of God.

The *other* service one should perform for another person in a Christian community is active helpfulness. To begin with, we have in mind simple assistance in minor, external matters. There are many such things wherever people live together. Nobody is too good for the lowest service. Those who worry about the loss of time entailed by such small, external acts of helpfulness are usually taking their own work too seriously. We must be ready to allow ourselves to be interrupted by God, who will thwart our plans and frustrate our ways time and again, even daily, by sending people across our path with their demands and requests. We can, then, pass them by, preoccupied with our more important daily tasks, just as the priest—perhaps reading the Bible—passed by the man who had fallen among robbers.[12] When we do that, we pass by the visible sign of the cross raised in our lives to show us that God's way, and not

---

11. On the theme of a "secular form of pastoral care" and its relationship to psychotherapy and existential philosophy, see Bonhoeffer, *SPC*, 35–38. Bonhoeffer's negative attitude toward these "secular forms" of pastoral care is never so emphatically stated as in his letter from Tegel Prison, June 8, 1944 (*LPP*, 326–29). [GK]

12. Luke 10:31.

our own, is what counts. It is a strange fact that, of all people, Christians and theologians often consider their work so important and urgent that they do not want to let anything interrupt it. They think they are doing God a favor, but actually they are despising God's "crooked yet straight path" (Gottfried Arnold).[13] They want to know nothing about how human plans are thwarted. But it is part of the school of humility that we must not spare our hand where it can perform a service. We do not manage our time ourselves but allow it to be occupied by God. In the monastery, the monk's vow of obedience to the abbot takes away his right to do what he likes with his time. In Protestant community life, voluntary service to one another takes the place of the vow. One can joyfully and authentically proclaim the Word of God's love and mercy with one's mouth only where one's hands are not considered too good for deeds of love and mercy in everyday helpfulness.

*Third,* we speak of the service involved in bearing with others. "Bear one another's burdens, and in this way you will fulfill the law of Christ" (Gal. 6:2). Thus the law of Christ is a law of forbearance. Forbearance means enduring and suffering. The other person is a burden to the Christian, in fact for the Christian most of all. The other person never becomes a burden at all for the *pagans.* They simply stay clear of every burden the other person may create for them. However, Christians must bear the burden of one another. They must suffer and endure one another. Only as a burden is the other really a brother or sister and not just an object to be controlled. The burden of human beings was even for God so heavy that God had to go to the cross suffering under it.[14] God truly suffered and endured human beings in the body of Jesus Christ. But in so doing, God bore them as a mother carries her child, as a shepherd the lost lamb. God took on human nature. Then, human beings crushed God to the ground. But God stayed with them and they

---

13. "Your ways are often crooked, yet still are they straight / whereby you lead your children to come unto you." Bonhoeffer quotes here from the hymn, "So Führst du doch recht selig, Herr, die Deinen" (Thus You Truly Bless and Guide Those Who Belong to You, O Lord), *Evangelisches Gesangbuch*, no. 230, v. 1; it is also found in the *Evangelisches Kirchengesangbuch*, 472. This hymn, based on Ps. 4:4, was written in 1697 by Gottfried Arnold (1666–1714). [GK]

14. The sufferings of God in Jesus Christ and Jesus' sufferings in and for God's people are major themes in Bonhoeffer's theology. See Geffrey B. Kelly, "Sharing in the Pain of God: Dietrich Bonhoeffer's Reflections on Christian Vulnerability." [GK]

with God. In suffering and enduring human beings, God maintained community with them. It is the law of Christ that was fulfilled in the cross. Christians share in this law. They are obliged to bear with and suffer one another; but what is more important, now by virtue of the law of Christ having been fulfilled, they are also able to bear one another.

It is remarkable that the Scriptures talk so often about "forbearance." They are capable of expressing the whole work of Jesus Christ in this one word. "Surely he has borne our infirmities and carried our diseases . . . upon him was the punishment that made us whole" (Isa. 53).[15] Therefore, the Bible can characterize the whole life of the Christian as carrying the cross. It is the community of the body of Christ that is here realized, the community of the cross in which one must experience the burden of the other. If one were not to experience this, it would not be a Christian community. One who refuses to bear that burden would deny the law of Christ.

First of all, it is the *freedom* of the other, mentioned earlier, that is a burden to Christians.[16] The freedom of the other goes against Christians' high opinions of themselves, and yet they must recognize it. Christians could rid themselves of this burden by not giving other persons their freedom, thus doing violence to the personhood of others and stamping their own image on others. But when Christians allow God to create God's own image in others, they allow others their own freedom. Thereby Christians themselves bear the burden of the freedom enjoyed by these other creatures of God. All that we mean by human nature, individuality, and talent is part of the other person's freedom—as are the other's weaknesses and peculiarities that so sorely try our patience, and everything that produces the plethora of clashes, differences, and arguments between me and the other. Here, bearing the burden of the other means tolerating the reality of the other's creation by God—affirming it, and in bearing with it, breaking through to delight in it.

86

This will be especially difficult where both the strong and the weak in faith are bound together in one community. The weak must not judge the strong; the strong must not despise the weak. The weak must guard against pride, the strong against indifference. Neither must seek their own rights. If the strong persons fall, the weak ones must keep their hearts from gloating over the misfortune. If the weak fall, the strong

---

15. Bonhoeffer cites from Isa. 53: 4a, 5b.
16. See above, 36–38, 43–45.

must help them up again in a friendly manner. The one needs as much patience as the other. "Woe to the one who is alone and falls and does not have another to help!" (Eccles. 4:10).[17] No doubt, when Scripture admonishes us to "bear with one another" (Col. 3:13), and to do so "with all humility and gentleness, with patience, bearing with one another in love" (Eph. 4:2), it is talking about this bearing of the other in freedom.

Then, along with the other's freedom comes the abuse of that freedom in *sin*, which becomes a burden for Christians in their relationship to one another. The sins of the other are even harder to bear than is their freedom; for in sin, community with God and with each other is broken. Here, because of the other, Christians suffer the breaking of the community with the other established in Jesus Christ. But here, too, it is only in bearing with the other that the great grace of God becomes fully apparent. Not despising sinners, but being privileged to bear with them, means not having to give them up for lost, being able to accept them and able to preserve community with them through forgiveness. "My friends, if anyone is detected in a transgression, you who have received the Spirit should restore such a one in a spirit of gentleness" (Gal. 6:1). As Christ bore with us and accepted us as sinners, so we in his community may bear with sinners and accept them into the community of Jesus Christ through the forgiveness of sins. We may suffer the sins of one another; we do not need to judge. That is grace for Christians. For what sin ever occurs in the community that does not lead Christians to examine themselves and condemn themselves for their own lack of faithfulness in prayer and in intercession, for their lack of service to one another in mutual admonition and comforting, indeed, for their own personal sin and lack of spiritual discipline by which they have harmed themselves, the community, and one another? Because each individual's sin burdens the whole community and indicts it, the community of faith rejoices amid all the pain inflicted on it by the sin of the other and, in spite of the burden placed on it, rejoices in being deemed worthy of bearing with and forgiving sin. "Behold, you bear with them all and likewise all of them bear with you, and all things are in common, both the good and the bad" (Luther).[18]

87

---

17. See editorial note 7 above. [GK]

18. Martin Luther, "A Treatise Concerning the Blessed Sacrament of the Holy and True Body of Christ and Concerning the Brotherhood," 1519, *LW*, 35/1: 54 (*WA*, 2:745) [trans. GK]. See 83, editorial note 4. [GK]

The service of forgiveness is done by one to the other on a daily basis. It occurs *without words* in intercessory prayer for one another. And all members of the community who do not grow tired of doing this service can depend on the fact that this service is also being offered to them by other Christians. Those who bear with others know that they themselves are being borne. Only in this strength can they themselves bear with others.

Wherever the service of listening, active helpfulness, and bearing with others is being faithfully performed, the ultimate and highest ministry can also be offered, the service of the Word of God.

This service has to do with the free word from person to person, not the word bound to a particular pastoral office, time, and place. It is a matter of that unique situation in which one person bears witness in human words to another person regarding all the comfort, the admonition, the kindness, and the firmness of God. This word is threatened all about by endless dangers. If proper listening does not precede it, how can it really be the right word for the other? If it is contradicted by one's own lack of active helpfulness, how can it be a credible and truthful word? If it does not flow from the act of bearing with others, but from impatience and the spirit of violence against others, how can it be the 88 liberating and healing word? On the contrary, the person who has really listened, served, and patiently borne with others is the very one who can easily stop talking. A deep distrust of everything that is merely words often stifles a personal word to another Christian. What can a powerless human word accomplish for others? Why add to the empty talk? Are we, like those experienced spiritual "experts," to talk past the real needs of the other person? What is more perilous than speaking God's Word superfluously? But, on the other hand, who wants to accept the responsibility for having been silent when we should have spoken? The orderly word spoken in the pulpit is so much easier than this totally free word, standing responsibly between silence and speech.

Added to the fear of one's own responsibility to speak the word, there is the fear of the other. At what a cost do we bring ourselves to say the name of Jesus Christ even in the presence of another Christian. Here, too, right and wrong approaches are mixed together. Who has permission to force oneself on one's neighbor? Who is entitled to corner and confront one's neighbor in order to talk about ultimate issues? It would not be a sign of great Christian insight if one were simply to say at this point that everybody has this right, indeed, this obligation. Again here the spirit of doing violence to others could insinuate itself in the worst way. In fact, others have their own right, responsibility, and even duty to defend themselves against unauthorized intrusions. Other persons have their own secrets that may not be violated without the infliction of great harm. Nor can they divulge them without destroying themselves. They are not secrets based on knowledge or emotion, but secrets of their freedom, their redemption, their being. And yet this good insight lies perilously close to Cain's murderous question: "Am I my brother's keeper?"[19] Our seemingly spiritually based respect for the freedom of the other can be subject to the curse of God. "I will hold you responsible for their blood" (Ezek. 3:18).[20]

89

When Christians live together, at some time and in some way it must come to the point that one Christian personally declares God's Word and will to another. It is inconceivable that the things that are most important to each individual should not be discussed with one another. It is unchristian when one person knowingly denies another this decisive service. If we cannot bring ourselves to say the necessary word, we will have to ask ourselves whether we are not still seeing other Christians clothed in a human dignity that we think we dare not touch, and thus whether we are not forgetting the most important thing—that they, too, no matter how old or high ranking or distinguished they may be, are still persons like us, sinners crying out for God's grace. They have the same great troubles that we have, and need help, comfort, and forgiveness as we do. The basis on which Christians can speak to one another is that each knows the other as a sinner who, even given all one's human renown, is forlorn and lost if not given help. This does not mean that the others are being disparaged or dishonored. Rather, we are paying them the only real honor a human being has, namely, that as sinners they share in God's grace and glory, that they are children of God. This realization gives our mutual speech the freedom and openness it needs. We talk to one another about the help we both need. We admonish one another to go the way Christ bids us to go. We warn one another against the disobedience that is our undoing. We are gentle and we are firm with one another, for we know both God's kindness and God's firmness.[21]

---

19. Gen. 4:9.

20. [Trans. GK] Cf. the NRSV, "their blood I will require at your hand." [GK]

21. This thought is probably drawn from Rom. 11:22, which in the NRSV

Why should we be afraid of one another since both of us have only God to fear? Why should we think that another Christian would not understand us when we understood very well what was meant when somebody spoke God's comfort or God's admonition to us, even in words that were inept and awkward? Or do we really believe there is a single person in this world who does not need either comfort or admonition? If so, then why has God given us the gift of Christian community?

The more we learn to allow the other to speak the Word to us, to accept humbly and gratefully even severe reproaches and admonitions, the more free and to the point we ourselves will be in speaking. One who because of sensitivity and vanity rejects the serious words of another Christian cannot speak the truth in humility to others. Such a person is afraid of being rejected and feeling hurt by another's words. Sensitive, irritable people will always become flatterers, and very soon they will come to despise and slander other Christians in their community. But humble people will cling to both truth and love. They will stick to the Word of God and let it lead them to others in their community. They can help others through the Word because they seek nothing for themselves and have no fears for themselves.

When another Christian falls into obvious sin, an admonition is imperative, because God's Word demands it. The practice of discipline in the community of faith begins with friends who are close to one another. Words of admonition and reproach must be risked when a lapse from God's Word in doctrine or life endangers a community that lives together, and with it the whole community of faith. Nothing can be more cruel than that leniency which abandons others to their sin. Nothing can be more compassionate than that severe reprimand which calls another Christian in one's community back from the path of sin. When we allow nothing but God's Word to stand between us, judging and helping, it is a service of mercy, an ultimate offer of genuine community. Then it is not we who are judging; God alone judges, and God's judgment is helpful and healing. After all, we can only serve other Christians; we can never place ourselves above them. We serve them even when we must speak the judging and sundering Word of God to them, even when in obedience to God we must break off community with them. We know

90

---

reads, "Note then the kindness and the severity of God." The Luther translation of the Bible has "Drum schau die Güte und den Ernst Gottes" ("Consider, therefore, God's goodness and firmness."). [GK]

that it is not our human love that enables us to remain devoted to others, but God's love that comes to them only through judgment. God's Word serves humankind by judging it. Those who allow God's judgment to serve themselves are helped. This is the place where the limitation of all human action toward one another becomes obvious. "Truly, no ransom avails for one's life, there is no price one can give to God for it. For the ransom of life is costly, and can never suffice" (Ps. 49:8f. [7-8]). This renunciation of our own ability is precisely the prerequisite for, and the

91   acknowledgment of, the redeeming help that only the Word of God can give to others. The ways of other Christians are not in our hands; we cannot hold together what is going to break into pieces. We cannot keep alive what is intent on dying. But God joins together in breaking, creates community in division, confers grace through judgment. However, God has put God's own Word in our mouth. God wants it to be spoken through us. If we hinder God's Word, the blood of the other who sins will be upon us. If we carry out God's Word, God wants to save the other through us. "Whoever brings back a sinner from wandering will save the sinner's soul from death and will cover a multitude of sins" (James 5:20).

"Whoever wishes to become great among you must be your servant" (Mark 10:43). Jesus tied all authority in the community to service, one to another. Genuine spiritual authority is to be found only where the service of listening, helping, forbearing, and proclaiming is carried out. Every personality cult that bears the mark of the distinguished qualities, outstanding abilities, powers, and talents of an other, even if these are of a thoroughly spiritual nature, is worldly and has no place in the Christian community of faith; indeed, it poisons that community. The longing we so often hear expressed today for "episcopal figures," "priestly people," "authoritative personalities" often enough stems from a spiritually sick need to admire human beings and to establish visible human authority because the genuine authority of service appears to be too insignificant. Nothing contradicts such a desire more sharply than the New Testament itself in its description of a bishop (1 Tim. 3:1ff.). None of the magic of human talents or the brilliant qualities of a spiritual personality is to be found there. Bishops are those unpretentious persons who are sound and loyal in faith and life and who properly carry out their ministry to the community of faith. The authority of bishops lies in accomplishing the tasks of their service. There is nothing to admire in the person himself. Ultimately, the craving for inauthentic authority reasserts its desire to reestablish some kind of immediacy, a commitment to a human figure in the church. Genuine authority knows, however, that all immediacy is disastrous, particularly in matters of authority. Genuine authority knows that it can only exist in the service of the One who alone has authority. Genuine authority knows that it is bound in the strictest sense by the words of Jesus, "You have one teacher, and you are all brothers" (Matt. 23:8). The community of faith does not need brilliant personalities but faithful servants of Jesus and of one another. It does not lack the former, but the latter. The community of faith will place its confidence only in the simple servant of the Word of Jesus, because it knows that it will then be guided not by human wisdom and human conceit, but by the Word of the Good Shepherd. The question of spiritual trust, which is so closely connected with the question of authority, is decided by the faithfulness with which people serve Jesus Christ, never by the extraordinary gifts they possess. Authority in pastoral care can be found only in the servants of Jesus who seek no authority of their own, but who are Christians one to another, obedient to the authority of the Word.

# Confession and
# the Lord's Supper

---

93   "Confess your sins to one another" (James 5:16). Those who remain alone with their evil are left utterly alone. It is possible that Christians may remain lonely in spite of daily worship together, prayer together, and all their community through service—that the final breakthrough to community does not occur precisely because they enjoy community with one another as pious believers, but not with one another as those lacking piety, as sinners. For the pious community permits no one to be a sinner. Hence all have to conceal their sins from themselves and from the community. We are not allowed to be sinners. Many Christians would be unimaginably horrified if a real sinner were suddenly to turn up among the pious. So we remain alone with our sin, trapped in lies and hypocrisy, for we are in fact sinners.

However, the grace of the gospel, which is so hard for the pious to comprehend, confronts us with the truth. It says to us, you are a sinner, a great, unholy sinner. Now come, as the sinner that you are, to your God who loves you. For God wants you as you are, not desiring anything from you—a sacrifice, a good deed—but rather desiring you alone. "My child, give me your heart" (Prov. 23:26). God has come to you to make the sinner blessed. Rejoice! This message is liberation through truth. You cannot hide from God. The mask you wear in the presence of other people won't get you anywhere in the presence of God. God wants to see you as you are, wants to be gracious to you. You do not have to go on lying to yourself and to other Christians as if you were without sin. You are allowed to be a sinner. Thank God for that; God loves the sinner but hates the sin.

Christ became our brother in the flesh in order that we might believe in him. In Christ, the love of God came to the sinner. In the presence of Christ human beings were allowed to be sinners, and only in this way could they be helped. Every pretense came to an end in Christ's presence. This was the truth of the gospel in Jesus Christ: the misery of the sinner and the mercy of God. The community of faith in Christ was to live in this truth. That is why Jesus gave his followers the authority to hear the confession of sin and to forgive sin in Christ's name. "If you forgive the sins of any, they are forgiven them; if you retain the sins of any, they are retained" (John 20:23).[1]

When he did that, Christ made us into the community of faith, and in that community Christ made the other Christian to be grace for us. Now each stands in Christ's place. In the presence of another Christian I no longer need to pretend. In another Christian's presence I am permitted to be the sinner that I am, for there alone in all the world the truth and mercy of Jesus Christ rule. Christ became our brother in order to help us; through Christ other Christians have become Christ for us in the power and authority of Christ's commandment. Other Christians stand before us as the sign of God's truth and grace. They have been given to us to help us. Another Christian hears our confession of sin in Christ's place, forgives our sins in Christ's name. Another Christian keeps the secret of our confession as God keeps it. When I go to another believer to confess, I am going to God.[2]

Thus the call within the Christian community to mutual confession and forgiveness goes out as a call to the great grace of God in the congregation.

94

---

1. This passage from John's Gospel often is used as a basis for the long-standing Christian practice of confessing one's sins either in public or in private, either in a general ceremony or to an individual representing the Christian community. Other passages similarly invoked are Matt. 16:19, 18:18, 21-22; 1 Cor. 5:3-5; 2 Cor. 2:10-11; Eph. 4:32; and, of course, James 5:16, with which Bonhoeffer begins this chapter. [GK]

2. One finds the clearest example of his teaching on private confession and forgiveness in the way that Bonhoeffer makes this the centerpiece of his lectures on pastoral care. "If I go to confession I go to God. I am not confiding to a human being, rather this person stands wholly in God's stead. What I say to that person I say to God. He will guard it as God's secret" (*SPC,* 61; cf. 63). Also see Bethge's *Dietrich Bonhoeffer* (384), where he cites a sermon in which Bonhoeffer describes private confession as an "experience of being wrested away from grave sin by God and then receiving God's forgiveness" (384). [GK]

In confession there takes place a *breakthrough to community*. Sin wants to be alone with people. It takes them away from the community. The more lonely people become, the more destructive the power of sin over them. The more deeply they become entangled in it, the more unholy is their loneliness. Sin wants to remain unknown. It shuns the light. In the darkness of what is left unsaid sin poisons the whole being of a person. This can happen in the midst of a pious community. In confession the light of the gospel breaks into the darkness and closed isolation of the heart. Sin must be brought into the light. What is unspoken is said openly and confessed. All that is secret and hidden comes to light. It is a hard struggle until the sin crosses one's lips in confession. But God breaks down gates of bronze and cuts through bars of iron (Ps. 107:16). Since the confession of sin is made in the presence of another Christian, the last stronghold of self-justification is abandoned. The sinner surren-

95     ders, giving up all evil, giving the sinner's heart to God and finding the forgiveness of all one's sin in the community of Jesus Christ and other Christians. Sin that has been spoken and confessed has lost all of its power. It has been revealed and judged as sin. It can no longer tear apart the community. Now the community bears the sin of the individual believer, who is no longer alone with this evil but has "cast off" this sin by confessing it and handing it over to God. The sinner has been relieved of sin's burden. Now the sinner stands in the community of sinners who live by the grace of God in the cross of Jesus Christ. Now one is allowed to be a sinner and still enjoy the grace of God. We can admit our sins and in this very act find community for the first time. The hidden sins separated the sinner from the community and made the sinner's apparent community all a sham. The sins that were acknowledged helped the sinner to find true community with other believers in Jesus Christ.

In this connection, we are talking exclusively about confession between two Christians. A confession of sin in the presence of all the members of the congregation is not required to restore one to community with the entire congregation.[3] In the one other Christian to whom I

---

3. This, too, echoes the passage in *Spiritual Care* where Bonhoeffer states categorically that "the whole community is contained in those two people who stand next to one another in confession" (63). See also Luther's comment on the various ways to confess one's sins and to receive forgiveness in *The Large Catechism*, sections 1–22, incorporated into *The Book of Concord: The Confessions of the Evangelical Lutheran Church*, 457–59. [GK]

confess my sins and by whom my sins are declared forgiven, I meet the whole congregation. Community with the whole congregation is given to me in the community which I experience with this one other believer. For here it is not a matter of acting according to one's own orders and authority, but according to the command of Jesus Christ, which is intended for the whole congregation, on whose behalf the individual is called merely to carry it out. So long as Christians are in such a community of confession of sins to one another, they are no longer alone anywhere.

In confession there occurs a *breakthrough to the cross.* The root of all sin is pride, *superbia.*[4] I want to be for myself; I have a right to be myself, a right to my hatred and my desires, my life and my death. The spirit and flesh of human beings are inflamed by pride, for it is precisely in their wickedness that human beings want to be like God. Confession in the presence of another believer is the most profound kind of humiliation. It hurts, makes one feel small; it deals a terrible blow to one's pride. To stand there before another Christian as a sinner is an almost unbearable disgrace. By confessing actual sins the old self dies a painful, humiliating death before the eyes of another Christian. Because this humiliation is so difficult, we keep thinking we can avoid confessing to one another. Our eyes are so blinded that they no longer see the promise and the glory of such humiliation. It is none other than Jesus Christ who openly suffered the shameful death of a sinner in our place, who was not ashamed to be crucified for us as an evildoer. And it is nothing else but our community with Jesus Christ that leads us to the disgraceful dying that comes in confession, so that we may truly share in this cross. The cross of Jesus Christ shatters all pride. We cannot find the cross of Jesus if we are afraid of going to the place where Jesus can be found, to the public death of the sinner. And we refuse to carry the cross when we are ashamed to take upon ourselves the shameful death of the sinner in confession. In confession we break through to the genuine community of the cross of Jesus Christ; in confession we affirm our cross. In the profound spiritual and physical pain of humiliation before another believer,

96

---

4. *Superbia* is translated as "pride," "arrogance," "haughtiness." It is generally considered that Sir. 10:13-14 provides the scriptural basis for the classical theological tradition that pride is the root of the evil in the rebellion against God. See also Gen. 3:5. Thomas Aquinas is likewise insistent on this point (*Summa Theologica*, 2a–2ae, q.162, a.7), as had been Augustine of Hippo before him.

which means before God, we experience the cross of Jesus as our deliverance and salvation. The old humanity [Mensch] dies, but God has triumphed over it. Now we share in the resurrection of Christ and eternal life.

In confession there occurs a *breakthrough to new life*. The break with the past is made when sin is hated, confessed, and forgiven. "Everything old has passed away." But where there is a break with sin, there is conversion. Confession is conversion. "Everything has become new" (2 Cor. 5:17). Christ has made a new beginning with us. As the first disciples [die Jünger] left everything behind and followed Jesus' call, so in confession the Christian gives up everything and follows. Confession is following after [Nachfolge].[5] Life with Jesus Christ and the community of faith has begun. "No one who conceals transgressions will prosper, but one who confesses and *forsakes* them will obtain mercy" (Prov. 28:13). In confession, Christians begin to renounce their sins. The power of sin is broken. From now on, the Christian gains one victory after another. What happened to us in baptism is given to us anew in confession. We are delivered from darkness into the rule of Jesus Christ. That is joyful news. Confession is the renewal of the joy of baptism. "Weeping may linger for the night, but joy comes with the morning" (Ps. 30:6 [5]).

In confession there occurs a *breakthrough to assurance*.[6] Why is it often easier for us to acknowledge our sins before God than before another believer? God is holy and without sin, a just judge of evil, and an enemy of all disobedience. But another Christian is sinful, as are we, knowing from personal experience the night of secret sin. Should we not find it easier to go to one another than to the holy God? But if that is not the case, we must ask ourselves whether we often have not been deluding

---

5. Cf. the extended discussion of *Nachfolge* in CD. *Nachfolge* literally means "following after." Bonhoeffer's book *The Cost of Discipleship* was titled in German simply *Nachfolge*. German has a separate term for "discipleship" [*Jüngerschaft*], referring specifically to the calling of the original disciples [*die Jünger*] of Jesus. The word *Nachfolge*, to the contrary, does not refer to a person, but to an action; it connotes no status, but rather the activity one undertakes in responding to the call of God. [GK]

6. Bonhoeffer likewise discusses in *CD* the bestowal of this assurance or certitude [*Gewißheit*] as a benefit of personal confession of sins. There he writes: "In addition to the examination of one's faith there is also the confession of sins whereby Christians seek and find reassurance [*Gewißheit*] that their sins are forgiven" (*DBW* 4:287; trans. GK). [GK]

ourselves about our confession of sin to God—whether we have not instead been confessing our sins to ourselves and also forgiving ourselves. And is not the reason for our innumerable relapses and for the feebleness of our Christian obedience to be found precisely in the fact that we are living from self-forgiveness and not from the real forgiveness of our sins? Self-forgiveness can never lead to the break with sin. This can only be accomplished by God's own judging and pardoning Word. Who can give us the assurance that we are not dealing with ourselves but with the living God in the confession and the forgiveness of our sins? God gives us this assurance through one another. The other believer breaks the circle of self-deception. Those who confess their sins in the presence of another Christian know that they are no longer alone with themselves; they experience the presence of God in the reality of the other. As long as I am by myself when I confess my sins, everything remains in the dark; but when I come face to face with another Christian, the sin has to be brought to light. But because the sin must come to light some time, it is better that it happens today between me and another believer, rather than on the last day in the bright light of the final judgment. It is grace that we can confess our sins to one another. Such grace spares us the terrors of the last judgment. The other Christian has been given to me so that I may be assured even here and now of the reality of God in judgment and grace. As the acknowledgment of my sins to another believer frees me from the grip of self-deception, so, too, the promise of forgiveness becomes fully certain to me only when it is spoken by another believer as God's command and in God's name. Confession before one another is given to us by God so that we may be assured of divine forgiveness.

But it is precisely for the sake of this assurance that confession is about admitting *concrete* sins. People usually justify themselves by making a general acknowledgment of sin. But I experience the complete forlornness and corruption of human nature, insofar as I ever experience it at all, when I see my own specific sins. Examining myself on the basis of all Ten Commandments will therefore be the right preparation for confession. Otherwise, it might happen that I could still become a hypocrite even in confessing to another Christian, and then God's comfort would continue to be remote from me. Jesus dealt with people whose sins were obvious, with tax collectors and prostitutes. They knew why they needed forgiveness, and they received it as forgiveness of their specific sins.

98

Jesus asked blind Bartimaeus, "What do you want me to do for you?"[7] Before confession we must have a clear answer to this question. In confession we too receive the forgiveness of particular sins that come to light at that time. And it is in confessing these particular sins that we receive the forgiveness of all our sins, both known and unknown.

Does all this mean that confession to one another is a divine law? No, confession is not a law; rather, it is an offer of divine help for the sinner. It is possible that by God's grace a person may break through to assurance, new life, the cross and community without benefit of confession to another believer. It is certainly possible that a person may never come to know what it means to doubt one's own forgiveness and question one's own confession of sin, that one may be given everything in one's solitary confession in the presence of God. We have spoken here for those who cannot say that about themselves. Luther himself was one of those for whom the Christian life was unthinkable without confession to one another. In *The Large Catechism* he said, "Therefore when I urge you to go to confession, I am urging you to be a Christian."[8] The divine offer that is made to us in the form of confession to one another should be shown to all those who, despite all their searching and struggling, cannot find the great joy of community, the cross, the new life and assurance. Confession stands in the realm of the freedom of the Christian. But who could, without suffering harm, turn down that help which God considered it necessary to offer?

To whom should we make a confession? According to Jesus' promise every Christian believer can hear the confession of another. But will the other understand us? Might not another believer be so far beyond us in the Christian life that she or he would only turn away from us without understanding our personal sins? Whoever lives beneath the cross of Jesus, and has discerned in the cross of Jesus the utter ungodliness of all people and of their own hearts, will find there is no sin that can ever be unfamiliar. Whoever has once been appalled by the horror of their own sin, which nailed Jesus to the cross, will no longer be appalled by even the most serious sin of another Christian; rather they know the human heart from the cross of Jesus. Such persons know how totally lost is the

99

---

7. Mark 10:51; Luke 18:41.

8. From Luther's *The Large Catechism*, sec. 32, as incorporated into *The Book of Concord*, 460. Bonhoeffer's quotation of Luther here comes from *WA*, 30/1: 238.

human heart in sin and weakness, how it goes astray in the ways of sin—and know too that this same heart is accepted in grace and mercy. Only another Christian who is under the cross can hear my confession. It is not experience with life but experience of the cross that makes one suited to hear confession. The most experienced judge of character knows infinitely less of the human heart than the simplest Christian who lives beneath the cross of Jesus. The greatest psychological insight, ability, and experience cannot comprehend this one thing: what sin is. Psychological wisdom knows what need and weakness and failure are, but it does not know the ungodliness of the human being. And so it also does not know that human beings are ruined only by their sin and are healed only by forgiveness. The Christian alone knows this. In the presence of a psychologist I can only be sick; in the presence of another Christian I can be a sinner. The psychologist must first search my heart, and yet can never probe its innermost recesses. Another Christian recognizes just this: here comes a sinner like myself, a godless person who wants to confess and longs for God's forgiveness.[9] The psychologist views me as if there were no God.[10] Another believer views me as I am before the judging and merciful God in the cross of Jesus Christ.[11] When we are so piti- 100

---

9. This distinction between the confession of sins to one another in the Christian community and the discussion of one's inner psychological troubles in psychotherapy is brought out clearly in Bonhoeffer's lectures on pastoral care (*SPC*, 61–62). [GK]

10. On Bonhoeffer's negative attitude toward psychology and the psychologist, see 99, editorial note 11. Bonhoeffer here asserts that the psychologist regards a client as if there were no God or apart from any reference to God. The German editors of *LT* point out that the wording of the latter half of Bonhoeffer's statement here is, in fact, close to that passage in the prison letters where he, in writing of what led to affirmation of the world's autonomy, mentions the contribution of Hugo Grotius (*LPP*, 359). In *LPP* his point is that the laws that govern society need not have reference to or validation from God for them to be applicable at a human level independent from the dictates of the churches and their clergy. Such a dependence would infringe on the world's acknowledged autonomy. It does not mean, as asserted by some critics of Bonhoeffer's thought, that one should act in the modern world *as if* God did not exist. See Geffrey B. Kelly, "Revelation in Christ: A Study of Bonhoeffer's Theology of Revelation," 56–60. [GK]

11. The need for Christians to have this attitude toward one another and to live in the spirit of reconciliation emanating from their profession of faith in the

ful and incapable of hearing the confession of one another, it is not due to a lack of psychological knowledge, but a lack of love for the crucified Jesus Christ. If Christians seriously deal on a daily basis with the cross of Christ, they will lose the spirit of human judgmentalism, as well as weak indulgence, receiving instead the spirit of divine firmness and divine love. The death of the sinner before God, and the life that comes out of death through grace, becomes a daily reality for them. So they love the other believers with the merciful love of God that leads through the death of the sinner to the life of the child of God.[12] Who can hear our confession? Those who themselves live beneath the cross. Wherever the Word of the Crucified is a living reality, there will be confession to one another.

A Christian community that practices confession must guard against two dangers. The first concerns the one who hears confessions. It is not a good thing for one person to be the confessor for all the others. All too easily this individual will become overburdened, one for whom confession becomes an empty routine, giving rise to the unholy misuse of confession for the exercise of spiritual tyranny over souls. Those who do not practice confession themselves should be careful not to hear the confessions of other Christians, lest they succumb to this most frightening danger for confession. Only those who have been humbled themselves can hear the confession of another without detriment to themselves. The second danger concerns those who confess. For the well-being of their soul they must guard against ever making their confession into a work of

101 piety. If they do so, it will become the worst, most abominable, unholy, and unchaste betrayal of the heart. Confession then becomes sensual prattle [wollüstiges Geschwätz]. Confession understood as a pious work is the devil's idea. We can dare to enter the abyss of confession only on the basis of God's offer of grace, help, and forgiveness; only for the sake of the promise of absolution can we confess. Confession as a work is spiritual death; confession in answer to God's promise is life. The forgiveness of sins is alone the ground and goal of confession.

Although confession is an act in the name of Christ that is truly com-

---

saving power of the cross of Jesus Christ is emphasized by Bonhoeffer in his sermon of November 4, 1934, "Reformation Sunday," in *TF,* 250 [GK]

12. Here Bonhoeffer echoes the theme of the child, with which he ended his book *Act and Being:* 161.

plete in itself and is practiced in the community as often as there is a desire for it, confession serves the Christian community especially as a preparation for participation together in the *Lord's Supper*.[13] Reconciled to God and human beings, Christians desire to receive the body and blood of Jesus Christ. It is the command of Jesus that no one should come to the altar with a heart unreconciled to another Christian.[14] If this command applies to all worship, indeed, to every prayer we offer, then it applies all the more to receiving the sacrament. The day before the Lord's Supper together will find the members of a Christian community with one another, each asking of the other forgiveness for wrongs committed. Anyone who avoids this path to another believer cannot go to the table of the Lord well prepared. All anger, strife, envy, malicious gossip, and conduct to the detriment of one another must have been done away with if all wish to receive together the grace of God

---

13. Bethge mentions that it was in preparation for the communion service that Bonhoeffer introduced the practice of confession of sins to his seminarians. See editorial note 2 above. The connection between the confession of sins and participation in the Lord's Supper, or the use of confession as preparation for the reception of Jesus' body and blood under the species of bread and wine, has an intriguing liturgical history that dates to the medieval period. In the early church the confession of sins was generally reserved to a once in a lifetime act and sometimes was restricted to the reconciliation of a sinner on her or his deathbed. The shift to the eventually dominant system of private confession and penance is traceable to the movement away from the severity of earlier penitential practices by Irish monks of the sixth century. It was not until the eleventh century, however, that it became more customary to grant absolution immediately after the recounting of sins and before the expiatory penance was accomplished. By the time of the systematizing theologians of the Middle Ages, the theology of the sacrament of penance seemed to turn on the basic elements of the penitent's sorrow for having sinned and the minister's juridical power to absolve. The Fourth Lateran Council in 1215 decreed confession of sins for all the faithful at least once a year. By 1518 Luther had denied the prevailing theological notion that confession functioned solely as a purifying rite whose cleansing effects provided sinners their justification for receiving the Holy Communion. Instead, confession was to be approached as part of the whole complex of the faith and freedom of the Christian, who is invited to partake at the Lord's table. See Luther's *The Large Catechism* in *The Book of Concord*, 457–61. For a history of the sacrament of penance and the practice of confession with specific emphasis on Luther's attempt to reform the practice, see Thomas N. Tentler, *Sin and Confession on the Eve of the Reformation*, 345–70 *et passim*. See also John M. T. Barton, *Penance and Absolution*. [GK]

14. Matt. 5:23-24.

in the sacrament. But apologizing to another Christian is still not confession. Only the latter stands under the express command of Jesus. But preparation for the Lord's Supper will also awaken in individuals the desire to be completely certain that the particular sins which frighten and torment them, which are known to God alone, are forgiven. The offer of confession and absolution with one another is proclaimed to fulfill this desire. Whenever anxiety and worry over one's own sins has become intense and the assurance of forgiveness is sought, the invitation to come to confession is extended in the name of Jesus. What brought the accusation of blasphemy against Jesus was that he forgave sinners;[15] this is what now takes place in the Christian community [Bruderschaft] in the power of the present Jesus Christ. One forgives all the sins of the other in the name of Jesus and the triune God.[16] And among the angels in heaven there is joy over the sinner who returns to God.[17] Thus the time of preparation prior to the Lord's Supper will be filled with admonition and consolation of one another, with prayers, anxiety, and joy.

102

The day of the Lord's Supper is a joyous occasion for the Christian community. Reconciled in their hearts with God and one another, the community of faith receives the gift of Jesus Christ's body and blood, therein receiving forgiveness, new life, and salvation. New community with God and one another is given to it. The community of the holy Lord's Supper is above all the fulfillment of Christian community. Just as the members of the community of faith are united in body and blood at the table of the Lord, so they will be together in eternity. Here the community has reached its goal. Here joy in Christ and Christ's community is complete. The life together of Christians under the Word has reached its fulfillment in the sacrament.

---

15. Mark 2:7; Matt. 9:3; Luke 5:21.

16. The following scriptural passages are sometimes cited in support of Bonhoeffer's counsel here, although the actual invocation of the name of Jesus, or of God as triune, is merely implied, not explicitly stated: Matt. 6:14; 18:21, 35; Luke 6:37; James 5:16. [GK]

17. Luke 15:7.

GERHARD LUDWIG MÜLLER
AND
ALBRECHT SCHÖNHERR

# EDITORS' AFTERWORD TO THE GERMAN EDITION

## Ecclesiastical and Historical Background

IN *LIFE TOGETHER* Bonhoeffer describes what he experienced with the candidates of the Finkenwalde Seminary and those who lived in the Brothers' House from 1935 to 1937. Questions about the shape and significance of Christian community had, of course, occupied his attention long before this. Soon after he had begun teaching as a lecturer at the Berlin theological faculty, he invited his students to weekend retreats. Considering how universities were run at that time, this was an unusual occurrence.[1] They would meet in the Prebelow Youth Hostel near Rhinesberg in the northern part of Berlin or in an arbor on a piece of meadowland property near Biesenthal. In the form taken by these retreats one can find an outline of the basic community life in Finkenwalde: daily morning and evening worship, quiet time, much singing, and lots of theological conversation. The discussions carried on in Prebelow during those years made it easy later on for several of those participants in Berlin to have a positive attitude toward the strict order of the Finkenwalde seminary. Out of these Berlin retreats of 1931 and 1932 a circle was formed that stayed together even after Bonhoeffer began to serve the London parish. Their theme was the Christian life; and in their discussions, Bonhoeffer was always interested in its concrete realization. "The invisibility is killing us," he wrote to a friend in 1931.[2]

---

1. See Bethge, *Dietrich Bonhoeffer*,156–60.
2. Letter to Helmut Rössler, *GS* 1:61.

During his stay in England Bonhoeffer visited Anglican monasteries and free-church communities to study how an ordered life in a regular Christian community might look. Through the mediation of Bishop George Bell he got to know, among others, the Society of the Sacred Mission in Kelham and the Community of the Resurrection in Mirfield, in 134   whose company he came to love the 119th Psalm. Beyond that, he also visited the Methodist College in Richmond and Woodbrooke College, the Quaker center in the Selly Oak Colleges in Birmingham.[3] Prepared in this way, he took over one of the seminaries of the Confessing Church in April 1935. The Confessing Church had established seminaries and church-related schools in 1935 as a result of the decisions made the previous year at the Dahlem Synod. They made great sacrifices in order to implement those decisions. From the outset these schools were subject to constant restrictions and harassment by branches of the government and party. On the one hand, the Confessing Church wanted to demonstrate the sovereignty it was claiming for itself in the matter of training students. On the other hand, it wanted to create a counterbalance to those theological faculties that were no longer acceptable to the Confessing Church due to the infiltration of these institutions by the German Christians and their allies. A special significance was thus attached to the seminaries in the church struggle.

Bonhoeffer placed great value on establishing an immediate connection with practice. A nucleus of former seminarians who remained together in the Brothers' House stood ready to represent the spiritual tradition they cherished in the church struggle; the Old Prussian Provincial Councils of the Brethren had released a few of their young pastors specifically for this ministry. One sentence in the application to establish the Brothers' House could be considered the heading for the entire spiritual life of Finkenwalde: "The goal is not cloistered isolation, but the most intense concentration for ministry outside the seminary."[4] "Ministry outside the seminary" meant at that time "to preach the Word of God toward the goal of commitment and discernment of spirits in the

---

3. Bethge, *Dietrich Bonhoeffer*, 334–36.

4. "An den Rat der Evangelischen Kirche der Altpreußischen Union, Berlin-Dahlem. Betrifft: Einrichtung eines Bruderhauses im Predigerseminar Finkenwalde" (To the council of the Protestant Church of the Old Prussian Union, Berlin-Dahlem. Concerning: the establishment of a Brothers' House in the preachers seminary of Finkenwalde), September 6, 1935, see *WF,* 30 (*GS* 2:449).

current and coming church struggles, and to be prepared to assume immediately the ministry of preaching in any new crisis that may emerge."[5]

At any rate it was not "cloistered isolation" that Bonhoeffer had in mind when he wrote to his Swiss friend Erwin Sutz, in a letter dated September 11, 1934: "I am struggling over a decision on whether I should go back to Germany as director of the new Preachers' Seminary . . . or whether I should remain here or whether I should go to India. . . . The entire training of the new generation of seminarians belongs today in church-monastic schools in which the pure doctrine, the Sermon on the Mount, and worship are taken seriously."[6]

What stood behind the attempt at a life together in the Finkenwalde seminary becomes even more apparent from Bonhoeffer's letter to Karl Barth dated September 19, 1936.

> I am firmly convinced that in view of what the young seminarians bring with them from the university and in view of the independent work which will be demanded of them in the parishes—particularly here in the East— they need a completely different kind of training which such a life together in a seminary unquestionably gives. You can hardly imagine how empty, how completely burned out, most of the brothers are when they come to the seminary. Empty not only as regards theological insights and still more as regards knowledge of the Bible, but also as regards their personal life. . . . But there are very few who recognize this sort of work with young seminarians as a task of the church and do something about it. And it is really what everyone is waiting for. Unfortunately, I too am not able to do it properly, but I show them by having them practice with one another. That seems to be the most important thing to me.[7]

Not just theological work, but also a community of pastoral care can only develop

> in a life that is governed by gathering around the Word morning and evening and by fixed times of prayer. . . . The accusation that such practices are legalistic does not really bother me at all. What is really so legalistic

5. Ibid., trans. altered.

6. Letter to Erwin Sutz, September 11, 1934, in *TF,* 412 (*GS* 1:42).

7. Letter to Karl Barth, September 19, 1936, in *WF,* 117, and *TF,* 431 (*GS* 2:285), trans. altered.

136  about Christians beginning to learn what it means to pray and spending a good part of their time on this learning process? When a leading man of the Confessing Church said to me recently, "We don't have any time now for meditation; the candidates should learn to preach and teach the catechism," that is either total ignorance of what a young seminarian is today, or it is culpable ignorance about how a sermon or catechism lesson comes to life. The questions that are seriously put to us today by young seminarians are the following: How do I learn to pray? How do I learn to read the Bible? If we cannot help them in this, we do not help them at all. . . . It is clear to me that all these things have a place only when really accurate theological, exegetical, and doctrinal work is done together with, and at the very same time as, these spiritual exercises. Otherwise, all these questions

137  are given a false emphasis.[8]

The candidates of the Confessing Church were, in fact, looking forward to a table set with theological riches, "in the face of their enemies." For several of them had already made acquaintance with prisons and expulsions, and all of them had endured various forms of discrimination and flagrant abuse. Having been constantly dismissed as fanatics or contentious types they were looking forward to a community of like-minded people. They came from the small groupings of confessing congregations that had lost contact with one another and were looking forward to exchanging views and experiences. They gladly let Bonhoeffer draw their attention to the fact—at least, the majority did—that all the struggles and suffering of the church could only be overcome if they trusted absolutely in Christ's presence in the Word and in the communion of saints. Of course, there was also opposition.[9]

In those days they also clearly understood why Bonhoeffer drew such a sharp contrast between spiritual [pneumatisch] and "self-centered" [psychisch] relationships in the community of brothers. He was solely interested in the community established by Christ alone and not in any human charisms or human claims to authority, solidarity, or friendship. He believed in the Word that calls into being and creates the communion of saints. Bonhoeffer's sharpness and clarity is all the more understandable in light of the groups that were being formed at that time which, fleeing into psychological and liturgical forms of inwardness,

---

8. Letter to Barth, in *WF,* 117–18, and *TF,* 431–32, trans. altered.

9. See especially the testimonials of two of Bonhoeffer's seminarians, Otto Dudzus and Albrecht Schönherr, in *I Knew Dietrich Bonhoeffer,* ed. Wolf-Dieter Zimmermann and Ronald Gregor Smith, 82–90, 126–29.

shied away from the necessity of engaging in the church struggle and
seduced others to take flight as well.[10]

138

## What Was the Practice at Finkenwalde?

God's Word was to be the first word spoken each day. The candidates
committed themselves to silence until the worship [Andacht] that started
their day together. That was not an easy undertaking in the primitive
conditions of the former teacher-training school that had prepared students for admission to a career in education. The seminary was housed
in its classrooms. Most of the seminarians slept in halls. There were far
too few bathing facilities.

Daily worship was comprised of a long prayer from the Psalms in addition to the regular hymn verses and those selected in a random and ad
hoc manner. As in the monasteries, it was their goal to pray through the
whole Psalter every week. The readings comprised a whole chapter of
the Old Testament and a rather long section of the New Testament.
Only on Saturdays did Bonhoeffer deliver a commentary; he offered an
extemporaneous prayer every day. Both the prayer and the commentary
were of great spiritual significance for the seminary. At the end of the
service, after a regular hymn verse was sung, came the benediction. Following the modest breakfast (the daily allowance for food amounted to
one Reichsmark) came a half-hour of quiet for meditation alone in one's
room. This followed a text that had been issued for the whole week. A
remedy for distracting thoughts was recommended: seek to transform
them into intercessory prayer. During the quiet time no conversation or
movement of any kind was allowed to disturb the peace in the entire
house. Telephone calls were not accepted.

After the period of meditation came the theological work that was
normal for a seminary. In the first course Bonhoeffer presented his lectures on "discipleship" [Nachfolge]. Before lunch a half-hour of singing
was scheduled. At this time the unison singing was practiced that Bonhoeffer valued so highly,[11] but choral singing with new and old compo-
sitions was also given a chance. Above all, songs and canons were sung
from the hymnbook for Protestant youth entitled *Ein neues Lied* (A new

---

10. See Bethge, "Afterword," 3–7.
11. See above 66–68.

139   song), edited by Otto Riethmüller in 1933. The seminarians frequently read aloud during the mealtimes. After an evening together with games and music came the daily evening worship, in the same form as that in the morning. These were the last words of the day. It was customary for daily worship to last forty-five minutes; after 10 o'clock it was often felt to be a real strain.

The monthly celebrations of the Lord's Supper were the high point of the community. They were carefully prepared. Bonhoeffer encouraged the seminarians to make personal confessions to one another. He himself went to confession to one of his candidates. The "Finkenwalde Rule" proved to be especially important for the community: the brothers obliged themselves not to talk about a brother who was absent.

This life together was also continued outside of the seminary. The former students were committed to visiting one another. Moreover, they were supposed to participate regularly in the annual retreats of their class in Finkenwalde. Bonhoeffer insisted that participation in this event should take priority over all their other commitments. Even in the final circular letters that have been preserved, Bonhoeffer reminded them of the community that is present in hearing the Scriptures and praying for one another. Of course, during wartime, with its inhuman demands on the individual, he did not want such commitments to wear out his former candidates. In the rough draft of a speech that was to be delivered to the pastors in the event of a successful coup d'etat, Bonhoeffer wrote:

> We call you to order your lives anew. We have suffered long enough from the desire of individuals to go their own way and separate themselves from their brothers. That was not the spirit of Jesus Christ, but the spirit of individualism, indolence, and defiance. To a great extent it has done serious harm to our preaching. Pastors cannot perform the duties of their office
>
140   > alone. They need their brothers. We call you faithfully to keep regular times for prayer and for the contemplation and study of scripture every day. We ask you to claim the help of brothers who can discuss matters of concern with you and receive your personal confession. We impose on each of you the sacred duty to be available to your brother for this ministry. We ask you to come together to pray as you prepare your sermons and to help one another find the proper words. . . .[12]

---

12. Bonhoeffer, "Incomplete Draft from the Year 1942 of a Proclamation from the Pulpit after a Political Overthrow," in *ILTP*, 45–48 (*GS* 2:439–40), trans. altered.

## Success and Influence

*Life Together* was published in 1939, the first year of the war. Amazingly, it has been reprinted again and again since the end of the war. Of all Bonhoeffer's publications, it has the greatest number of copies in print. For many at that time it must have been an aid for reflection and stock-taking. It encouraged Christians to embrace brotherly and sisterly community, particularly in view of the frightful destruction of human ties. Christians reached for this book wherever they endeavored to live and work together in responsible, Christ-centered communities of faith.

Bonhoeffer's ideas about this-worldliness, worldly Christianity, and the world come of age in his prison letters—*Letters and Papers from Prison,* which appeared in German in 1951—cast new light on the work *Life Together.* Only a superficial, eclectic reading of this work could lead one to draw the hasty conclusion that insurmountable contradictions between two periods in Bonhoeffer's thought had now come to light. How could one overlook the fact that the basic concern of *Life Together* was found again in the words about "prayer and action for justice on behalf of people" and in remembering the "discipline of the secret" [Arkandisziplin] of the early church?[13] The words so frequently quoted from the period of the Third Reich, "Only those who cry out for the Jews may also sing Gregorian chants,"[14] became the motto of all those who saw the task of the church not in looking out for itself and reproducing itself but in defending the weak.

141

## The Spirit and Content of *Life Together*

142

Whoever wants to become familiar with *Life Together* will discover in a first reading how Bonhoeffer reveals essential elements of his understanding of the origin and essence, the position and task, of the church of Jesus Christ. He understands the form of Christian life in the church as an answer to the challenge of any secular mentality that stands against Christianity, either in the form of the terror of an all-powerful state

---

13. *LPP,* 300, trans. altered.

14. Bethge, *Dietrich Bonhoeffer,* 512. Bethge has since corrected the date of this statement by Bonhoeffer from 1938 to the end of 1935. See his essay, "Dietrich Bonhoeffer and the Jews," 71–72.

ideology or in the form of a society's paralyzing indifference, which does not allow any decisive significance to be attached to questions about God and truth. If one understands the secular world, as Bonhoeffer does, as being accepted by God precisely in its secularity, and if one sees the church, as he does, wherever people are serious about a form of Christian discipleship that demands one's whole life—wherever faith is lived in practice—then the center of one's attention becomes the question: How does one give a Christian form to daily life that does justice to its origins and to the challenges of the present day? The nature of the church as community (*koinonia/communio*) should become a present reality in the experience of faith. Of course, this does not mean reducing the concept of the church to a natural longing for the experience of community and security. The church is to be understood as a reality that has already been established by God's action in word and grace. Christians associate themselves with this reality in faith and love. Individual, smaller communities of Christians—such as local parishes, congregations at Sunday worship, pastors' gatherings, lay groups, and Christian families—thus do not appear as groups alongside the church. Rather, they *are* practical expressions of the one church, concrete social forms in which the nature of the church as *communio Christi* becomes visible. They are the church at the local level.

Here Bonhoeffer begins to lay the theological foundations of community, not from an analysis of the natural sociological forms or from the romantic insistence on being secure in the feeling of oneness. Rather, he begins this theological work on the basis of revelation and the Bible. The church of Jesus knows it is in diaspora in the midst of the world and in the midst of its enemies. However, in this way it understands itself as anticipating the eschatological community of salvation in the reign of God. And, for that reason, the church of Jesus Christ becomes a sign of hope. The perspective of eschatology is grounded in the incarnation of God in Jesus Christ and in the mission of the Holy Spirit. Thus Bonhoeffer understands the church, following an old patristic idea, as a created image of the community of divine persons in the tri-unity of their infinite love. Yet, only in the incarnation of the eternal Word does the church, as a creature of the Word, receive the dynamism engendered of the Spirit of God. This enables the church to aim to be the epitome of close human companionship with God, which is dynamically realized in a continuous process of uniting brothers and sisters into a living community as members of the ecclesial body of Christ. That is why a strong emphasis is placed on experiencing the physical closeness of one's brothers. The church is the gift of visible community—the embodiment of its unity with the triune God, who meets us in the humanity of Jesus.

The tendency to unite with others for a life together—under and from the creative and uniting Word of God—emerges from the center of Christian existence. The community of Jesus Christ that is thus continually being reformed in the correlation of Word and faith contains three essential requirements for a life together.

*First*, Christians need brothers and sisters because they represent and authenticate the origin of salvation outside of myself (*extra me*), as those who are given to me and yet are not under my control. Christians need their brothers and sisters as the objective bearers and proclaimers of the divine Word of forgiveness and grace. They are dependent on them solely for the sake of Jesus Christ. "The Christ in their own hearts is weaker than the Christ in the word of other Christians. Their own hearts are uncertain; those of their brothers and sisters are sure."[15] Therefore, the goal of community among Christians comes fully into view when they encounter one another as bearers of the message of salvation.

*Second*, just as salvation comes from Jesus Christ alone—and the community of brothers and sisters is to be understood as an expression of God's nearness that has become flesh, as the mode of God's appearance—so the broken original-community with God and human beings is restored only through Christ. As the origin and source of all community, Christ remains the mediator between God and human beings. In that capacity, Christ is also the mediator between human beings themselves.

*Third*, the nature of the church as community is encountered in the 146 Bible under the metaphor of the "body of Christ." However, this presupposes that all Christians are chosen and called to community with God in and through Jesus Christ, the one who initiates and represents the new humanity. As those who, as members of this body, share the humanity of the Word, the Logos, Christians are oriented toward Christ for close companionship with the triune God. In their familial togetherness they are a hopeful sign of the unity between the freedom and love that constitutes the essence of God, in which the diversity of personal relations is the prerequisite for the community of their love. 153

15. See 32 above.

## *Life Together* in the Genre of Spiritual Literature

*Life Together* can be interpreted within the total context of Bonhoeffer's theology only after grasping the meaning of its central ideas. Without a doubt it belongs to the most valuable of Christianity's spiritual literature. Bonhoeffer's renunciation of an academic style of language and a scholarly form of argumentation clears the way for a spiritual intensity that also appeals to the reader on an existential-personal level. However, his commitment to Jesus Christ, revealed here in all its passion, keeps the book from becoming blurred by any romantic sense of community or pietistic fanaticism that would desire first and foremost to enjoy the mood created by religious, self-centered feelings.

Such commitment to Jesus Christ opens up a number of elementary Christian concepts: community, solitude, service, Scripture reading, prayer, intercession, meditation, the ability to listen, forgiveness, confession and forgiveness of sins, Christians' breaking of bread together, the celebration of the Lord's Supper in the church of Christ, as well as the
154    hope of breaking bread together eternally.

Bonhoeffer wants to lend support to Christians who are learning to spell out Christianity anew. Thus we may surely count *Life Together* as one of those basic teachings on Christian faith and life that have become the classics of Christian spirituality, such as the *Rule of St. Benedict*,[16] *The Imitation of Christ* by Thomas à Kempis,[17] or Luther's sermon, "A Treatise Concerning the Blessed Sacrament of the Holy and True Body of Christ and Concerning the Brotherhood."[18] They possess a lasting validity independent of a more detailed knowledge of the theology and biography of their authors.

Nevertheless, one can ask with good reason whether *Life Together* can be isolated from the whole of Bonhoeffer's theology as a merely edifying work, or whether it does not, in fact, emphasize in an essential way many of the great themes of his thought on the issues of "Christ-church-world." One of the standards of Bonhoeffer interpretation for quite

---

16. On this point, see Hans Urs von Balthasar, *Die grossen Ordensregeln*, 173–259.

17. On Bonhoeffer's fondness for and use of *The Imitation of Christ*, see 85, editorial note 10. See also Ignatius of Loyola, *The Spiritual Exercises*, NL 6 B 26.

18. *LW*, 35/1: 54 (*WA*, 2:742–58). Bonhoeffer likes to quote from this work in his early writings; e.g., see *CS*, 126–35, and *Das Wesen der Kirche* (The nature of the church), *GS* 5:263.

some time has been the recognition that in his case theology and biography cannot be separated.[19] However, if this consensus is to signify more than the trivial insight that every theology is always somehow dependent on the personality of the theologian—his or her life experiences and gifts, as well as that theology's location in the history of ideas and the contemporary situation—then this basic hermeneutical rule needs to be stated more precisely with regard to *Life Together*.

155

## *Life Together* in the Context of Bonhoeffer's Theology

The basic starting point for understanding Bonhoeffer's theology is related to his characteristic turning away from a certain prior type of academic theology. Eberhard Bethge has called this "the theologian turning into a Christian."[20] From the perspective of intellectual history, the change resulted from an inner decision corresponding to the loss of Christianity's dominance over the spiritual self-understanding and lifestyle of Western people.[21] In a Christianized society, a pure devotion to the infinite relationships of the *mysterium* produced the theological type of a Thomas Aquinas, an almost iconlike vision of divine truth. Martin Luther's profound existential emotion visualized the divine-human relationship as a drama of grace and sin. Bonhoeffer, however, understood theology primarily as an aid in determining the position of the church, and the Christian life, within a secular world.

More and more, Bonhoeffer was gripped by the conviction, as he wrote in a letter to his brother Karl Friedrich in January 1934, "that Christianity is coming to its end in the West—at any rate in its present form and its present interpretation."[22] Liberal theology had found a position for theology that classified it in the canon of university disci-

---

19. On this point see Gerhard L. Müller, *Für Andere da. Christus–Kirche–Gott in Bonhoeffers Sicht der mündig gewordenen Welt*, 13–43.

20. Bethge, *Dietrich Bonhoeffer*, 153–56.

21. Bonhoeffer attempted to analyze this situation in his lectures at Berlin University, "Die Geschichte der systematischen Theologie des 20. Jahrhunderts" (The history of systematic theology in the twentieth century"), winter semester 1931–32, *GS* 5:181–227. For Bonhoeffer's views on secularization see also the section "Inheritance and Decay," in *E*, 88–109.

22. Bonhoeffer, letter to his brother, Karl Friedrich, January 1934, *GS* 2:158.

plines along with the empirical-monistic [empirisch-monistisch] ideal, as
seen from the perspective of the philosophy of science. Bonhoeffer
declared as unacceptable this attempt by liberal theology to generate a
contemporary theological position by acting as a mediator. Liberal theology, in turn, wanted to reconstitute theology as philosophy, psychology, ethics, or history of religions. In this way, following the Enlighten-
ment, especially since Friedrich Schleiermacher, "religion" had become
a mediating concept between Christianity and modern culture. Basi-
156  cally, liberal theology attempted to root historical and empirical Christianity in a "religious a priori" of human self-consciousness and to
understand Christianity as the highest form of its historical development. Within the unified whole of culture, "religion" was based on what
was rational, affective, transcendental, or pragmatic, but only insofar as
it related to an aptitude, province, and region of the spirit in meta-
physics, individualism, and inwardness. Thus "religion" was, in Bonhoeffer's judgment, only anthropology, which was in the final analysis
incapable of overcoming the immanence of the spirit.[23]

But how does one come to genuine transcendence?[24] This question
always moved Bonhoeffer. It also remains a key problem in his *Letters and
Papers from Prison*. In his attempt to give reasons for the Christian faith
without the help of the idea of the "religious a priori," the young Bonhoeffer first of all encountered Karl Barth. The distinctive mark of the
starting point of Bonhoeffer's early theology was that there can be no a
priori, immediate awareness of God and God's revelation, either tran-
scendentally or ontologically. There only can be an a posteriori, contin-
gent process of being addressed by the Word of God—both in the historical Christ-event and in the current working of the Spirit that gives it
meaning in the midst of the community of faith of the church. This was
worked out especially as a theological epistemology in *Act and Being*.[25]

---

23. See Bonhoeffer's lectures, "Die Geschichte der systematischen Theologie
des 20. Jahrhunderts," *GS* 5:184–95; see also his lectures, "Das Wesen der
Kirche," summer semester 1932, *GS* 5:231–39, and *LPP*, 279–81, 286.

24. See Bonhoeffer's Christology lectures of the summer semester 1933 (*CC*,
30–31); his essay, "Concerning the Christian Idea of God"; and his biblical exposition written in Tegel Prison, "The First Table of the Ten Commandments,"
found in *PTB*, 60–61.

25. A basic feature of the Lutheran doctrine of justification, according to
which human beings in their natural state and in the condition of original sin

"Revelation" meant for Bonhoeffer a reality beyond human control that descends to sinful humanity from above, demanding a response. "Religion," however, meant the attempt to ascend through pious experience and conceptual abstractions. Throughout his entire career, Bonhoeffer considered these to be the all-determining, yet mutually exclusive, options for theology.[26]

157

Transcendence originates, then, only in the concrete act of being addressed from without. In the *Letters and Papers from Prison*, Bonhoeffer speaks of the inability to be in control of the other whom one encounters (the boundary).[27] Transcendence in the direction of God does not occur by means of transcendental reflection and a placing of oneself into the truth. It originates only in the encounter with the person of Jesus Christ, for this initiates "being in Christ" as a being towards God, naturally including an existence in the congregation of Jesus as well.[28] An encounter with Christ, as Lord (head) and body of the church, places us in the reality of God. For in Christ—the incarnate Word of God's freedom—God's being for us, and thus the fact of the covenant, the forgiveness of sins, and the grace of the new life, becomes real in faith.[29]

With this reference to the congregational structure of Christian faith, Bonhoeffer wants to go beyond the actualism of (the early) Barth. Bonhoeffer seeks to show a continuity in the event of revelation, both by grounding the concrete community in the reality and activity of Christ and by seeing it become actual through Christ in the present through Word and Spirit. This idea finds expression in frequently occurring phrases such as "Christ existing as community"[30] or "the community is

---

can reach God neither through their works nor by their reflection, is decisive here. The *cor curvatum in se* (the "heart turned in on itself") can be opened up only by God's action and can be placed in truth and in reality only by God's word. See *AB*, 83–85.

26. On the problematic of Bonhoeffer's concept of religion, see Ernst Feil, *The Theology of Dietrich Bonhoeffer*, 160–202; see also Feil's "*Ende oder Wiederkehr der Religion?*" 27–49.

27. See *LPP*, 387, 381–82.

28. See *AB*, 99–134; see also Bonhoeffer's lectures on "Das Wesen der Kirche," *GS* 5:236; and *LPP*, 282.

29. See "Das Wesen der Kirche," *GS* 5:245, 247–49.

30. See *SC*, 85, 100–102, 135–36; see also "Das Wesen der Kirche," *GS* 5:245.

the present Christ himself."[31] The church, understood as the form of revelation, overcomes from the outset the atomistic misunderstanding of the church as a secondary association of religiously or ethically motivated individuals. Therefore, the way of access to transcendence must include the church in its specific structure, its mission, and the form it takes to carry out its mission.

158

In its unity, as "Christ existing as community," the church recognizes its character as person. The Christ who has ascended to heaven faces the community of faith as its Lord, making intercession for its members in the presence of his Father, acting on them in the Holy Spirit through Word, sacrament, and the community of other Christians. By taking on our humanity, by taking our place, Christ became a brother to us. That is why every other brother has become Christ for us.

By grounding the church in revelation, and opening up transcendence from the point of view of an empirical personal encounter,[32] the church's difference from a "religious community" becomes clear, whether it be conceptually based on the idea of the holy, psychologically based on the human desire for companionship and communication, or developed on the basis of a philosophy of history which posits the idea that the whole of culture reaches its culmination through religion. In such approaches the church is always derived from a "religious a priori" and is thereby distorted into a "religious" community.

> A concept of community cannot be gained from the concept of religion. It will always remain individualistic and atomistic. Religious community is the form of humanity in Adam, the last futile attempt to get beyond the loneliness for which he himself is to blame, to redeem oneself. Presently there is an abundance of proposals to renew and activate life in community in the church, in the youth movement, in the ecumenical world. Everywhere the basis for this is pious experience. At any rate, they don't mean the church of faith. The church is present before we desire it. It is Christ acting on our behalf, it is actualization and application by the Holy Spirit. It cannot be

---

31. See Bonhoeffer's essay, "What Is the Church?" in *NRS*, 153–57 (*GS* 3:288, 292). See also "Das Wesen der Kirche," *GS* 5:251; "On the Theological Basis of the Work of the World Alliance," in *NRS*, 161–62; and "Acht Thesen über Jugendarbeit der Kirche" (Eight theses on youth work of the church), *GS* 3:292.

32. See Bonhoeffer's inaugural lecture at the University of Berlin, July 31, 1930, "Man in Contemporary Philosophy and Theology," in *NRS*, 50–69 (*GS* 3:62–84).

experienced. What we see are only the works, not the persons who are in God. We walk by faith and not by sight.[33]

159

These theological starting points that we have only briefly surveyed here can be recognized clearly in *Life Together*: the grounding of genuine transcendence in the verbal character of revelation; God's personal claim on us in Jesus Christ and Christ's community; and the criticism of a "religious" misunderstanding of church and community life and thus religion's classification in the structure of an autonomous culture or in the immanence of human consciousness.

That is why only a "practical" interest in the church could arise at the time of the church struggle and the resistance to the dictatorship. What is missing, as Bonhoeffer realized in retrospect in 1944, is "personal" *faith* in Christ.[34] That is why to a great extent the church has become incapable of carrying out its own ministry of being "the bearer of the reconciling and redeeming Word for humanity and for the world."[35] This requires a return to the basic functions of the church in "prayer and

160

doing justice,"[36] a focused restriction to "work and prayer."

Thus we discover a conceptual link between his starting point in 1931 and 1932 and his later reflections in 1943–44 from *Letters and Papers from Prison*. But also, from a material point of view, both ends of Bonhoeffer's theology can be held together to form one bow. We come across *Life Together* chronologically and materially in the middle. Is it situated like an arrow in the middle of the bow? Or do we have to move this work to one side, as a reflection on the depressing experiences and set-

---

33. "Das Wesen der Kirche," *GS* 5:254. See also "The Visible Church in the New Testament," in *WF*, 47–48 : "Therefore, a new religion is not being established, rather a part of the world is being recreated. That is the founding of the church. . . . The religious community has its end in itself, in "religion" as the highest—one can also say God-given—value. The church, as the part of the world and humanity recreated from the Spirit of God, cares about total obedience to the Spirit who recreates what is religious and profane. . . . It is not the religious question or the religious concern that constitutes the church humanly speaking, but obedience to the Word of the gracious, new creation" [trans. altered]. See also *LPP*, 281–82.

34. See *LPP*, 380–81.

35. *LPP*, 300.

36. Bonhoeffer addresses the double function of prayer and work above, 74–76. This may be a conscious echo of the Benedictine motto, *"ora et labora"* (pray and work).

backs in the church struggle, because they supposedly made Bonhoeffer retreat into pious assemblies [fromme Konventikel] for religious worship in the face of the world's superior strength?

Do we have to construe this middle phase of Bonhoeffer's theological development merely as a narrowing of his thought compared to its original width and breadth, a phase marked by his experiences in Finkenwalde, by *The Cost of Discipleship* and *Life Together*, a phase that can be interpreted in light of his opposition to the German Christian infiltration of the church and National Socialism's totalitarian battle against the church? Was not his negative and defensive relationship to the world further developed in *Letters and Papers from Prison* and there turned into a positive understanding of the world?[37]

## The Continuity of Bonhoeffer's Theological Approach through the Changing Demands of the Times

It is undeniable that a development took place in Bonhoeffer's theology which is connected with the intellectual and political history of the church in Germany. Bonhoeffer mentions the experience he had in his final years of the profound worldliness of Christianity, an experience that only strengthened his resistance to all that was "religious" in it.[38]

161

---

37. In his *Von der Kirche zur Welt*, Hanfried Müller has advocated this thesis. Recently, however, he has modified his views. See Hanfried Müller, "Stationen auf dem Wege zur Freiheit," 221–42. See also Tiemo R. Peters, *Die Präsenz des Politischen in der Theologie Dietrich Bonhoeffers*, 57–60. Peters criticizes Müller's original classification of *The Cost of Discipleship* in its relationship to Bonhoeffer's theological development.

38. See *LPP*, 369–70, 135. In a letter to Eberhard Bethge on June 25, 1942, Bonhoeffer remarks: "But I acknowledge how resistance against everything religious is growing within me. Often even to the point of an instinctive repugnance—which is certainly not good. I am not religious by nature. But I must think ever so strongly about God and Christ; I acknowledge, too, that authenticity, life, freedom, and compassion mean a great deal to me. It is just their religious garments that disquiet me so much" (*GS* 2:420) [trans. GK]. In a journal entry on January 31, 1944, he confessed that he sometimes read only a little in the Bible for weeks on end. Something seemed to prevent him from doing it, but when he would again reach for the Bible, it captivated him even more intensely. He wondered whether these human foibles were also accepted by God's Word (*TP*, 88).

However, he does not link this experience with precise information about the time or circumstances. Nevertheless, one may assume, in view of the *Ethics*, that his encounter with the members of the political and military resistance, and thus with a mentality no longer directly shaped by the church, resulted in an intensified confrontation with problems of modern culture in law, economics, science, ethics, and politics.[39] His experience of Christianity's worldliness goes along with his early criticism of *homo religiosus* and the religious a priori. And this goes back to his early approach in which Christianity is not the highest form of a religious inclination, but a process of being included in the reality of God in Christ, who has laid claim to the *whole* world with *all* its spheres of activity. That is why being a Christian means living from the vantage point of God's comprehensive "yes" to the world and this earthly existence; but being a Christian also means sharing in God's sufferings in and at the hands of the world. "Jesus does not call us to a new religion, but to life."[40]

162

Religious individualism—including its limitation to partial aspects of life, its retreat into pious inwardness, and its interest in institutional self-preservation—is overcome and becomes a participation in God's being-for-us in revelation, in Christ and Christ's church being-for-the-world.[41] Thus it becomes clear that "the whole world is its territory," as Bonhoeffer had put it as early as 1932, in lecture he delivered at Cernohorske Kupele on July 26. No longer does a gap in the natural autonomy of the world need to be maintained for God.[42]

Thematically, the connection with his early theology is obvious. By contrasting "religious" interpretation with God's free disclosure in Jesus' being for the world, Bonhoeffer opened new horizons for seeing how theology is related to the world. This perspective can best be seen in Bonhoeffer's commitment to the concrete form of the church in the

---

Finally, in *LPP*, Bonhoeffer inquired as to the role of liturgy and worship in a "religionless" Christianity (*LPP*, 281–82, 382–83). In this connection, it is essential to maintain that in Bonhoeffer's theology, prayer, worship, and the sacraments are not necessarily merely identical to the "religious" even if they can appear in religious garb as all aspects of Christianity do.

39. On this point, see *E*, 188–213.

40. *LPP*, 362, trans. altered.

41. *LPP*, 281–82, 285–86, 301–2, 360–61, 381–82.

42. See NRS, 262–64.

triad of peace, ecumenism and international relations, a commitment that is fully in line with his initial concept of revelation, church, and world. Yet an eschatological difference remains; that is, God's reign and the church are not identical.[43]

163

The church claims no totality in relation to the world. Even if it assumes the wholeness of God's Word, nevertheless it recognizes the relative autonomy of the state, and of the world of industry, culture, and family through which God's governance of the world gets asserted in God's own way. A tension characteristic of the church emerges precisely in its relatedness to the world. On the one hand, it is the place of God's presence in the world that has appeared in Christ once and for all. On the other hand, it serves God in the world as an instrument by which God desires to become active on behalf of the world. This is the functional purpose of the church. In his 1932 lectures on "The Nature of the Church" Bonhoeffer depicted this polarity by using the key words *worldliness* and *Christ-likeness* to describe the church.[44] In the *Ethics*, he speaks of the church as a *means to the end* of carrying out the proclamation of Christ to the world, and of the church as an *end in itself* precisely in this proclamation of Christ (as the goal of God's action).[45] Finally, in the *Letters and Papers from Prison*, this duality appears as the "church for others" and as the "discipline of the secret" [Arkanum], in worship, prayer, and confession.[46] Therefore, materially there is no contradiction; rather, in keeping with its purpose, this dual emphasis expresses a complementarity between the church's inner being in God's presence and its function of service to God's world. The central theme of continuity emerges in the process, from his early ecclesiology in *The Communion of Saints* via *Life Together* to *Ethics* and *Letters and Papers from Prison*. Yet this does not mean we have to overlook Bonhoeffer's breakthrough into a worldliness that now is no longer formally defined as the place to which God's attention turns, but is included in Bonhoeffer's theological thought in its multidimensional phenomenality.[47]

---

43. See *CS*, 198–204; "Das Wesen der Kirche," *GS* 5:272–75; and *E*, 207–13.

44. *"Das Wesen der Kirche,"* *GS* 5:270–72.

45. See *E*, 301–2.

46. See *LPP*, 280–81, 282.

47. One should not speak of *praxis pietatis* in the sense of cultivating a pious inwardness with regard to prayer and liturgy in Bonhoeffer's theology, that is, with regard to the discipline of the secret. Instead, Bonhoeffer brings worldliness and the discipline of the secret into a strong relationship with each other.

In the next to last surviving letter written to Eberhard Bethge, dated August 28, 1944, Bonhoeffer reveals the three structural elements of his thought that decisively shaped his theology in all its stages: first, the full [164] and exclusive presence of God in the life, suffering, death, and resurrection of Jesus Christ; second, the believers' assurance that they live their new life in the nearness and presence of God; and third, "that in all this we are in a community that sustains us."[48]

According to Bonhoeffer's statements in *Life Together*, Christians do not belong in the seclusion of a cloistered life or in pious assemblies for worship [Konventikel]. Their place is in the midst of their enemies. Thus the experiment of *Life Together* must prove successful in everyday life.[49] [165]

One would miss the truth of the matter by a considerable margin if one wanted to understand *Life Together* merely as an offshoot of the communitarian movement after World War I, as Bonhoeffer encountered it in the Berneuchen Movement and the Sydow Brotherhood, or as a kind of monastic romanticism.[50] In the Preface to *Life Together* Bonhoeffer expressly distinguishes his understanding from the idea of its being "a concern of some private circles."[51] He is not interested in establishing a [166] movement, order, club, or *collegium pietatis*.[52] Rather, he places the diversity of ecclesiastical forms of community within the context of the life of the one, holy, universal, Christian church.[53] Thus he wants *Life Together* to be taken as one individual contribution to a more comprehensive question and as an aid to practice.[54] [167]

## The Christological Grounds
## for Christians' Life Together

Concrete community is ultimately a vicarious living out of the relationship to Christ accepted in faith, a relationship that always includes

---

48. *LPP*, 391.

49. See 27–31 above.

50. See Bethge, *Dietrich Bonhoeffer*, 379–80. Johannes Halkenhäuser clarifies the interrelationships and the differences in his *Kirche und Kommunität*, 201–5.

51. See Bonhoeffer's "Preface," 25 above.

52. See 45 above.

53. See 45 above.

54. See Bonhoeffer's "Preface," 25 above.

the necessity of relating to the church founded in Christ as the new humanity. "Christian community means community through Jesus Christ and in Jesus Christ."[55] This basic sentence may also mute those critical voices that claimed to see non-Protestant ideas at work in Finken-walde[56] and wanted to relativize the experiment with certain negative judgments such as "catholicizing tendencies," "religious fanaticism," "legalism," or "monastic atmosphere."[57] Because Christian community is the gift and grace of God in Jesus, it is based on the righteousness of Christ which is imputed to the believer "from the outside," just as is our whole salvation.

Since the Word of God goes out through the human mouth, we need our brothers as the proclaimers of the divine Word of salvation. That is the reason Bonhoeffer can see the origin of Christian community and our longing for it rooted in justification by grace alone.

Christ is the mediator between God and human beings, making possible the new being of the justified sinner in the Christ-humanity. Christ is thus the center and the mediator in this encounter with human beings, who live isolated from one another in their "being in Adam," caught in hopeless egocentricity. As members of the body of Christ, however, we find our loneliness overcome, even if, of course, our existence as individuals is not. Therefore, Bonhoeffer is not driving into the opposite ditch of collectivism to escape individualism. The connecting bridge between God and humanity, as well as between one person and another, 168 proves to be Christ as the basis of the new humanity. Yet this also means that I first encounter Christ in my brother and sister. In them, I meet God in Christ. The community of faith and the community of love belong together. They show the vertical and horizontal dimensions of the congregation, which are both rooted in the love of God. Faith establishes unity; love establishes community.[58] The clear christological and

---

55. See 31 above.

56. On this point, see Bethge, *Dietrich Bonhoeffer*, 386.

57. Karl Barth spoke in this way, undoubtedly in view of the instructions for meditation written not by Bonhoeffer but by Bethge. He spoke of a "hard to define odor of monastic ethos and pathos" (*GS* 2:290). Hanfried Müller took a reserved approach to *Life Together* since he regarded it as catholic and legalistic (*Von der Kirche zur Welt*, 257–60). Bonhoeffer himself came to grips with the charge of legalism on 91 above.

58. This aspect of the Lutheran doctrine of justification serves Bonhoeffer's purpose of resisting theologically the attempt by the German Christians and

ecclesial interpretation of the idea of *communio* does not allow a congregational formation that starts with a pious and "religious" desire for the other instead of starting with the Word of God, or that centers itself on the dream of extraordinary experiences in the community.

171

## Christian Life in the Church Community

In that Bonhoeffer justifies the forms that Christian community takes as life in community under and from the Word, these forms are always considered "a part of the one, holy, universal, Christian Church." In their "actions and sufferings" they participate in the distress, promise, and struggle of the whole church.[59]

Living on the basis of its "discipline of the secret" [Arkanum], the church for others can participate in the worldly tasks of human life in society, "not by dominating but by helping and serving."[60] By delineating the church's intensive relationship with the world and giving its ministry an external orientation, Bonhoeffer distinguishes his idea of community from a *collegium pietatis* interested merely in its own piety. The dual purpose of the community's work on behalf of the world [*Stellvertretung*] consists of its being, on the one hand, the goal of all God's ways, and, on the other hand, its standing in the place where the world should be standing. The church is thus completely led into the community and discipleship of the Lord "who was the Christ precisely because he was there totally for the sake of the world and not for himself."[61]

As a post-Christian society develops, the various forms of community

---

other Protestant schools of thought to derive the church from below (orders of creation, votes by race, etc.). "What is church community? Is church community the unity created by the Holy Spirit and the community in Word and sacrament, or is it the community of well-dispositioned, honest, pious Christians, whether their observance be that of German Christians, that of the church committees, or that of the Confessing Church?" (*WF*, 112 [*GS* 2:261]), trans. altered. "God probably intends for only one thing to remain with us, God's Word, sacrament, and promise. We ask for nothing else, because from giving us this there springs the incomparable gift of genuine community in faith, prayer, intercession, in mutual ministry, forgiveness, confession, discipline, and recognizing our sins and the mercy of Jesus Christ" (*WF*, 114 [*GS* 2:263]), trans. altered.

59. See 45 above.
60. *LPP*, 382–83.
61. *E*, 301, trans. altered.

life in the local congregation and in the larger church take on especially increasing significance as intensive means by which to encounter the sources of Christian life in Word, sacrament, and faithful life in community.[62] They fortify the Christian, who is threatened with isolation, to proclaim the gospel and to take an active part in the autonomous life of society in the Spirit of Christ. The polarity between the discipline of the secret and the worldliness of Christianity is rooted in the eschatological structure of Christian revelation. One could say that Bonhoeffer rediscovered this polarity and tried to express it in concrete terms relevant to the post-Christian situation.

172

Bonhoeffer's rediscovery in prison of this polarity may explain why he could say to his fiancée, Maria, then having difficulty reading his more complex theological books, that the only book "of concern to him at that moment was *Life Together,* and he preferred that I [Maria] wait until he was around to read it."[63]

---

62. See 28, 45–47 above. Bonhoeffer notes that there are also mixed forms of the spiritual-natural, such as the family.

63. Maria van Wedemeyer-Weller, "The Other Letters from Prison," in *LPP,* 416.

DIETRICH BONHOEFFER

# *Prayerbook of the Bible*
# *An Introduction to the Psalms*

*Translated from the German Edition*
*Edited by*
GERHARD LUDWIG MÜLLER AND ALBRECHT SCHÖNHERR

*English Edition*
*Edited by*
GEFFREY B. KELLY

*Translated by*
JAMES H. BURTNESS

FORTRESS PRESS          MINNEAPOLIS

PRAYERBOOK OF THE BIBLE

New English-language edition translation with new supplementary material published by Fortress Press in 1996 as part of *Dietrich Bonhoeffer Works*.

First published in English as *Psalms: The Prayer Book of the Bible* copyright © 1970 Augsburg Publishing House. First published in German as *Das Gebetbuch der Bibel* by MBK Verlag in 1940.

GEFFREY B. KELLY

# EDITOR'S INTRODUCTION TO THE ENGLISH EDITION

ONE SHOULD MAKE no mistake about it; in the context of Nazi Germany's bitter opposition to any manner of honoring of the Old Testament, this book, at the time of its publication, constituted an explosive declaration both politically and theologically. It came as no surprise, therefore, that its appearance led to an unpleasant exchange of letters between Bonhoeffer and the Reich Board for the Regulation of Literature, which had seen fit to fine him thirty Reichsmarks for violating the obligation already imposed on him to report his writing activity to the proper authorities. The board added a prohibition against any further publications. Bonhoeffer appealed this punishment on the grounds that he was only doing "scientific exegesis." He argued, moreover, that the prohibitions against his religious writings were so vague that he was unable to discern whether this particular work should have been submitted to the board or not. The head of this censorship board was not fully taken in by Bonhoeffer's disingenuous protest. Although he repealed the fine, he strengthened the prohibition against any further publishing on Bonhoeffer's part, adding that there were enough dangerous dogmatic and spiritual connections in the book to make it impossible for the board to declare it "scientific," or to accept Bonhoeffer's reasoning.

This book could hardly qualify as "scientific exegesis." In fact, Bonhoeffer was fully aware that his writings on themes of the Old Testament, which occupied him during this period, would be part of the church struggle in which theologians debated the value of the Hebrew Bible and the "Old Testament people of God" for the Christian church. This was a conflict aggravated by the anti-Judaism of the German Christians in the German Reich Church which, in Bonhoeffer's opinion, had sold its soul to Nazism. He was particularly troubled by their clumsy, ideologically based attempt to eliminate the Jewish heritage from Christianity. So-called "neutrals" among the scholars in the schools of theology were also criticized by Bonhoeffer for their pusillanimity in refusing to take sides in the church struggle. Many among them, to avoid antagonizing the Nazi government, had abandoned studies of the Old Testament. The hard-core Nazis in the German Reich Church had dismissed the Old Testament as a Jewish book already supplanted by the New Testament.

It was in the context of the German church struggle, therefore, that Bonhoeffer desired to retrieve the Psalms as the prayerbook of Jesus Christ himself. Hence his approach to this book is not that of historical, literary exegesis searching for the human motivation, cultural milieu, historical conditioning, Hebrew usage, or even the psychological disposition of the authors. With due regard to the merits of other approaches, Bonhoeffer declared his intention to go beyond these scholarly analyses in order to offer, instead, a *theological* interpretation of the Psalter. In doing so, he set himself squarely in the tradition of Luther's style of exegesis. Luther had himself interpreted the Psalms christologically; he not only searched for the moral point of a text but also saw in the Old Testament personages and prophetic utterances both types of, and references to, the Christ who speaks even before his advent in New Testament times. Although this approach renders his exegesis somewhat dated and, from a modern, scholarly point of view, debatable, Bonhoeffer seemed much more content to explore the deeper theological meaning that he felt was more congruent with the needs of people in Nazi Germany.

From the very outset, Bonhoeffer made it clear that the Christian use of the Psalms as a prayerbook goes back to the plea of Christ's followers: "Lord, teach us to pray!" For Bonhoeffer, in the manner of Luther, the Psalter is of a piece with the Lord's Prayer of the Gospels. The essence of the Psalms is distilled into this prayer of Jesus; likewise the Christian can see the Lord's Prayer itself as the lens through which one reads the Psalter. And Jesus, Bonhoeffer points out, wants not only to teach his followers how to pray but also to pray with them, and he has them pray along with him. It is, Bonhoeffer says, like children learning to speak the language of their parents. The Psalms are God's way of enabling people to speak in the language of Jesus who invites people to enter into these prayers and thus enter into a relationship with God that is akin to his own union with the Father.

Although Bonhoeffer acknowledges the authorship of King David and others, he reads more into David's role than modern exegetes would concede by insisting that, in the Psalms, David the prophet is consciously attesting to the coming of Jesus Christ, that is, the Messiah. The New Testament itself, he claims, ties the Psalms in a definitive way to Jesus. In that perspective the Psalms become not only a written testimony to the prophetic foresight of the Jewish king and of the people's hopes for Jesus, their Messiah to come, but also the way in which both Jesus and other human beings can pour out their hearts to God. Jesus who has known human weakness and borne pain, suffering, guilt, and death thus expresses himself in the name of all peoples. And the people in turn make his prayer their own. God who, as Bonhoeffer says here, knows us better than we know ourselves, makes us aware in the Psalms of the wonderful ways in which we can pray the prayer of Christ. Through the Psalter, Christ's followers are enabled at times even to pray against the whims of their own hearts. In their rhythmic repetitiveness, these psalms, whether sung or read in the Christian community, constitute for Bonhoeffer the privileged center of the church's spiritual life and a means of regenerating a community's flagging spirits.

## The Psalms in Bonhoeffer's Prayer Life

Personal and communal prayer had a regular, firmly set place in Bonhoeffer's life. He once wrote from the Benedictine monastery at Ettal that "a day without [their] morning and evening prayers and personal intercessions was a day without meaning or importance."[1] Like Luther and in keeping with the monastic tradition, Bonhoeffer saw prayer as the "day's first worship service to God."[2] As a seminary director and a pastor himself, he urged his seminarians, as preachers of the Word, to be mindful of the urgency of letting the Word of God speak to them daily. "Pastors," he said, "must pray more than others, and they have more to pray."[3] The context of that remark was a written introduction to the

---

1. *TP,* 89 (*GS* 2:398), trans. altered.
2. *WF,* 58 (*GS* 2:479), trans. altered.
3. Ibid., trans. altered.

practice of daily meditation in which God's Word in Christ could become God's Word to the praying pastor and to the prayerful community.

Bonhoeffer emphasized the need for regularity in structuring this prayer into one's day. He was especially insistent on morning prayer. His account of "The Day Together" in his Christian community at Finkenwalde is replete with the scripturally based conviction that they must begin the day with prayer. "Life together under the Word begins at an early hour of the day with a worship service together. A community living together gathers for praise and thanks, Scripture reading, and prayer. The profound silence of morning is first broken by the prayer and song of the community of faith. After the silence of the night and early morning, hymns and the Word of God will be heard all the more clearly." Citing a string of verses from the Psalms, Bonhoeffer adds, "Along these lines the Holy Scriptures tell us that the first thought and the first word of the day belong to God."[4] In speaking of the individual components of such a morning worship service, Bonhoeffer, in keeping with his own biblical approach to prayer, begins with the Psalms. Indeed, Bethge, then his student at the seminary, notes that Bonhoeffer put all his heart into their common worship services. Even in the extemporized prayers he composed at these services, the model was the language of the Psalms, with which he tried to harmonize his own prayers.[5]

While such regular prayer had a meaningful purpose in Bonhoeffer's own experience, conveying this to his seminarians was not without its difficulties. Bethge relates that in their first encounter with Bonhoeffer in 1935 and, despite their Bible-centered backgrounds, Bonhoeffer's mandate of a daily schedule of prayer seemed to them an imposition. They too had heard the rumors that Bonhoeffer was turning the seminary into something resembling more a Catholic monastery than a training ground for Protestant pastors. At the least, it was clear that Bonhoeffer was trying something foreign to their experience. With Bonhoeffer in charge, he says, the day would open with a half-hour worship service begun with long readings from the Psalms and from both the

---

4. *See* above, 51. Bonhoeffer cites here Pss. 5:3, 88:13, 57:8f. [7-8], 119:147, 63:1, and 46:5, in addition to the Wisdom of Solomon, Sirach [Ecclesiasticus], and Lam. 3:23.

5. Bethge, *Dietrich Bonhoeffer*, 382–83.

Old and the New Testaments. They would then meditate in their rooms for a half-hour. It was only with the introduction of a common meditation time every Saturday, in which they could share their prayers and concerns, that their resistance toward this routine broke down. They had come to realize that this form of prayer was a profound help in their forming an independent relationship with God and with God's Word.[6] The seminary was to become not just a protracted series of lessons on how to preach and catechize, but an occasion for the ordinands to steep themselves in prayer and meditation in order themselves to become bearers of God's Word, the absolute precondition for being a good preacher or teacher.[7]

In forming Christian community and in developing a prayerful relationship with God and God's Word, praying the Psalter was paramount in importance for Bonhoeffer. Nor would he hear of shortening the Psalms or omitting some of the more problematic of these prayers, for example, those that proclaim one's innocence (un-Lutheran!) or those that clamor for vengeance (un-Christian!). Instead, he claimed that the Psalms need to be prayed in their entirety since they "mirror life with all its ups and downs, its passions, and discouragements." As can be seen from the text of this book, Bonhoeffer gave unique interpretations to these "difficult" psalms. In encouraging this form of prayer, Bonhoeffer cited Luther to the effect that the Psalms, once taken to heart and incorporated into a daily program of prayer, make all other prayers seem so bloodless. "Whoever has begun to pray the Psalter earnestly and regularly, will soon give leave to those other, easy, little prayers of their own" because they lack the "power, passion, and fire" to be found in the Psalter.[8]

In any number of significant passages from his correspondence, sermons, and biblical commentaries, one can see that in pondering the Psalms, Bonhoeffer both encountered the power of God and experienced the passion within his own heart. To give but one illustration of this, Bethge's description of Bonhoeffer's solidarity with the Jews on Crystal Night is significant. In relating Bonhoeffer's reaction to the

---

6. Bethge, *Dietrich Bonhoeffer*, 382; Bethge, "Der Ort des Gebets in Leben und Theologie Dietrich Bonhoeffers," 162–63.

7. *WF*, 117 (*GS* 2:285–86), trans. altered.

8. Bethge, "Der Ort des Gebets in Leben und Theologie Dietrich Bonhoeffers," 163–64.

burning of the synagogues, the breaking of the windows of Jewish shops, and the brutalization of Jews all over Germany, Bethge pointed to the Bible that Bonhoeffer used for daily reading and meditation. There at Psalm 74, verse 8, Bonhoeffer had jotted in the margin the date of Crystal Night, "9.11.38" (November 9, 1938). These verses read: "They say to themselves, 'Let us plunder them.' They have set afire all the houses of God in the land." The following two verses are also marked with a stroke and an exclamation point: "Our signs we do not see; there is no longer a prophet to preach; there is nobody among us who knows how long. How long, O God, shall the foe blaspheme? Shall the enemy revile thy name forever?"[9] A little later Bonhoeffer incorporated his reactions to these destructive acts of racist hatred in his circular letter to the former seminarians now living their separate lives as pastors in small parishes. "During the past few days I have been thinking a great deal about Psalm 74, Zechariah 2:12 (2:8 'he who touches you touches the apple of his eye!'), Romans 9:4f. (Israel, to whom belongs the sonship, the glory, the covenant, the law, the service, the promises); Romans 11:11-15. That takes us right into prayer."[10] For Bethge, this was a typical instance of how Bonhoeffer prayed the Psalms and meditated on them in a way that linked them to life, in this case a most tragic event in Germany, opening that event itself up to the kind of prayer that could lead to protest and counteraction.

For Bonhoeffer, psalmodic prayer was never meant to be encased in little modules of time with little or no reference to the events of life. In the circular letter to which Bethge alluded, Bonhoeffer wanted his seminarians to look up the passages in question and to take to heart God's own word about never having repudiated the Jews. In meditating on these Bible verses Bonhoeffer was also able to express his solidarity with, and affirm God's continuing predilection for, the Jewish people now being persecuted.[11] It is important to note that Bonhoeffer had taught these seminarians that they were to pray these psalms with Jesus Christ, who, in this case, was being brutalized anew in the person of the Jewish victims of Nazi ideology.

---

9. These biblical quotations in this section are taken from Eberhard Bethge's essay, "Dietrich Bonhoeffer and the Jews." The wording of the Bible used by Bonhoeffer differs from the NRSV text.

10. *WF,* 202 (*GS* 2:544), trans. altered.

11. Bethge, "Dietrich Bonhoeffer and the Jews," 74–75.

Christian prayer for Bonhoeffer was, in fact, always prayer mediated through Jesus Christ and the spirit of Jesus. He acknowledged Jesus as one with the community, interceding for the community in all biblically based prayers, especially those of the Psalter. In a memorable lecture on "Christ in the Psalms," Bonhoeffer depicted the action of Christ as the prayer of one "who, like us, is tempted on all sides, who has endured sin and death, as our brother who knows us. He prays this prayer for us, but not as one who does not belong to us, or would not stand by us. He has made our prayer his prayer and does this daily in everlasting intercession for his own wherever they pray *in his name*."[12] It is clear from this essay and his *Prayerbook of the Bible* that Bonhoeffer construes the Psalms as expressive of the special presence of Christ—alive, praying, enjoying blessings, suffering, and even crucified anew. The verses, in turn, become a continuum mirroring one's own life.

Bonhoeffer loved to pray the Psalms because they offered him the sustaining and liberating power of God's own words in coping with the vicissitudes of everyday living. These prayers seemed so well to express not only the moods of an individual's relationship with God but also the turns of love and heartbreak, of joy and sorrow, that are themselves the Christian community's path to God.[13] For this reason he believed they were suited to the liturgical prayer of the Christian churches. Hence he could tell his seminarians that "the prayer of the Psalms teaches us to pray as a community."[14]

These same Psalms, prayed privately, also provided Bonhoeffer with a rich source of solace and inspiration. In the early days of his imprisonment he wrote these words to his parents: "I read the Psalms every day, as I have done for years; I know them and love them more than any other book. I cannot now read Psalms 3, 47, 70, and others without hearing them in the settings by Heinrich Schütz. It was Renate who introduced me to his music, and I count it one of the greatest enrichments of my life." In that same letter he described a poignant statement scribbled over his cell door by a previous prisoner: "In 100 years it will all be over." It was a complaint that life in prison was bereft of any saving worth. But Bonhoeffer told his parents, too, that the answer to such a thought lies in

---

12. "Christus in den Psalmen" (Christ in the Psalms), *GS* 3:296; emphasis Bonhoeffer's [trans. GK].

13. Geffrey B. Kelly, *Liberating Faith*, 148–49.

14. See 57 above.

Psalm 31 where one reads the Bible's answer to the anguish of a prisoner: "My times are in your hands" (Ps. 31:15). Another psalm raised "the question that threatens to dominate everything here: 'How long, O Lord?'" (Psalm 13).[15]

It comes as no surprise, then, that the prayers Bonhoeffer composed at Tegel Prison for his fellow prisoners were closely allied with the wording and spirit of the Psalms. To cope with the discouragement and the somber atmosphere of his incarceration, Bonhoeffer had put himself into a daily discipline of prayer nourished by moments of solitude and readings from the Scriptures. One student of Bonhoeffer's spirituality has remarked that a perusal of his prayers in prison made him begin "to realize with new appreciation the source of Bonhoeffer's spiritual stamina and vitality—his constant, daily, childlike relationship to God."[16] There are no masks in Bonhoeffer's communing with God. His written prayers are often poetic. But the beauty of his words comes not so much from the artistic quality of his poetry as from the grace and simplicity of his prayer life. "Before I go to sleep I repeat to myself the verses that I have learned during the day, and at 6 a.m. I like to read psalms and hymns, think of you all, and know that you are thinking of me," he told his parents in the early days of his imprisonment.[17] And at the end, the prison doctor who attended his execution was to write: "I was most deeply moved by the way this extraordinary, lovable man prayed, so resigned and so certain that God heard his prayer."[18]

## Content and Form
## of "The Prayerbook of the Bible"

Much of the "way" in which Bonhoeffer prayed comes through in this commentary on the Psalms. Bonhoeffer organizes the subject matter according to those psalms that praise God as creator, those that exalt God's will and law, those that trace the history of salvation, those that prophesy of the Messiah, those that rejoice in the presence of God in the church, those that petition for life and life's blessings, those that cry out

---

15. Bonhoeffer, *LPP,* 39–40.

16. F. Burton Nelson, "Bonhoeffer and the Spiritual Life: Some Reflections," 36.

17. *LPP,* 27.

18. Recounted in Bethge, *Dietrich Bonhoeffer,* 830, trans. corrected.

in anguish, those that cope with guilt and celebrate the preservation of innocence, those that imprecate the enemies of God, and those that point to the ultimate triumph of good and the promised resurrection.

There is a common element in all these diverse turns of Christ's and the Christian's common, psalmodic journey through life to God. It is the buoyant hope that springs from the faith-filled awareness of sharing in Christ's own communion with his Father through these prayers. In the midst of all the turmoil besetting a world plunged in war, one can still praise the splendor of God's creation and proclaim one's love for God's will and Word. In a country in thrall to idols, one can recognize and renew allegiance to the only true Messiah, whose victory is already won and whose kingdom is that of justice and peace. In a church torn between persecution and divisiveness, one can thank God that this church and its Christian community will endure. In a historic period in which people are threatened by death on all sides, one can petition for life, happiness, peace, and the positive signs of God's gracious community with all people.

In the final four dramatic sections, Bonhoeffer addresses the problems of suffering, guilt, the imprecation of enemies, and the hope of resurrection. The meaning of these psalms for a people living under the heartlessness and militaristic nationalism of Nazi rule is not to be missed.

Bonhoeffer invokes the psalms of lamentation as expressive of the anguish of the entire Christian community facing the ordeal of persecution, imprisonment, and death. These psalms encourage the Christian to relive the experience of Jesus' passion in all those events in which good people suffer misfortune while the godless seem to be free do their evil with impunity. Bonhoeffer observes that, in this, God's ways are just too difficult to fathom, especially as the cries of the innocent seem to pit God's honor and promises against the apparent signs of God's wrath. For Bonhoeffer, the question of why God does not alleviate the torment of the just becomes, in turn, the plea of Christ for deliverance. He who bore human affliction is God's enfleshed answer to the cry of abandonment. Christ's anguished cry from the cross is the divine way of telling people that God suffers with them in the bleakest moment of a heart broken by the forces of evil.

It is obvious here that Bonhoeffer is alluding to the anguish of Christians. It is equally obvious that Bonhoeffer felt that there could be no specific mention of the Jews, given the rigorous censorship to which his book was submitted. To sympathize with the plight of the Jewish people in any public way could only have brought down the wrath of the Gestapo on the Confessing Church and on those with whom Bonhoeffer was involved in 1940. But it is equally clear that even when he speaks openly only of the suffering of Christians, he is likewise describing the crucifixion of the Jews of Europe to whom he was viscerally bound during the church struggle.

No one is without sin in this time of distress. But innocence and righteousness are, Bonhoeffer insists here, the work of God through the merits of Jesus alone. In this world of rampant self-deception and nationalistic self-righteousness, it is heartening to see Bonhoeffer's spirited defense of the innocent in the context of a realistic appraisal of the psalmist's confession of guilt. The innocent plead for vindication in the midst of their oppression. But Bonhoeffer reiterates his conviction that those forced to suffer, though they be innocent, suffer with God. God is their vindication. One should, he declares, hold one's head high with joy, because the victims of injustice and those who suffer for the sake of justice are drawn into God's own cause.

From this declaration of the communion of the "innocent" with God, Bonhoeffer adds a word about the most troublesome aspect of the Psalter, the psalms of imprecation of enemies. Can Christians, told to forgive their enemies, pray these verses? Bonhoeffer replies in the affirmative, stating his belief that the grievances uttered with such fierceness are really directed against the very enemies of God. In praying these psalms, one shifts the desire for vengeance to God alone. These psalms become for Bonhoeffer an act of trust that God will ultimately vindicate the just against the injustices they endure. Bonhoeffer sees these psalms converging at the cross of Christ. As such, they must be set in the context of Christ's own experience of God's wrath, which he transformed with his moving prayer that his Father forgive even his executioners. Bonhoeffer uses Christ's example to challenge the surface impression of these psalms, making it possible to see that it is the crucified Jesus who leads victimized Christians to turn their outrage at injustice into the prayers of forgiveness and confidence in their eventual vindication.

This confidence is of a piece with the hope for resurrection that Bonhoeffer claims is a constant refrain in the Psalms. What appears to be defeat and death from the viewpoint of the evil forces of this world becomes, in the loving power of God in Christ, the victory of God and the victory of Christians united with their suffering-triumphant Christ.

Bonhoeffer thus ends this remarkable little book on an optimistic note. Against the quasi-apocalyptic background of Europe at war, a church divided, and his own nation engaged in a malignant national policy of genocide, Bonhoeffer's study of the Psalms offers protest and hope. This book, coming from one who is representative of that small group of resisters acting at great risk and seemingly in vain to restore true Christianity in Germany, stands in sobering contrast to the blind, flag-waving patriotism and nationalistic sloganeering that cheered on senseless violence against innocent peoples. The Nazi censor was not deceived; he saw the political implications of this book and its exposé of the suffering inflicted by Nazism on so many. This book not only is a commentary on the Psalter; it also taps into the strength of one's personal communion with Christ that is the sustenance of the faith of Christians caught in a life-and-death struggle against evil.[19]

## The Text

Bonhoeffer published *The Prayerbook of the Bible: An Introduction to the Psalms* through the Verlag Bad Salzuflen, Verlag für Missions- und Bibel-Kunde (Bad Salzuflen publishers, Publishing house for mission and Bible information). It appeared in 1940 and was the last of his books to be published during his lifetime. Reprinted after the war, it went through twelve reprintings up until 1986. The new German critical edition, on which this English language edition is based, was published in 1987 by Kaiser Verlag, as part of volume 5 of the *Dietrich Bonhoeffer Werke* series. The German text of the critical edition contains references at the top of each page to the pagination found in the previous reprint of this work in the *Gesammelte Schriften*.[20] There are two prior English translations of this text, one published by Augsburg Publishing House in 1970, and another published by SLG Press in 1982.

This new, annotated translation owes much to the valuable services of Prof. James H. Burtness, the present vice-president of the International Bonhoeffer Society, English Language Section, and himself a noted

---

19. The preceding sections are drawn from Geffrey B. Kelly, "The Prayerbook of the Bible: Dietrich Bonhoeffer's Introduction to the Psalms," 36–41.

20. *GS* 4:544–69, translated in *PB*, 9–63.

Bonhoeffer scholar. Prof. Burtness was also the translator of the first English version of the book, and so as translator of the new edition was asked to accept an even more difficult task: that of improving on his own critically acclaimed translation. That he accomplished this with considerable skill and admirable patience, even as his efforts went through the long process of editorial revision, is a tribute to his mastery of Bonhoeffer's German text. I am indebted to him for making my work as editor of this volume much easier.

A word of gratitude is also due to Wayne Whitson Floyd, Jr., the general editor of the *Dietrich Bonhoeffer Works*. Dr. Floyd spent countless hours with me going over the text in his usual meticulous fashion, word by word, phrase by phrase, in consultation with the other editors and translators of the first four volumes of the series, in order to accomplish the main aims of the new critical editions—fidelity to the German text and consistency in rendering Bonhoeffer's language and style from one volume to another. The result is, I believe, a very readable text that is faithful to the original wording and instructive for Bonhoeffer's ultimate aim in writing the book, to assist people to pray the Psalms in union with Jesus Christ.

# INTRODUCTION

"LORD, TEACH US TO PRAY!"[1] So spoke the disciples to Jesus. In doing so, they were acknowledging that they were not able to pray on their own; they had to learn. "To learn to pray" sounds contradictory to us. Either the heart is so overflowing that it begins to pray by itself, we say, or it will never learn to pray. But this is a dangerous error, which is certainly very widespread among Christians today, to imagine that it is natural for the heart to pray. We then confuse wishing, hoping, sighing, lamenting, rejoicing—all of which the heart can certainly do on its own—with praying. But in doing so we confuse earth and heaven, human beings and God. Praying certainly does not mean simply pouring out one's heart. It means, rather, finding the way to and speaking with God, whether the heart is full or empty. No one can do that on one's own. For that one needs Jesus Christ.

The disciples want to pray, but they do not know how they should do it. It can become a great torment to want to speak with God and not to be able to do it—having to be speechless before God, sensing that every cry remains enclosed within one's own self, that heart and mouth speak a perverse language which God does not want to hear. In such need we seek people who can help us, who know something about praying. If someone who can pray would just take us along in prayer, if we could pray along with that person's prayer, then we would be helped! Certainly, experienced Christians can help us here a great deal, but even they can do it only through the one who alone must help them, and to

---

1. Luke 11:1.

whom they direct us if they are true teachers in prayer, namely through Jesus Christ. If Christ takes us along in the prayer which Christ prays, if we are allowed to pray this prayer with Christ, on whose way to God we too are led and by whom we are taught to pray, then we are freed from the torment of being without prayer. Yet that is what Jesus Christ wants; he wants to pray with us. We pray along with Christ's prayer and therefore may be certain and glad that God hears us. When our will, our whole heart, enters into the prayer of Christ, then we are truly praying. We can pray only in Jesus Christ, with whom we shall also be heard.

Therefore we must learn to pray. The child learns to speak because the parent speaks to the child. The child learns the language of the parent. So we learn to speak to God because God has spoken and speaks to us. In the language of the Father in heaven God's children learn to speak with God. Repeating God's own words, we begin to pray to God. We ought to speak to God, and God wishes to hear us, not in the false and confused language of our heart but in the clear and pure language that God has spoken to us in Jesus Christ.

108

God's speech in Jesus Christ meets us in the Holy Scriptures. If we want to pray with assurance and joy, then the word of Holy Scripture must be the firm foundation of our prayer. Here we know that Jesus Christ, the Word of God, teaches us to pray. The words that come from God will be the steps on which we find our way to God.

Now there is in the Holy Scriptures one book that differs from all other books of the Bible in that it contains only prayers. That book is the Psalms.[2] At first it is something very astonishing that there is a prayerbook in the Bible. The Holy Scriptures are, to be sure, God's Word to us. But prayers are human words. How then do they come to be in the Bible? Let us make no mistake: the Bible is God's Word, even in the Psalms. Then are the prayers to God really God's own Word? That seems difficult for us to understand. We grasp it only when we consider that we can learn true prayer only from Jesus Christ, and that it is, there-

---

2. On the question of how Bonhoeffer understands and interprets the Psalms, see the Editor's Introduction, 150–53 above. Some of Bonhoeffer's analysis here dovetails with what he states in *LT*, 53–58. See also Bonhoeffer's address to the seminarians of the Confessing Church in Pomerania, July 31, 1935, "Christus in den Psalmen" (Christ in the Psalms), in *GS* 3:294–302; his meditation on Psalm 119, from 1939–40, in *MW*, 103–44 (*GS* 4:505–43); and Martin Kuske, *The Old Testament as the Book of Christ*, 62–67. [GK]

fore, the word of the Son of God, who lives with us human beings, to God the Father who lives in eternity. Jesus Christ has brought before God every need, every joy, every thanksgiving, and every hope of humankind. In Jesus' mouth the human word becomes God's Word. When we pray along with the prayer of Christ, God's Word becomes again a human word. Thus all prayers of the Bible are such prayers, which we pray together with Jesus Christ, prayers in which Christ includes us, and through which Christ brings us before the face of God. Otherwise there are no true prayers, for only in and with Jesus Christ can we truly pray.

If we want to read and to pray the prayers of the Bible, and especially the Psalms, we must not, therefore, first ask what they have to do with us, but what they have to do with Jesus Christ. We must ask how we can understand the Psalms as God's Word, and only then can we pray them with Jesus Christ. Thus it does not matter whether the Psalms express exactly what we feel in our heart at the moment we pray. Perhaps it is precisely the case that we must pray against our own heart in order to pray rightly. It is not just that for which we ourselves want to pray that is important, but that for which God wants us to pray. If we were dependent on ourselves alone, we would probably often pray only the fourth petition of the Lord's Prayer. But God wants it otherwise. Not the poverty of our heart, but the richness of God's word, ought to determine our prayer. 109

Thus if the Bible contains a prayerbook, we learn from this that not only the word which God has to say to us belongs to the Word of God, but also the word which God wants to hear from us, because it is the word of God's dear Son. It is a great grace that God tells us how we can speak with, and have community with, God. We can do so because we pray in the name of Jesus Christ. The Psalms have been given to us precisely so that we can learn to pray them in the name of Jesus Christ.

At the request of the disciples, Jesus gave them the Lord's Prayer.[3] In it every prayer is contained. Whatever enters into the petitions of the Lord's Prayer is prayed aright; whatever has no place in it, is no prayer at all. All the prayers of the Holy Scriptures are summed up in the Lord's Prayer and are taken up into its immeasurable breadth. They are, therefore, not made superfluous by the Lord's Prayer, but are rather the inexhaustible riches of the Lord's Prayer, just as the Lord's Prayer is their

---

3. See Matt. 6:9-13; Luke 11:2-4.

crown and unity. Luther says of the Psalter: "It runs through the Lord's Prayer and the Lord's Prayer runs through it, so that it is possible to understand one on the basis of the other and to bring them into joyful harmony."[4] The Lord's Prayer thus becomes the touchstone for whether we pray in the name of Jesus Christ or in our own name. It makes good sense, then, that the Psalter is very often bound together with the New Testament. It is the prayer of the church of Jesus Christ. It belongs to the Lord's Prayer.

110

## Those Who Pray the Psalms

Of the 150 psalms, 73 are attributed to King David, 12 to the choirmaster Asaph appointed by David, 12 to the levitical family of the children of Korah working under David, 2 to King Solomon, and one to each of the master musicians, Heman and Ethan, probably working under David and Solomon. So it is understandable that the name of David has been connected with the Psalter in special ways.

It is reported that after his secret anointing as king, David was called to play the harp for King Saul, who was abandoned by God and plagued with an evil spirit. "And whenever the evil spirit from God came upon Saul, David took the lyre and played it with his hand, and so Saul would be relieved and feel better, and the evil spirit would depart from him" (1 Sam. 16:23). That may have been the beginning of David's composition of the psalms. In the power of the spirit of God, which had come upon him with his anointing as king, he drove away the evil spirit through his song. No psalm from the time before the anointing has been handed down to us. David first prayed the songs, which were later taken up into the canon of Holy Scripture, after he was called to be the messianic king—from whose lineage the promised king, Jesus Christ, was to come.

According to the witness of the Bible, David, as the anointed king of the chosen people of God, is a prototype of Jesus Christ. What befalls David occurs for the sake of the one who is in him and who is to proceed from him, namely Jesus Christ. David did not remain unaware of this, but "being therefore a prophet, and knowing that God had sworn with an oath to him that he would set one of his descendants upon his throne,

---

4. Martin Luther, "Vorrede zur Neuburger Psalterausgabe" (Foreword to the Neuburg edition of the Psalms), 1545, *WA, Deutsche Bibel,* 10/2: 155.

he foresaw and spoke of the resurrection of the Christ" (Acts 2:30f.).[5] David was a witness to Christ in his kingly office, in his life, and in his words. And the New Testament says even more. In the Psalms of David it is precisely the promised Christ who already speaks (Heb. 2:12; 10:5) or, as is sometimes said, the Holy Spirit (Heb. 3:7). The same words that David spoke, therefore, the future Messiah spoke in him. Christ prayed along with the prayers of David or, more accurately, it is none other than Christ who prayed them in Christ's own forerunner, David.

111

This short observation about the New Testament sheds significant light on the entire Psalter. It refers the Psalter to Christ. How that is to be understood in detail is something we still have to consider. It is important for us that even David prayed not only out of the personal raptures of his heart, but from the Christ dwelling in him. To be sure, the one who prays these psalms, David, remains himself; but Christ dwells in him and with him. The last words of the old man David express the same thing in a hidden way: "The oracle of David, son of Jesse, the oracle of the man whom God exalted, the anointed of the God of Jacob, the dear psalmist of Israel: 'The Spirit of the Lord speaks through me, his word is upon my tongue.'" Then follows a final prophecy of the coming king of righteousness, Jesus Christ (2 Sam. 23:2ff.).[6]

With this we are led once again to the realization that we had affirmed earlier. Certainly not all the Psalms are from David, and there is no word of the New Testament that places the entire Psalter in the mouth of Christ. Nevertheless, the hints already stated must be sufficiently important to us to apply to the entire Psalter what is decisively linked to the name of David. Jesus himself says of the Psalms in general that they announced his death and resurrection and the preaching of the gospel (Luke 24:44ff.).

How is it possible that a human being and Jesus Christ pray the Psalter simultaneously? It is the incarnate Son of God, who has borne all human

---

5. Bonhoeffer's text here differs significantly from NRSV. [GK]

6. The NRSV begins this quotation at verse 1b; trans. altered [JB]. The reader needs to keep in mind that *Christ* is the Greek form of the Hebrew word for "messiah"; when read is this sense, Bonhoeffer's exegesis may be less a supersessionist reading of Hebrew Scripture than it at first appears. It may be read more as a messianic interpretation of these texts, that is, placing them in a conscious relation to the traditions of messianic expectation of some Jews in Jesus' own day. Still, it remains clear that for Bonhoeffer Jesus of Nazareth was to be interpreted unequivocally as the fulfillment of this messianic expectation. [GK]

weakness in his own flesh, who here pours out the heart of all humanity before God, and who stands in our place and prays for us. He has known torment and pain, guilt and death more deeply than we have. Therefore it is the prayer of the human nature assumed by Christ that comes before God here. It is really our prayer. But since the Son of God knows

112   us better than we know ourselves, and was truly human for our sake, it is also really the Son's prayer. It can become our prayer only because it was his prayer.

Who prays the Psalter? David (Solomon, Asaph, etc.) prays. Christ prays. We pray. We who pray are, first of all, the whole community of faith in which alone the entire richness of the Psalter can be prayed. But those who pray are also, finally, all individuals insofar as they have a part in Christ and in their congregation and share in the praying of their prayer. David, Christ, the congregation, I myself—wherever we consider all these things with one another, we become aware of the wonderful

113   path that God follows in order to teach us to pray.

## Names, Music, Verse Form

The Hebrew title of the Psalter means much the same as the word "Hymns." Ps. 72:20 calls all preceding psalms "prayers of David." Both terms are surprising and yet understandable. To be sure, at first glance the Psalter does not contain exclusively either hymns or prayers. In spite of this, the didactic poems or the songs of lamentation are basically hymns, for they serve to praise God's glory. Even those psalms that do not address God a single time (e.g. 1, 2, 78) may be called prayers, for they serve to submerge us in God's purpose and will. A "psalter" was originally a musical instrument, and only in a metaphorical sense is the word used for the collection of prayers that were offered to God as songs.

The Psalms, as they have been handed down to us today, were for the most part set to music for use in worship. Singing voices and instruments of all kinds work together. Again it is David to whom the specific liturgical music is traced. As his playing upon the harp once drove away the evil spirit, so holy and worshipful music is such an active power that occasionally the same word can be used for it as for the prophetic proclamation (1 Chron. 25:2). Many of the headings of the psalms that are difficult to understand are actually directions for the choirmaster. Likewise, the word *selah*, which often occurs within a psalm, probably indicates an interlude inserted at this point. "The Selah indicates that one must be still and quickly reflect on the words of the Psalm; for they demand a quiet and restful soul, which can grasp and hold to that which the Holy Spirit there presents and offers" (Luther).[7]

The Psalms were probably most often sung antiphonally. They were    114
also specifically suited for this through their verse form, according to which the two parts of each verse are so bound to one another that they express essentially the same thought in different words. This is the so-called structural parallelism. This form is not accidental, rather it summons us not to break off our prayer. It invites us to pray together with one another. That which seems to be unnecessary repetition to us, who are accustomed to praying too hurriedly, is in fact true submersion in, and concentration on, the prayer. It is at the same time the sign that many, indeed all, believers pray with different words one and the same prayer. So the verse form specifically summons us to pray the Psalms together.    115

## The Worship Service and the Psalms

In many churches psalms are read or sung every Sunday, or even daily, according to a regular pattern. These churches have preserved for themselves a priceless treasure, for only with daily use does one become immersed in that divine prayerbook. With only occasional reading these prayers are too overwhelming for us in thought and power, so that we again and again turn to lighter fare. But whoever has begun to pray the Psalter earnestly and regularly will "soon take leave" of those other light and personal "little devotional prayers and say: Ah, there is not the juice, the strength, the passion, the fire which I find in the Psalter. Anything else tastes too cold and too hard" (Luther).[8]

---

7. Luther's interpretation of *selah* is one among several possible meanings of the word; however, there is little consensus among modern biblical scholars about what this term means. Bonhoeffer quotes here the Erlanger Ausgabe (Erlangen edition) of Luther's "Auslegung des 67 Psalms" (Interpretation of Psalm 67), 1521, 39, 220. The Weimar Edition offers a slightly different wording, *WA*, 8:25. The main point of this interpretation of "Selah" is also found in Luther's "Operationes in Psalmos" (Works on the Psalms), 1519–21, *WA*, 5:81. [GK]

8. Luther, "Vorrede zur Neuburger Psalterausgabe" (Foreword to the Neuburg Edition of the Psalms), 1545, *Deutsche Bibel*, *WA*, 10/2: 157.

Where we no longer pray the Psalms in our churches, we must take the Psalter that much more into our daily morning and evening worship. Every day we should read and pray several psalms, if possible with others, so that we read through this book repeatedly during the year and continue to delve into it ever more deeply. We also ought not to select psalms at our own discretion, exhibiting disrespect to the prayerbook of the Bible and thinking that we know better than even God does what we should pray. In the early church it was nothing unusual to know "the entire David" by heart. In one eastern church this was a prerequisite for an ecclesiastical office. The church father Jerome says that in his time one could hear the Psalms being sung in the fields and gardens.[9] The Psalter filled the life of early Christianity. But more important than all of this is that Jesus died on the cross with words from the Psalms on his lips.[10]

Whenever the Psalter is abandoned, an incomparable treasure is lost to the Christian church. With its recovery will come unexpected power.

## Classification

We will organize the subject matter of the psalm-prayers in the following way: creation, law, the history of salvation, the Messiah, the church, life, suffering, guilt, enemies, the end. It would not be difficult to arrange all of these according to the petitions of the Lord's Prayer, and thus to show how the Psalter is entirely taken up into the prayer of Jesus. But in order not to anticipate the result of our observations, we want to retain the division taken from the Psalms themselves.

---

9. See Jerome, *Epistola ad Marcellam*, 24.4 (*Patrologiae Cursus Completus Series Latina*, ed. J. P. Migne [Paris, 1844–64], 22:428) and *Epistola ad Marcellam*, 43.3 (*PL*, 22:479), which Bonhoeffer simply took over from Franz Delitzsch, *Die Psalmen*, vol. 5 (revised), 43. See also Delitzsch's *Biblischer Kommentar über die Psalmen*. The 1873 edition of Delitzsch's commentary was in Bonhoeffer's possession and is underlined in the section dealing with Psalm 119. NL 1 C 2.

10. See Matt. 27:46 and Mark 15:34, where the words of Jesus are derived from Ps. 22:2: "My God, my God, why have you forsaken me?" See also Luke 23:46, which cites the words of Jesus derived from Ps. 31:6: "Father, into your hands I commend my spirit."

## Creation

Scripture proclaims God as the creator of heaven and earth. Many psalms call upon us to bring God honor, praise, and thanksgiving. There is, however, not a single psalm that speaks only of the creation.[11] It is always the God who has already revealed the divine self to God's people in the Word who is to be acknowledged as the creator of the world. Because God has spoken to us, because God's name has been revealed to us, we can believe in God as the creator. Otherwise we could not know God. The creation is a picture of the power and the faithfulness of God, demonstrated to us in God's revelation in Jesus Christ. We worship the creator, revealed to us as redeemer.

Psalm 8 praises the name of God and God's gracious deed to humanity as the crown of God's work, something which is impossible to grasp on the basis of the creation alone. Ps. 19 cannot speak of the splendor of the course of the stars without at the same time, in sudden and unexpected interjections, reflecting on the much greater splendor of the revelation of God's law, and calling us to repentance. Ps. 29 allows us to wonder at the fearful power of God in the thunder, and yet its goal lies in the power, the blessing, and the peace which God sends to God's people. Ps. 104 fixes our eyes upon the fullness of the work of God and

118

---

11. Bonhoeffer came out against the idea of a revelation in creation alone, independent of or disconnected from a revelation in Christ, such as was advocated by a theology oriented toward nationalism or infiltrated by racist ideology. In place of this he proposed an interpretation of creation mediated by a christological-eschatological perspective. See "On the Theological Basis of the World Alliance," in *TF*, 96–101. In this lecture from 1932 Bonhoeffer reiterated his attack on the concept of "orders of creation" and the reasoning of its principal advocate, Prof. Wilhelm Stahlin of Münster, that Bonhoeffer had made earlier that year at the Berlin Youth Conference. Bonhoeffer argued that the advocates of "orders of creation" had made it easy for the churches to overlook the evidence of individual and corporate evil in government policies, indeed to claim that such evil may have God's own blessing. The structures of society are not grounded in orders created by God, according to Bonhoeffer, but are to be seen as "orders of preservation" of a fallen world. It is because an "order" of the state can be so anti-Christ that the church in the name of Christ must oppose it. Bonhoeffer makes a similar point in his lectures on Genesis, *CF/T*, 25–26, 88–89. See also *AB* 12, 131; Floyd, "The Search for an Ethical Sacrament"; Kelly, "Bonhoeffer's Theology of History and Revelation," in *A Bonhoeffer Legacy: Essays in Understanding*, ed. A. J. Klassen, 109–10; and Bethge, *Dietrich Bonhoeffer*, 621. [GK]

sees it at the same time as nothing before the one whose honor alone remains forever, and who finally must blot out sins.

The creation psalms are not lyrical poems, but provide guidance for the people of God by which they are to find and honor the creator of the world in the grace of salvation that they have experienced. The creation serves those who believe, and everything created by God is good when we receive it with thanksgiving (1 Tim. 4:3f.). But we can give thanks only for that which stands in harmony with the revelation of God in Jesus Christ. The creation with all its gifts is there for the sake of Jesus Christ. So we thank God with, in, and through Jesus Christ to whom we belong, for the splendor of God's creation.

### The Law

The three psalms (1, 19, 119) that in a special way make the law of God the object of thanksgiving, praise, and petition, wish above all to make clear to us the blessing of the law. Under "law," then, is to be chiefly understood the entire redemptive act of God and direction for a new life in obedience. Joy in the law, in the commandments of God, fills us when God has given to our life the great transformation that comes through Jesus Christ. That God might sometimes hide God's own command from me (Ps. 119:19), that God might someday not let me recognize the divine will, is the deepest anxiety of the new life.

It is grace to know God's commands. They free us from self-made plans and conflicts. They make our steps certain and our way joyful. We are given God's commands so that we may fulfill them, and "[God's] commandments are not burdensome" (1 John 5:3) for those who have found all salvation in Jesus Christ. Jesus himself was under the law and fulfilled it in total obedience to the Father. God's will became his joy, his
119     food. So in us he gives thanks for the grace of the law and grants us joy in its fulfillment. Now we confess our love for the law. We affirm that we hold it dear, and we ask that we continue to be preserved blameless in it. We do not do this in our own power, but we pray it in the name of Jesus Christ, who is for us and in us.

Psalm 119 becomes especially difficult for us perhaps because of its length and uniformity.[12] Here a rather slow, quiet, patient movement

---

12. See Bonhoeffer, "Meditation on Psalm 119," 1939–40, in MW, 101–45 (*GS* 4:505–43). Bonhoeffer worked on this commentary only sporadically, never polishing it into finished form. [GK]

from word to word, from sentence to sentence is helpful. We recognize, then, that the apparent repetitions are in fact always new variations on one theme, the love of God's word. As this love can have no end, so also the words that confess it can have no end. They want to accompany us through all of life, and in their simplicity they become the prayer of the child, the adult, and the elderly.

### The History of Salvation

Psalms 78, 105, and 106 tell us about the history of the people of God on earth, the electing grace and faithfulness of God and the faithlessness and ingratitude of God's people. Ps. 78 is not addressed to God at all. How ought we to pray these psalms? Ps. 106 summons us to thanksgiving, praise, commitment, and petition, to the confession of sin and to the cry for help in the light of the past history of salvation. Thanksgiving for the goodness of God, which continues for God's people into eternity, which we also today experience as did our parents; praise for the wonderful works which God accomplished for our sake, from the redemption of God's people out of Egypt all the way to Golgotha; commitment to keep the command of God more faithfully than before; petition for the grace of God to keep it according to God's promise; confession of our own sin, faithlessness, and unworthiness in the face of so great a mercy; crying out for the final gathering together and redemption of the people of God.

We pray these psalms when we look upon everything that God once did for God's people as having been done for us, when we confess our   120
guilt and the divine grace, when on the basis of God's former wonderful works we hold God to promises made and pray for their fulfillment, and when we finally see the entire history of God's people with their God fulfilled in Jesus Christ, through whom we have been helped and will be helped. For the sake of Jesus Christ we bring God thanksgiving, petition, and confession.

### The Messiah

God's history of salvation comes to fulfillment in the sending of the Messiah.[13] According to Jesus' own exposition, the Psalter prophesied

---

13. On the christological interpretation, see Bonhoeffer's essay, "Christus in

about this Messiah (Luke 24:44). Psalms 22 and 69 are known to the Christian community as the psalms of the passion of Christ.

Jesus himself prayed the beginning of Psalm 22 on the cross, and thus clearly made it his prayer. Heb. 2:12 places verse 23 [22] in the mouth of Christ. Verses 9 [8] and 19 [18] are direct prophecies of the crucifixion of Jesus. If David himself once prayed this psalm in his own suffering, he did it as the king anointed by God and therefore persecuted by men. From this king, Christ was to come. He did it as the one who bore in himself the Christ. But Christ appropriated this prayer, and for the first time it acquired its full meaning. We can pray this psalm only in community with Jesus Christ as those who have participated in the suffering of Christ. We pray this psalm not out of our random personal suffering, but out of the suffering of Christ that has also come upon us. But we always hear Jesus Christ praying with us and through him that Old Testament king. Repeating this prayer, without ever being able to measure or experience it in its entire depth, we walk with Christ praying before the throne of God.

In Psalm 69, verse 6 [5] tends to present certain difficulties, for here Christ complains about his foolishness and guilt to God. Certainly David spoke here of his own guilt. But Christ is speaking of the guilt of all people, also David's guilt and my own, which he has taken upon himself and borne, and for which he now suffers the wrath of the Father. The truly human Jesus Christ prays in this psalm and takes us into his prayer.

Psalms 2 and 110 testify to the victory of Christ over his enemies, the establishment of his reign, the worship of him by the people of God. Here also the prophecy links up with David and his kingdom. But we already recognize in David the coming Christ. Luther calls Psalm 110 "the truly supreme, main Psalm of our dear Lord Jesus Christ."[14]

Psalms 20, 21, and 72 no doubt referred originally to the earthly kingdom of David and Solomon. Psalm 20 asks for the victory of the messianic king over his enemies, for the acceptance by God of his sacrifice; Ps. 21 gives thanks for the victory and the crowning of the king; Ps. 72

121

den Psalmen," *GS* 3:294–302. See also Ernst Georg Wendel, *Studien zur Homiletik Dietrich Bonhoeffers. Predigt–Hermeneutik–Sprache,* 87–88 and 135–37; and Kuske, *The Old Testament as the Book of Christ,* 62–67. [GK]

14. Luther, "Predigt über den 110 Psalm" (Sermon on Psalm 110), 1535, *WA,* 41:79.

asks for justice and help for the poor, for peace, stable government, and eternal honor in the king's realm. We pray in these psalms for the victory of Jesus Christ in the world, we give thanks for the victory already won, and we pray for the establishment of the kingdom of justice and of peace under the king Jesus Christ. To this group also belong Ps. 61:7ff. [6-8] and Ps. 63:12 [11].

The much debated Psalm 45 speaks about love for the messianic king, about his beauty, his wealth, his power. At her marriage to this king the bride is to forget her people and her father's house (v. 11 [10]) and swear allegiance to the king. For him alone she is to adorn herself and come to him with joy. That is the song and prayer of the love between Jesus, the king, and his church, which belongs to him.

### *The Church*

Psalms 27, 42, 46, 48, 63, 81, 84, 87, and others sing of Jerusalem, the city of God, of the great festivals of the people of God, of the temple and the glorious services of worship. It is the presence of the God of salvation in the midst of God's people for which we here give thanks, about which we rejoice, for which we long. What Mount Zion and the temple were for the Israelites is for us the church of God in all the world, where God always dwells with the people of God in word and sacrament. This church will endure in spite of all its enemies (Ps. 46); its captivity under the powers of the godless world will come to an end ([Pss.] 126, 137). The gracious God who is present in Christ to the congregation is the fulfillment of all thanksgiving, all joy and yearning in the Psalms. As Jesus, in whom God truly dwells, longed for community with God because he had become human like us (Lk. 2:49), so he prays with us for the fullness of God's nearness and presence with those who are his.

God has promised to be present in the worship service of the congregation. So the congregation conducts its worship service according to God's order. But Jesus Christ himself has offered the perfect worship service, in that he fulfilled all the ordained sacrifices in his own voluntary, sinless sacrifice. In his own person Christ offered God's sacrifice for us and our sacrifice for God. For us there remains only the sacrifice of praise and thanksgiving in prayers, songs, and in a life lived according to God's commands (Ps. 15, Ps. 50). So our entire life becomes the worship service, the thank-offering. God wishes to acknowledge such a thank-offering and to show salvation to those who are thankful (Ps. 50:23). These psalms wish to teach us to become thankful to God for the sake of Christ and to praise him in the congregation with heart, mouth and hands.

## Life

It is striking to many earnest Christians as they pray the Psalms how frequently there occurs a petition for life and good fortune. When looking at the cross of Christ there arises in many the unhealthy thought that life and the visible earthly blessings of God are in themselves certainly a questionable good and in any case not to be desired. They then take the corresponding prayers of the Psalter as an early first stage of Old Testament piety that is overcome in the New Testament. But in doing so they want to be even more spiritual than God is.

123   As the petition for daily bread includes the entire sphere of the needs of bodily life, so the prayer that is directed to the God who is the creator and sustainer of this life necessarily includes the petition for life, health, and the visible evidence of God's friendliness. Bodily life is not disdained. On the contrary, God has given us community in Jesus Christ precisely so that we can live in God's presence in this life and then certainly also in the life to come. For this reason God gives us earthly prayers so that we can know, praise, and love God all the more. It is God's will that it go well on earth for those who are devout (Ps. 37).[15] This desire is not set aside by the cross of Jesus Christ, but is established all the more. And precisely at the point where in following Jesus people must take on many privations, they will answer the question of Jesus, "Did you lack anything?" as the disciples answered it: "No, not a thing." (Luke 22:35).[16] The assumption behind this is the teaching of the psalm: "Better is a little that the righteous person has than the abundance of many wicked" (Ps. 37:16).

We really ought not to have a bad conscience in praying with the Psalter for life, health, peace, and earthly good, if only like the psalm itself we recognize all these as evidences of God's gracious community

---

15. The exact reference, not included in Bonhoeffer's text, is Ps. 37:3-4.

16. Bonhoeffer's quotation from Luke ends with the disciples' reply: "Never [*Niemals*]!" [GK]

with us and thereby hold fast to the knowledge that God's goodness is better than life (Ps. 63:4 [3], 73:25f.).

Psalm 103 teaches us to understand all the fullness of the gifts of God, from the preservation of life to the forgiveness of sins, as a great unity and to come before God with thanks and praise for it (cf. also Ps.65). For the sake of Jesus Christ, the Creator gives us life and sustains it. So God wants to make us ready, finally, through the loss of all earthly goods in death, to obtain eternal life. For the sake of Jesus Christ alone, and at his bidding, we may pray for the good things of life, and for the sake of Christ we should also do it with confidence. But when we receive what we need, then we should not stop thanking God from the heart for being so friendly to us for the sake of Jesus Christ.

124

## *Suffering*

"Where do you find more pitiful, miserable words of sadness than in the psalms of lamentation? There you see into the heart of all the saints as into death, even as into hell. How sad and dark it is there in every wretched corner of the wrath of God" (Luther).[17]

The Psalter has rich instruction for us about how to come before God in a proper way in the various sufferings that the world brings upon us. The Psalms know it all: serious illness, deep isolation from God and humanity, threats, persecution, imprisonment, and whatever conceivable peril there is on earth (13, 31, 35, 41, 44, 54, 55, 56, 61, 74, 79, 86, 88, 102, 105, and others). They do not deny it, they do not deceive themselves with pious words about it, they allow it to stand as a severe ordeal of faith, indeed at times they no longer see beyond the suffering (Ps. 88), but they complain about it all to God. No single human being can pray the psalms of lamentation out of his or her own experience. Spread out before us here is the anguish of the entire Christian community throughout all time, as Jesus Christ alone has wholly experienced it. Because it happens with God's will, indeed because God alone knows it completely and better than we ourselves, therefore only God can help. But then, all our questions must also again and again storm directly against God.

There is in the Psalms no quick and easy surrender [Ergebung] to suf-

---

17. Luther, "Vorrede auf den Psalter" (Foreword to the Psalter), 1545, *WA, Deutsche Bibel,* 10/1: 103.

fering. It always comes through struggle, anxiety, and doubt. Our confidence in God's righteousness and, indeed, in God's good and gracious will, is shaken, for it allows the pious to suffer misfortune but the godless to escape free (Pss. 44, 35).[18] God's ways are too difficult to grasp. But even in the deepest hopelessness, God alone remains the one addressed. Help is neither expected from other people, nor does the sufferer in self-pity lose sight of God, the origin and goal of all affliction. The one who suffers sets out to battle against God for God. God's promise, God's previous redemptive deeds, the honor of God's name among all people, are again and again held up before the wrathful God.

125

If I am guilty, why does God not forgive me? If I am not guilty, why does God not end my torment and demonstrate my innocence to my enemies (Pss. 38, 79, 44)? There is no theoretical answer to all these questions in the Psalms any more than in the New Testament. The only real answer is Jesus Christ. But this answer is already being sought in the Psalms. It is common to all of them that they cast every difficulty and tribulation [Anfechtung] upon God: "We can no longer bear them, take them away from us and bear them yourself, for you alone can handle suffering." That is the goal of all the psalms of lament. They pray about the one who took upon himself our sickness and bore our infirmities, Jesus Christ. They proclaim Jesus Christ as the only help in suffering, for in Christ is God with us.

The psalms of lament are concerned with full community with the God who is righteousness and love. But Jesus Christ is not only the goal of our prayer; he himself is also with us in our prayer. He, who bore every affliction[19] and brought it before God, prayed in God's name for our sake: "Not what I want, but what you want."[20] For our sake he cried out on the cross: "My God, my God, why have you forsaken me?"[21] Now we know that there is no longer any suffering on earth in which Christ, our only helper, is not with us, suffering and praying with us.

On the basis of this conviction, the great psalms of trust emerge.

---

18. Bonhoeffer lists the reference as "Ps. 44, 35," thus creating an ambiguity for German speaking readers for whom such a reference could also mean Ps. 44, verse 35. The German editors point out that Bonhoeffer undoubtedly meant both Psalm 44 and Psalm 35 seen in their entirety. [GK]

19. See Isa. 53:4; Matt. 8:17; John 1:29.

20. Matt. 26:39.

21. Matt. 27:46.

Trust in God without Christ is empty and without certainty; indeed it can only be another form of self-trust. But whoever knows that God has entered into our suffering in Jesus Christ himself may say with great confidence: "For you are with me, your rod and your staff, they comfort me"[22] (Pss. 23, 37, 63, 73, 91, 121).

126

## *Guilt*

There are fewer prayers for the forgiveness of sins in the Psalter than we expect. Most psalms presuppose complete certainty of the forgiveness of sins. That may surprise us. But even in the New Testament the same thing is true. Christian prayer is diminished and endangered when it revolves exclusively around the forgiveness of sins. There is such a thing as confidently leaving sin behind for the sake of Jesus Christ.

Yet in no way is the prayer of repentance absent in the Psalter. The seven so-called penitential psalms (6, 32, 38, 51, 102, 130, 143), yet not these alone (Pss. 14, 15, 25, 31, 39, 40, 41, etc.), lead us into the very depth of the recognition of sin before God. They help us in the confession of guilt. They turn our entire trust to the forgiving grace of God, so that Luther has quite rightly called them the "Pauline Psalms."[23] Usually a particular occasion leads to such a prayer. It may be heavy guilt (Pss. 32, 51); it may be unexpected suffering that drives us to repentance (Pss. 38, 102). In every case all hope is fixed on free forgiveness, as God has

---

22. Ps. 23:4.

23. This expression probably comes from Karl Holl's "Luthers Bedeutung für den Fortschritt der Auslegungskunst": "Briefly stated, it is the Pauline Gospel which Luther draws out of the Psalms as the tropological meaning" (546). "It is obvious that Luther bases his interpretation on the conviction that the Bible in all its parts has one and the same meaning. Under this constraint he points out that what had become for him the most significant feature of the Bible, the Pauline Gospel, was also integral to the Psalms. He did not realize that he was, thereby, doing very serious violence to the text. The Psalms, indeed, preach self-justification as does the entire Old Testament. . . . The meaning in the Pauline texts was somewhat the opposite of what the text [of the Psalms] implied. Only in the penitential psalms did such an interpretation find a real basis for Luther's conclusion" (549-50). Karl Holl (1866-1926) was considered the principal founder of the "Luther renaissance" in Germany. For Bonhoeffer's comments on Holl, including his critical reservations, see *CS*, 97, 127, 154-55, 185, 225, and *Jugend und Studium, 1918-1927 (DBW*, 9):305-6. See also Bethge, *Dietrich Bonhoeffer*, 46-47.

offered and promised it to us for all time in God's word about Jesus Christ.

The Christian will find scarcely any difficulty in praying these psalms. Nevertheless, the question could arise concerning how we are to under-127 stand the fact that Christ also prays these psalms with us. How can the sinless one ask for forgiveness? In the same way that the sinless one can bear the sins of the world and be made sin for us (2 Cor. 5:21). Jesus prays for the forgiveness of sins, yet not for his own but ours, which he has taken upon himself and for which he suffers. He puts himself completely in our place; he wants to be a human being before God as we are. So Jesus prays even the most human of all prayers with us and, precisely in this, shows himself to be the true Son of God.

It is often particularly striking and objectionable to the Protestant Christian that in the Psalter the innocence of the pious is spoken of at least as often as is their guilt (cf. Pss. 5, 7, 9, 16, 17, 26, 35, 41, 44, 59, 66, 68, 69, 73, 86, and others). Here seems to be evidence of a residue of the so-called Old Testament righteousness through works, with which the Christian can have nothing more to do. This point of view is completely superficial and knows nothing of the depth of the Word of God. It is certain that one can speak of one's own innocence in a self-righteous manner, but do we not realize that one can also pray the most humble confession of sin very self-righteously? Speaking of one's own guilt can be just as far from the Word of God as speaking of one's innocence.

But the question is not what possible motives stand behind a prayer, but whether the content of the prayer itself is true or false. Here it is clear that believing Christians have something to say not only about their guilt, but something equally important about their innocence and righteousness. To have faith as a Christian means that, through the grace of God and the merit of Jesus Christ, the Christian has become entirely innocent and righteous in God's eyes—that "there is therefore now no condemnation for those who are in Christ Jesus" (Rom. 8:1). And to pray as a Christian means to hold fast to this innocence and righteousness in which Christians share, and for which they appeal to God's Word and give God thanks. If in other respects we take God's action toward us at all seriously, then we not only may, but plainly must, pray in all humility and certainty: "I was blameless before [God], and I kept myself from guilt" (Ps. 18:24 [23]); "If you test me, you will find no

wickedness in me" (Ps. 17:3).[24] With such a prayer we stand in the center   128
of the New Testament, in the community of the cross of Jesus Christ.

The assertion of innocence comes out with particular emphasis in the psalms that deal with oppression by godless enemies. The primary thought here is of the justice of God's cause, which also, to be sure, vindicates the one who embraces it. The fact that we are persecuted for the sake of God's cause really places us in the right over against the enemy of God. Alongside objective innocence, which can of course never be really objective because the fact of the grace of God likewise always meets us personally, there can then stand in such a psalm the personal confession of guilt (Pss. 41:5 [4], 69:6 [5]). This is again only a sign that I really embrace God's cause. I can then ask even in the same breath: "Vindicate me, O God, and defend my cause against an ungodly people" (Ps. 43:1).

It is a thoroughly unbiblical and destructive idea that we can never suffer innocently as long as some kind of fault still remains in us. Neither the Old nor the New Testament makes such a judgment. If we are persecuted for the sake of God's cause, then we suffer innocently, and that means we suffer with God. That we really are with God and, therefore, really innocent is demonstrated precisely in this, that we pray for the forgiveness of our sins.

But we are innocent not only in relation to the enemies of God, but also before God, for we are now seen united with God's cause, into which it is precisely God who has drawn us, and God forgives us our sins. So all the psalms of innocence join in the hymn: "O blood of Christ, O Lord of Righteousness / my Robe of Honor, my Adorning dress, / Before God's throne I'll be clothed with you / When in heavenly glory I'll live anew."[25]

---

24. See Ps. 17:3 in the *Luther Bibel,* where one reads: "You test my heart and watch over it during the night; you try me and find nothing [of evil in me]."

25. [Trans. GK]. Bonhoeffer cites the *Evangelisches Gesangbuch für Brandenburg und Pommern,* no. 154, v. 1. An alternate English translation can be found in *The Service Book and Hymnal,* no. 376. This verse suggests Rev. 7:14. This hymn is also in the *Evangelisches Kirchengesangbuch,* no. 273, where the first verse is traced to Leipzig, 1638. *The Service Book and Hymnal* attributes the verse to Paul Eber (1511–69) and claims it was written earlier than 1638. [GK]

### Enemies

No part of the Psalter causes us greater difficulty today than the so-
129  called psalms of vengeance.[26] With shocking frequency their thoughts
penetrate the entire Psalter (5, 7, 9, 10, 13, 16, 21, 23, 28, 31, 35, 36, 40,
41, 44, 52, 54, 55, 58, 59, 68, 69, 70, 71, 137, and others). All attempts to
pray these psalms seem doomed to failure. They really seem to lay
before us the so-called preliminary religious stage [religiöse Vorstufe] in
relation to the New Testament. Christ prays on the cross for his enemies
and teaches us to do the same. How can we call down God's vengeance
upon our enemies with these psalms? The question is therefore: Can the
imprecatory psalms be understood as the Word of God for us and as the
prayer of Jesus Christ? Can we pray these psalms as Christians? Note
carefully that again we are not asking about possible motives, which we
cannot in any case discover, but about the *content* of the prayer.

The enemies referred to here are enemies of God's cause, who lay
hands on us because of God. Therefore it is nowhere a matter of personal conflict. Nowhere do those who pray these psalms want to take

---

26. It is important to note that in arguing for the need to integrate even these
seemingly atypically Christian passages into the Christian gospel, Bonhoeffer is
combating not only the tradition of Marcion, the second-century Christian who
rejected the Old Testament, but also the views of Emanuel Hirsch, whose exegesis of portions of the Old Testament seemed tainted with the regnant anti-Jewish,
Nazi ideology. Bonhoeffer's consistency on this point can be seen by examining
his "Predigt über einen Rachepsalm: Psalm 58" (Sermon on a Psalm of wrath:
Psalm 58), July 11, 1937, where he notes that the pleas of the innocent and the
avenging wrath of God converge in the cross of the innocent Jesus who suffers
for the just and unjust alike. Bonhoeffer declares toward the end of this sermon
that "in the midst of this distress, Christ prays this psalm vicariously as our representative. He accuses the godless, he calls down upon them God's vengeance
and justice, and he gives himself for all the godless with his innocent suffering on
the cross. And now we too pray this psalm with him, in humble thanks that we
have been granted deliverance from wrath through the cross of Christ, in our
fervent prayer that God will bring all our enemies under the cross of Christ and
grant them grace. . ." (*MW*, 96 [*GS* 4:422]). Earlier in that sermon Bonhoeffer
had interpreted the psalm in the context of Christ's prayer from the cross for
forgiveness of his enemies. Few exegetes today would agree from a historical
point of view with Bonhoeffer's attempt to interpret the psalms of wrath in
terms of the Christian gospel's insistence on forgiving one's enemies. On this
point and on Bonhoeffer's entire approach to Old Testament exegesis, see especially Kuske, *The Old Testament as the Book of Christ*, 60–144. [GK]

revenge into their own hands; they leave vengeance to God alone (cf. Rom. 12:19). Therefore they must abandon all personal thoughts of revenge and must be free from their own thirst for revenge; otherwise vengeance is not seriously left to God. Indeed only those who are themselves innocent in relation to the enemy can leave vengeance to God. The prayer for the vengeance of God is the prayer for the carrying out of God's righteousness in the judgment of sin. This judgment must be made known if God stands by God's Word, and it must be made known to those upon whom it falls; with my sin I myself belong under this judgment. I have no right to want to hinder this judgment. It must be fulfilled for God's sake. And it has certainly been fulfilled in a wonderful way.

God's vengeance did not fall on the sinners, but on the only sinless one, the Son of God, who stood in the place of sinners. Jesus Christ bore the vengeance of God, which the psalm asks to be carried out. Christ calmed God's anger against sin and prayed in the hour of the carrying out of the divine judgment: "Father, forgive them, for they do not know what they are doing!"[27] No one other than he, who himself bore the wrath of God, could pray like this. That was the end of all false thoughts about the love of a God who does not take sin very seriously. God hates and judges the enemies of God in the only righteous one, the one who prays for forgiveness for God's enemies. Only in the cross of Jesus Christ is the love of God to be found.

So the psalm of vengeance leads to the cross of Jesus and to the love of God that forgives enemies. I cannot forgive the enemies of God by myself, only the crucified Christ can; and I can forgive through him. So the carrying out of vengeance becomes grace for all in Jesus Christ.

Certainly it is important whether I stand with the psalm in the time of promise or in the time of fulfillment, but this distinction holds true for all the Psalms. I pray the psalm of wrath in the certainty of its wonderful fulfillment; I leave the vengeance in God's hands and pray for the carrying out of God's justice to all enemies. I know that God has remained true and has secured justice in wrathful judgment on the cross, and that this wrath has become grace and joy for us. Jesus Christ himself prays for the execution of God's vengeance on his body, and thus Christ leads me back daily to the gravity and the grace of his cross for me and all the enemies of God.

Even today I can believe God's love and forgive enemies only through

130

---

27. Luke 23:34.

the cross of Christ, through the carrying out of God's vengeance. The cross of Jesus applies to everyone. Whoever opposes him—whoever corrupts the word from the cross of Jesus, on whom God's vengeance had to be executed—must bear the curse of God either now or later. The New Testament speaks with great clarity, and in no way differs here from the Old Testament, about this curse that falls on those who hate Christ; but the New Testament speaks in addition about the joy of the Christian community on the day when God will carry out the final judgment (Gal. 1:8f.; 1 Cor. 16:22; Rev. 18:19; 20:11). In this way the crucified Jesus teaches us to pray truly the psalms of wrath.

### The End

The hope of Christians points to the coming again of Jesus and the
131  resurrection of the dead. In the Psalter this hope is not expressed in so many words. That which has been, since the resurrection of Jesus, spread out for the church as a long line of events of salvation history moving toward the end of all things, is from the viewpoint of the Old Testament still a single undivided whole. Life in community with the God of revelation, the final victory of God in the world, and the establishing of the messianic kingdom are all subjects of prayer in the Psalms.

There is no difference in this respect from the New Testament. To be sure, the Psalms pray for community with God in this earthly life, but they know that this community does not end with this earthly life but continues beyond it, even stands in contrast to it (Pss. 17:14f., 6, 34).[28] So life in community with God is certainly always directed beyond death. Death is indeed the irreversible bitter end for body and soul. It is the wages of sin, and this must not be forgotten (Pss. 39, 90). But on the other side of death is the eternal God (Pss. 90, 102). Therefore death will not triumph, but life will triumph in the power of God (Pss. 16:9ff., 56:14 [13], 49:16 [15], 73:24, 118:15ff.). We find this life in the resurrection of Jesus Christ, and we pray for it now and forever.

The psalms of the final victory of God and of God's Messiah (2, 96, 97, 98, 110, 148–150) lead us in praise, thanksgiving, and petition to the end of all things when all the world will give honor to God, when the

---

28. Bonhoeffer's reference (Ps. 6, 34) is to Psalms 6 and 34, not verse 34 of Psalm 6, an ambiguity that remains in the German mode of citing verses of Scripture. [GK]

redeemed community will reign with God eternally, and when the powers of evil will fall and God alone will retain power.

We have taken this brief journey through the Psalter in order to learn to pray better some of the psalms. It would not be difficult to arrange all the Psalms mentioned according to the petitions of the Lord's Prayer. We should need to change only slightly our arrangement of the order of the sections. But what alone is important is that we begin anew with confidence and love to pray the Psalms in the name of our Lord Jesus Christ. 132

"Our dear Lord, who has given to us and taught us to pray the Psalter and the Lord's Prayer, grant to us also the spirit of prayer and of grace so that we pray with enthusiasm and earnest faith, properly and without ceasing, for we need to do this; he has asked for it and therefore wants to have it from us. To him be praise, honor, and thanksgiving. Amen." (Luther).[29]

---

29. Luther, "Vorrede zur Neuburger Psalterausgabe" (Foreword to the Neuburg edition of the Psalter), 1545, *WA, Deutsche Bibel*, 10/2: 157.

GERHARD LUDWIG MÜLLER
AND
ALBRECHT SCHÖNHERR

# EDITORS' AFTERWORD
# TO THE GERMAN EDITION

172 *THE PRAYERBOOK OF THE BIBLE* serves the Christian as a profound guide into the Psalter considered as "the great school of prayer."[1] This little book takes its place in close connection with several expositions of individual psalms to which Bonhoeffer had increasingly devoted himself.[2]

However, *The Prayerbook of the Bible* should not be separated from a series of important biblical studies done at Finkenwalde on Old Testament themes.[3] In addition, there was the need to fight for the value of both the Old Testament and the Old Testament people of God within the Christian church. The problem was especially intensified by the anti-Semitism of the German Christians and their ideologically based attempts to eliminate from Christianity its Jewish heritage . This debate

---

1. See *LT,* 55 above. On the questions of Bonhoeffer's understanding of prayer, see especially Albert Altenähr, *Dietrich Bonhoeffer–Lehrer des Gebets*; see also Bethge, "Der Ort des Gebets," 159–77. It should be emphasized that Bonhoeffer brings out the trinitarian form in every Christian prayer composed by him. See, for example, Bonhoeffer's "Morning Prayers," written for his fellow prisoners for Christmas 1943, in *LPP,* 139–41.

2. See the following sermons and meditation in *MW:* "Sermon on Psalm 42: Sixth Sunday after Easter," June 2, 1935, 54–72 (*GS* 4:391–99); "Sermon on a Psalm of Vengeance: Psalm 58," July 11, 1937, 84–96 (*GS* 4:413–22); and "Meditation on Psalm 119," 1939–40, 103–44 (*GS* 4:505–43).

3. The following works belong to this series: "König David" (King David), October 8–11, 1935, *GS* 4:294–320, and "Der Wiederaufbau Jerusalems nach Esra und Nehemia" (The Rebuilding of Jerusalem according to Esra and Nehemia), April 21, 1936, *GS* 4:321–36.

moved to the level of a fundamental hermeneutical issue. The "neutrals" hid behind the theoretical distinction between pure scientific work and the taking of positions in church politics, and thus abandoned the Old Testament.

Can a purely historical-literary exegesis of the Old Testament satisfy a mere material and scientific interest? Or does the disclosure of the theological meaning that overlaps such interest also have its place, without its being set aside as merely nonbinding edification?[4] Bonhoeffer does not contest the relative legitimacy of historical-critical method, insofar as it must validate the "total *historicity* of the revelation."[5] If revelation as God's Word occurs only in human speech, the recognition of this can shed light on the way in which revelation is woven into the circle of human motives. It can likewise uncover links to the cultural milieu, take note of historical conditions and decisions, and illumine the psychic makeup of the biblical authors. Nonetheless, the one addressed by the Word can in faith take up and theologically assimilate what God intended to proclaim as well as the context for determining the meaning.[6] Under this rubric Bonhoeffer comes to a decisive theological interpretation of the Psalter.[7] The most important principles for interpretation he had already set forth in an essay, "Christ in the Psalms."[8] He had given them precise summary expression in *Life Together*.[9] To the extent that he goes beyond a purely historical-literary exposition, he places himself squarely within the great western tradition of the expositions of Augus-

173

---

4. On the problematic of historical and theological interpretation of the Scriptures, see Bonhoeffer's essay, "The Interpretation of the New Testament," August 23, 1935, in *NRS,* 308–25 (*GS* 3:303–24); selected parts of this text are also in *TF,* 168–71.

5. "Christus in den Psalmen" (Christ in the Psalms), July 31, 1935, *GS* 3:299.

6. Here Bonhoeffer gets involved in controversy with certain specialists in Old Testament exegesis. On this issue see D. Friedrich Baumgärtel, *Die Kirche ist Eine,* as this work relates to Bonhoeffer's study of Ezra and Nehemiah in *GS* 4:335–36. See also the exchange of letters between Baumgärtel and Eberhard Baumann, *GS* 4:335–43, and the exchange of letters between Baumgärtel and H. Strathmann, between Karl L. Schmidt and Strathmann, and between Gerhard Kittel and Strathmann, *GS* 6:401–2.

7. On this point, see Martin Kuske, *The Old Testament as the Book of Christ,* 60–96.

8. *GS* 3:294–300.

9. See *LT,* 53–60 above.

tine[10] and Luther,[11] who interpreted the Psalms christologically, tropologically, and typologically.[12] Bonhoeffer sets down the following basic hermeneutical rules.

## The Christological Mediation of Prayer

First of all, Christian prayer is not a natural self-expression directed at God, an uttering of spiritual needs, but rather a way to God. Only Jesus Christ can go this way. On the basis of his divine-humanity, Christ is the unity of the Word of God to us and our answer in prayer to God. He himself prays the Psalter in the humanity he has assumed. Thus we learn how to pray only from him. Only in him can we speak to God. At its core, then, prayer is a praying along with Jesus. Christians pray as members of the body of Christ, members of the new humanity in Christ their head. So once again application is given to the Augustinian idea of "head and body, one Christ."

## Scriptural Praying

Because Jesus in his humanity has taken upon himself all the distress, joy, burden, and hope of human existence, the Psalter can also stand in the Holy Scripture as a collection of human prayers. And thus it can at the same time be God's Word to us. In it a human word becomes God's Word and the Word of God becomes a human word. In the gift of the Lord's Prayer Jesus answers the request of the disciples for instruction in how to pray properly. And so all biblical prayers, including the Psalter, likewise find their direction and exposition in the Lord's Prayer. Christians, then, do not pray as their own spirit and feelings happen to dic-

---

10. Bonhoeffer had in his possession a copy of Aurelius Augustinus, *Über die Psalmen*, 1936. In this book, where Augustine comments on Psalm 118 (119), one finds numerous passages underlined.

11. See Karl Holl, "Luthers Bedeutung für den Fortschritt der Auslegungskunst," 544–82.

12. See Erwin Iserloh, "'Existentiale Interpretation' in Luthers erster Psalmenvorlesung?" 209–21. According to Iserloh, the "tropological" interpretation examines the text by seeking instructions for individual behavior. The "typological" interpretation analyzes characters and events of the text in terms of their representing later characters and events of salvation history.

tate. The Spirit of Christ in them teaches them how and why they ought to pray.

## The One Who Prays the Psalms

First of all, it is David himself who prays the Psalms. Yet, insofar as he bears the Messiah in himself in a prophetic-messianic way, Jesus Christ prays in him. Since Christ is not to be separated from his body, the church, and its members, it is in Christ that the church and individual Christians also pray the Psalter.

Bonhoeffer can now apply these basic hermeneutical principles to the individual genres and thematic areas of the Psalms. His original interpretation of the Psalms of vengeance should be of special help here. He does not with embarrassment interpret them away as a "preliminary stage of religion" [religiöse Vorstufe][13] that has been surpassed. He states that they never involve personal vengeance against one's enemies, but that the vengeance is directed to the enemies of the cause of God. But God takes vengeance by allowing God's wrath over sin and the sinner to come upon Christ. In Christ God has made the sinless one "to be made sin" [zur Sünde gemacht].[14] Thus the vengeance of God, with which the one who prays is allied, leads to the mystery of Christ's cross, where together the love of God, love for God's enemies, and God's merciful forgiveness of all guilt shine forth.

At issue in the prayers of the Psalms is the question of what is distinctively Christian in prayer. In this regard, the remark of Friedrich Christoph Ötinger (1702–1782), that basically the Psalter contains nothing other than the seven petitions of the Lord's Prayer, was key to Bonhoeffer's understanding of the Psalms. Of course, for Bonhoeffer this means not only that the Psalter is derived from Christ, but also the converse, namely, that the Psalter interprets the Christ-event. "In all our praying there remains only the prayer of Jesus Christ, which has the promise of fulfillment and frees us from the vain repetitions of heathen. The more deeply we grow into the Psalms, and the more often we have prayed them as our own, the more simple and rewarding will our prayer become."[15]

175

---

13. See the section entitled "Enemies," 174–76 above.
14. 2 Cor. 5:21.
15. *LT,* 58 above.

# CHRONOLOGY OF
## *LIFE TOGETHER* AND
## *PRAYERBOOK OF THE BIBLE*

4 February 1906
Dietrich Bonhoeffer and his twin sister, Sabine, born in Breslau, Germany

Summer semester 1923
Beginning of year of theological study at the University of Tübingen

Early summer 1924
Bonhoeffer travels to Rome and North Africa with his brother, Klaus

June 1924–July 1927
Theological studies at the University of Berlin

December 1927
Acceptance of *Sanctorum Communio*, Bonhoeffer's doctoral dissertation, at the University of Berlin

February 1928–February 1929
Curate for German congregations in Barcelona

July 1930
Acceptance of *Act and Being*, Bonhoeffer's *Habilitationsschrift* or qualifying thesis, at the University of Berlin

September
Publication of *Sanctorum Communio*

Academic year 1930–1931
Postgraduate year at Union Theological Seminary, New York

August 1931
Bonhoeffer begins his post as lecturer on the theological faculty of the University of Berlin

September 1931
Publication of *Act and Being*

November 1931
Bonhoeffer's ordination at St. Matthias Church, Berlin

Summer semester 1932
Lectures at Berlin University, "The Nature of the Church"

30 January 1933
Adolf Hitler made chancellor of Germany

Summer
Bonhoeffer's final lecture courses at Berlin

September
Preliminary work with Pastor Martin Niemöller to organize the Pastors' Emergency League

17 October
Beginning of Bonhoeffer's pastorate at the German Evangelical Church, Sydenham, and the Reformed Church of St. Paul in London

14 March 1934
Decree by Reich Bishop Müller to close the Old Prussian preachers' seminaries

29–31 May 1934
Organizational meeting of Confessing Church in Barmen, Germany; adoption of the Barmen Declaration

Autumn 1934
Opening of the first preachers' seminary of the Confessing Church at Bielefeld-Sieker

December 1934–March 1935
Bonhoeffer visits Anglican monasteries in Britain

10 March 1935
Bonhoeffer takes leave of his London parishioners

26 April 1935
Bonhoeffer travels to the site of the Confessing Church's seminary at Zingst by the Baltic Sea

24 June
Confessing Church Seminary relocated to Finkenwalde in Pomerania

15 September
Nuremberg Laws cancel citizenship for German Jews and prohibit marriage between Jews and Aryans

2 December
Confessing Church's training centers, examinations, and ordinations declared illegal by the state

5 August 1936
Bonhoeffer's authorization to teach on the faculty of the University of Berlin is withdrawn

Mid-October 1937
Finkenwalde Seminary closed by action of the Gestapo

November
Publication of [*The Cost of*] *Discipleship* [*Nachfolge*]

5 December
Collective pastorates begin in Köslin and Gross-Schlönwitz, replacing the Confessing Church seminaries

February 1938
Bonhoeffer makes initial contacts with leaders of the political resistance to Hitler: Canaris, Oster, Beck, and Sack

20 April
All pastors in Germany on active duty ordered to take the oath of allegiance to Hitler in recognition of his fiftieth birthday

9 September
Bonhoeffer and Bethge helped the family of Sabine and Gerhard Leibholz escape Germany into Switzerland

22 September
Sudetenland crisis reaches low point

30 September
Munich agreement between Hitler, Chamberlain, Daladier, and Mussolini

September-October
Bonhoeffer writes *Life Together* in four weeks while staying at the Leibholz's former home

9 November
*Kristallnacht* (Night of broken glass); destruction of hundreds of synagogues and thousands of Jewish-owned shops in Germany, arrests of an estimated 35,000 Jews

1939
Publication of *Life Together* as volume 61 of *Theologische Existenz heute* by Christian Kaiser Verlag, Munich

2 June–27 July
Bonhoeffer's second trip to the United States

1 September
German troops invade Poland; Great Britain and France declare war on Germany

1940
Publication of *Prayerbook of the Bible*

# BIBLIOGRAPHY

## 1. Literature Used by Bonhoeffer

Augustinus, Aurelius. *Über die Psalmen.* Selected and trans. Hans Urs von Balthasar. Leipzig, 1936. NL 1 C 1. English translation: Saint Augustine. *St. Augustine on the Psalms.* Trans. and annotated by Scholastica Hebgin and Felicitas Corrigan. Westminster: Newman Press, 1960–61.

Barth, Karl. *Der Römerbrief.* 2d ed. of the new, rev. version of 1922. Munich, 1923[3]. English translation: *The Epistle to the Romans.* Translated from the sixth German ed. by Edwin C. Hoskins. London: Oxford University Press, 1933, 1960[5].

*Die Bekenntnisschriften der evangelisch-lutherischen Kirche.* Edited and published in the anniversary year of the Augsburg Confession, 1930, vol. 2. Göttingen, 1930. NL 2 C 3. English translation: *The Book of Concord: The Confessions of the Evangelical Lutheran Church.* Ed. and trans. Theodore G. Tappert, in collaboration with Jaroslav Pelikan, Robert H. Fischer, and Arthur C. Piepkorn. Philadelphia: Muhlenberg, 1959.

Bezzel, Hermann. *Bezzel Brevier: Worte zur Besinnung und Vertiefung* (Bezzel breviary: Words for meditation and growth). Stuttgart, 1933. NL 5 F 2.

*Die Bibel oder die ganze Heilige Schrift des Alten und Neuen Testaments nach der deutschen Übersetzung D. Martin Luthers* (The Bible or the entire Holy Scriptures of the Old and New Testaments according to the German translation of Dr. Martin Luther). Supervised by the Commission of the Deutsche Evangelische Kirchenkonferenz. Mitteloktav ed. Munich, 1937. NL 1 A 6.

Bizer, Ernst. *Evangelisches Abendmahlsbüchlein: Das Heilige Abendmahl auf Grund von Luthers Lehre* (Protestant booklet for the Lord's Supper: The Holy Lord's Supper based on Luther's teaching). Munich, 1937. NL 5 D 3.

Bultmann, Rudolf. "Das christliche Gebot der Nächstenliebe." In Bultmann, *Glauben und Verstehen*, vol. 1. Tübingen, 1933. NL 3 B 20. English translation: "To Love Your Neighbor." In *Faith and Understanding*, trans. Louise Pettibone Smith. Philadelphia: Fortress Press, 1987.

Delitzsch, Franz. *Biblischer Kommentar über die Psalmen*. Leipzig, 3d printing, 1873. NL 1 C 2. English translation: *Biblical Commentary on the Psalms*, 3 vols. Trans. Francis Bolton. Edinburgh: T. & T. Clark, 1884.

———. *Die Psalmen*, 5. Rev. ed. Leipzig, 1894; Giessen, 1984.

Duhm, Bernhard. *Die Psalmen* (The Psalms). Freiburg, 1899. NL 1 C 8.

*Evangelisches Gesangbuch für Brandenburg und Pommern* (Protestant hymnbook for Brandenburg and Pomerania). Ed. the provincial councils of Brandenburg and Pomerania. Berlin/Frankfurt, 1931.

*Gebete* (Prayers). Edited by the Deutsche Christliche Studenten Vereinigung (German Christian Student Movement). Berlin-Lichterfelde, n.d. NL 5 F 7.

*Gebete der Väter: Eine Auswahl aus dem Gebetsschatz der Kirche für die Gegenwart* (Prayers of the fathers [of the church]: A selection from the church's treasury of prayers for the present time). Leipzig, 1930. NL 5 F 9.

Gunkel, Hermann. *Die Psalmen*. Göttingen, 1926. NL 1 C 9. English translation: *Psalms: A Form-Critical Introduction*. Trans. Thomas M. Horner. Philadelphia: Fortress Press, 1967.

Harnack, Adolf von. *Lehrbuch der Dogmengeschichte*, 3 vols. 4th rev. and enl. ed. Tübingen, 1909; Darmstadt, 1983. NL 2 C 17. English translation: *History of Dogma*. 4 vols. Trans. Neil Buchanan. New York: Russell & Russell, 1958.

———. "Was wir von der römischen Kirche lernen und nicht lernen sollten" (What we should and should not learn from the Roman church). In Harnack, *Reden und Aufsätze* (Speeches and essays) 2:247–64. Giessen, 1906².

Heiler, Friedrich. *Das Gebet: Eine religionsgeschichtliche und religionspsychologische Untersuchung*. Munich, 1921. NL 7 B 8a. English translation: *Prayer: A Study in the History and Psychology of Religion.* Trans. and ed. Samuel McComb with the assistance of J. Edgar Park. New York: Oxford University Press, 1958.

Hello, Ernest. *Worte Gottes* (Word of God). Leipzig, 1935. NL 5 F 10.

Herntrich, Volkmar, ed. *Ihr sollt meine Zeugen sein: Andachtsbuch der Bekennenden Kirche* (You must be my witness: Worship book of the Confessing Church). Gütersloh, 1935. NL 5 F 12.

Holl, Karl. "Luthers Bedeutung für den Fortschritt der Auslegungskunst" (The significance of Luther for the development of exegesis). In his *Gesammelte Aufsätze zur Kirchengeschichte.* Vol. 1, *Luther* (Collected essays on church history. Vol. 1, Luther). 4th and 5th ed. Tübingen, 1927.

Ignatius of Loyola. *Geistliche Übungen.* 5th ed. Translated from the original Spanish by A. Felder. Regensburg, 1932. NL 6 B 26. English translation: *The Spiritual Exercises of St. Ignatius.* Trans. Louis J. Puhl. Westminster: Newman Press, 1951.

Jung, Carl Gustav. *Die Beziehung der Psychotherapie zur Seelsorge.* Zurich, 1932. NL 5 E 7. English translation: *Modern Man in Search of a Soul.* Trans. W. S. Dell and Gary F. Baynes. New York: Harcourt, Brace and World, 1933; Harvest Books, 1955.

———. *Seelenprobleme der Gegenwart.* Zurich/Leipzig, Stuttgart, 1931. NL 11, 9. English translation: *Psychology and Religion.* Ed. Gerhard Adler et al. Trans. R. F. Hull. Princeton: Princeton University Press, 1969.

Köberle, Adolf, ed. *Das Brot des Lebens: Evangelische Abendandachten für jeden Tag nach der Ordnung des Kirchenjahres* (The bread of life: Protestant evening worship services for every day according to the order of the church year). Berlin, 1933. NL 5 F 4.

Kohlbrügge, Hermann Friedrich. *Quellwasser: Tägliche Andachten* (Water from the spring: daily worship services). Duisburg-Meiderich, 1931. NL 5 F 13.

*Die Komplet nach dem Benediktinischen und Römischen Brevier* (Compline according to the Benedictine and Roman breviary). 4th ed. Beuron, 1927. NL 5 F 14.

*Liber Usualis Missae et Officii pro Dominicis et Festis cum cantu Gregoriano quem ex editione typica in reccentioris Musicae* (Common book for the mass and office for Sundays and feasts with the Gregorian chant from the standard contemporary editions of the music). Paris, 1924. NL 5 F 16.

Lippert, Peter. *Einsam und gemeinsam* (Alone and together). 3d ed. Freiburg, 1932. NL 5 C 30.

Luther, Martin. *Der 118. Psalm: Klassische Erbauungsschriften des Protestantismus*, vol. 5 (Psalm 118: Classical edifying writings of Protestantism, vol. 5). 2d ed. Munich, 1934.

———. *Die Psalmen nach der deutschen Ubersetzung Martin Luthers* (The Psalms according to the German translation of Martin Luther). Stuttgart, 1936. NL 1 A 3.

———. *Sämtliche Werke* (*Erlanger Ausgabe*), *3. Abteil: Exegetische deutsche Schriften, vols. 5–10* (Collected works, Erlangen ed., Sec. 3: Exegetical writings in German, vols. 5-10.) Erlangen, 1845-47. NL 2 C 3, 21.

———. *Von der Bruderschaft Christi: Eine Predigt Luthers über das Wort des Auferstandenen an Maria Magdalena* (Concerning the brotherhood of Christ. A sermon of Luther on the word of the risen Christ to Mary Magdalene). Bad Salzuflen, 1935. NL C 3, 23.

———. *Werke*: *Kritische Gesamtausgabe* (*Weimarer Ausgabe*). Weimar, 1883ff. English translation: *Luther's Works*. Vols. 1–30 ed. Jaroslav Pelikan. St. Louis: Concordia, 1958-67. Vols. 31–55 ed. Helmut Lehmann. Philadelphia: Muhlenberg Press and Fortress Press, 1957-67.

*Ein neues Lied* (A new song). Ed. Otto Riethmüller. Berlin-Dahlem, 1932.

*Novum Testamentum Graece et Germanice: Das Neue Testament griechisch und deutsch* (The New Testament in Greek and German). 13th ed. Ed. Eberhard Nestle and rev. Erwin Nestle. Stuttgart, 1929. NL 1 A 4.

Nygren, Anders. *Eros und Agape. Gestaltwandlungen der christlichen Liebe.* 2 vols. Geneva, 1930, 1937. English translation: *Agape and Eros*. Trans. Philip S. Watson. Philadelphia: Westminster Press, 1953.

Ötinger, Friedrich Christoph. *Die Psalmen Davids nach den sieben Bitten des Gebets des Herrn in sieben Klassen dargebracht. Ein Wort zur Erbauung* (The Psalms of David arranged in the seven categories according to the seven petitions of the Lord's Prayer: a word for one's edification). In Ötinger, *Sämtliche Schriften* (Collected writings), 2/3. Ed. K. C. E. Ehmann. Stuttgart, 1860. New ed. E. Beyreuther, Stuttgart, 1977.

Parpert, Friedrich. *Das Mönchtum und die evangelische Kirche: Ein Beitrag zur Ausscheidung des Mönchtums aus der evangelischen Soziologie* (Monastery life and the Protestant church: An essay on the exclusion of monastery life from Protestant sociology). Munich, 1930. NL 2 C 16.

*Die Pommersche Kirchen-Ordnung und Agenda nebst den Legibus Praepositum, Statutis synodicis und der Visitations-Ordnung von 1736* (The

Pomeranian church order and agenda together with the proposal for laws, synodal statutes and the regulation of visitations of 1736). Ed. Superintendent (Bishop) Otto. Greifswald, 1854. NL 5 D 16.

Sasse, Hermann. *Kirche und Herrenmahl: Ein Beitrag zum Verständnis des Altarsakraments* (Church and the Lord's Supper: a contribution toward understanding the sacrament of the altar). Munich, 1938. NL 3 B 61.

Schott, Anselm. *Messbuch für die Sonn- und Feiertage im Anschluss an das grössere Messbuch* (Mass book for Sundays and feast days in conjunction with the larger mass book). Ed. the Arch Abbey of Beuron. Freiburg, 1935. NL 11, 7.

Seeberg, Reinhold. *Lehrbuch der Dogmengeschichte,* 4 vols. 3d reprinting. Leipzig, 1917–23. NL 2 C 44. English translation: *Textbook of the History of Doctrines.* 2 vols. in 1. Trans. Charles E. Hay. Grand Rapids: Baker Book House, 1956.

*Die täglichen Losungen und Lehrtexte der Brüdergemeine für das Jahr 1936–1944* (The daily texts and readings of the Church of the Brethren for the years 1936–44). Edited under the direction of the German Brüderunität. Herrnhut, 1936–44. NL 5 F 17.

Taube, Emil. *Praktische Auslegung der Psalmen zur Anregung und Förderung der Schrifterkenntniss* (Practical exposition of the Psalms for the purpose of stimulating and promoting knowledge of the Scriptures). Berlin, 1892. NL 1 C 24.

Thomas à Kempis. *Imitatio Christi. Werke,* vol. 2. Ed. M. J. Pohl. Freiburg, 1904. NL 11, 8. English translation: *The Imitation of Christ.* Ed. and with an introduction by Harold C. Gardner. Garden City: Doubleday, 1955.

Vogelsang, Erich. *Unbekannte Fragmente aus Luthers zweiter Psalmenvorlesung 1518* (Unknown fragments from Luther's second lecture on the Psalms, 1518). Berlin, 1940.

Witte, Karl. *Nun freut euch lieben Christen gmein: Luthers Wort in täglichen Andachten* (Now rejoice you dear Christians together: Luther's word in daily worship services). Berlin, 1934. NL 5 F 23.

## 2. Literature Consulted by the Editors

*The American Lutheran Hymnal.* Columbus, Ohio: The Lutheran Book Concern, 1930.

*The Australian Lutheran Hymnbook.* North Adelaide: Lutheran Publishing Company, 1940.

Balthasar, Hans Urs von. *Die grossen Ordensregeln: Lectio Spiritualis*, 12 (The great rules of order: spiritual reading series, no. 12). Einsiedeln, 1974.

Barth, Karl. *Church Dogmatics*. 4 vols. Ed. G. W. Bromiley and T. F. Torrance. Trans. G. T. Thomson. Edinburgh: T. & T. Clark, 1956–77.

Barton, John M. T. *Penance and Absolution*. New York: Hawthorn Books, 1961.

Baumgärtel, Friedrich. *Die Kirche ist Eine–die alttestamentlich-jüdische Kirche und die Kirche Jesu Christi: Eine Verwahrung gegen die Preisgabe des Alten Testaments* (The church is one–the Old Testament-Jewish church and the church of Jesus Christ: a protest against the abandonment of the Old Testament). Greifswald, 1936.

Bethge, Eberhard. "Afterword to the 1979 Edition of *Gemeinsames Leben*." *Newsletter*, International Bonhoeffer Society, English Language Section, no. 56 (1994): 10–14.

———. *Costly Grace: An Illustrated Introduction to Dietrich Bonhoeffer*. Trans. Rosaleen Ockenden. New York: Harper and Row, 1979.

———. "Dietrich Bonhoeffer and the Jews." In *Ethical Responsibility: Bonhoeffer's Legacy to the Churches*, 43–96. See Godsey and Kelly, eds., 1981.

———. *Dietrich Bonhoeffer: Man of Vision. Man of Courage*. Abridged from the 3d German ed. Trans. Eric Mosbacher, Peter and Betty Ross, Frank Clarke and William Glen-Doepel, under the editorship of Edwin R. Robertson. New York: Harper and Row, 1970.

———. "Der Ort des Gebets in Leben und Theologie Dietrich Bonhoeffers" (The place of prayer in the life and theology of Dietrich Bonhoeffer). In Bethge's *Bekennen und Widerstehen: Aufsätze–Reden–Gespräche* (Confessing and resistance: essays–talks–discussions), 159–77. Munich, 1984.

———. *Prayer and Righteous Action*. Ottawa: Canterbury House, 1979.

Bethge, Renate. "Bonhoeffer's Family and Its Significance for His Theology." In *Dietrich Bonhoeffer–His Significance for North Americans*, 1–30. See Rasmussen and Bethge, 1990.

———. "'Elite' and 'Silence' in Bonhoeffer's Person and Thoughts." In *Ethical Responsibility: Bonhoeffer's Legacy to the Churches*, 293–306. See Godsey and Kelly, eds., 1981.

Bonhoeffer, Dietrich. *Act and Being*. Translated by Bernard Noble. Introduction by Ernst Wolf. London: William Collins Sons, 1962; New

York: Harper and Row, 1961. (Reprinted by New York: Octagon Books, 1983.)

——. "The Causality and Finality of Preaching." In *Worldly Preaching: Lectures on Homiletics*, trans. and ed. Clyde E. Fant. Rev. ed. New York: Crossroad, 1991.

——. *Christ the Center*. A new translation by Edwin H. Robertson. San Francisco: Harper and Row, 1978.

——. *The Communion of Saints*. Trans. Ronald Gregor Smith, et al. London: Collins, 1963; New York: Harper and Row, 1964 [U.K. Title: *Sanctorum Communio: A Dogmatic Inquiry into the Sociology of the Church*.

——. "Concerning the Christian Idea of God." *Journal of Religion* 12, no. 2 (April 1932): 177–85.

——. *The Cost of Discipleship*. Trans. Reginald H. Fuller, revised by Irmgard Booth. New York: Macmillan, 1963.

——. *Creation and Fall/Temptation*. Trans. John C. Fletcher and Kathleen Downham. New York: Macmillan, 1966.

——. *Ethics*. Trans. Neville Horton Smith. New York: Macmillan, 1965.

——. *Gesammelte Schriften* (Collected writings). 6 vols. Ed. Eberhard Bethge. Munich, 1958–74.

——. *I Loved This People: Testimonies of Responsibility*. Ed. Hans Rothfels. Trans. Keith R. Crim. Richmond: John Knox Press, 1965.

——. "Incomplete Draft from the Year 1942 of a Proclamation from the Pulpit after a Political Overthrow." Ed. Hans Rothfels. Trans. Keith R. Crim. In *I Loved This People*, 45–48. Richmond: John Knox Press, 1965.

——. *Jugend und Studium 1918–1927* (Youth and education, 1918–27). *DBW* 9. Ed. Hans Pfeifer, with Clifford Green and Carl-Jürgen Kaltenborn. Munich, 1986.

——. *Letters and Papers from Prison*. 4th ed. Trans. Reginald H. Fuller, revised by Frank Clarke et al. Additional material trans. John Bowden for the enl. ed. New York: Macmillan, 1972.

——. *Life Together*. Trans. John W. Doberstein. New York: Harper & Row, 1954.

——. *Meditating on the Word*. Ed. and trans. David McI. Gracie. Cambridge, Mass., 1986; New York: Cowley Publications, 1987.

——. *No Rusty Swords: Letters, Lectures and Notes, 1928–1936*. Ed. Edwin H. Robertson. Trans. Edwin H. Robertson and John Bowden. New York: Harper and Row, 1965.

———. *Prayers from Prison*. Philadelphia: Fortress Press, 1979.

———. *Preface to Bonhoeffer: The Man and Two of His Shorter Writings*. Ed. John D. Godsey. Philadelphia: Fortress Press, 1965.

———. *Psalms: The Prayer Book of the Bible*. Trans. James H. Burtness. Minneapolis: Augsburg Publishing House, 1970.

———. *The Psalms: Prayer Book of the Bible*. Trans. Sister Isabel Mary SLG. Oxford: SLG Press, Convent of the Incarnation, 1982.

———. *Spiritual Care*. Ed., trans. and with an introduction by Jay C. Rochelle. Philadelphia: Fortress Press, 1985.

———. *A Testament to Freedom: The Essential Writings of Dietrich Bonhoeffer*. Ed. Geffrey B. Kelly and F. Burton Nelson. San Francisco: Harper Collins, 1990. Rev. and expanded ed., 1995.

———. *True Patriotism: Letters and Notes, 1939–1945*. Ed. Edwin H. Robertson. Trans. Edwin H. Robertson, and John Bowden. New York: Harper and Row, 1973.

———. *The Way to Freedom: Letters, Lectures and Notes, 1935–1939*. Ed. Edwin H. Robertson. Trans. Edwin H. Robertson and John Bowden. New York: Harper and Row, 1966.

———. *Worldly Preaching*. Trans. Clyde E. Fant. New York: Crossroad, 1991.

Brunner, Emil. *Eros und Liebe* (Eros and love). Berlin, 1936.

Burtness, James H. *Shaping the Future: The Ethics of Dietrich Bonhoeffer*. Philadelphia: Fortress Press, 1985.

Chapman, Clarke G., Jr. "What Would Bonhoeffer Say to Christian Peacemakers." In *Theology, Politics, and Peace*, ed. Theodore Runyon, 167–75. Maryknoll, N.Y.: Orbis, 1989.

Clements, Keith. *What Freedom? The Persistent Challenge of Dietrich Bonhoeffer*. Bristol: Bristol Bible College, 1990.

Day, Thomas I. *Dietrich Bonhoeffer on Christian Community and Common Sense*. Lewiston, N.Y.: Edwin Mellen Press, 1982.

De Gruchy, John. "Bonhoeffer's English Bible." *Dialog* 17, no. 3 (Summer 1978): 211–15.

*Evangelisches Kirchengesangbuch* (Protestant church hymnbook). Munich, n.d.

Feil, Ernst. *The Theology of Dietrich Bonhoeffer*. Trans. H. Martin Rumscheidt. Philadelphia: Fortress Press, 1985.

———. "Ende oder Wiederkehr der Religion? Zu Bonhoeffers umstrittener Prognose eines 'religionslosen Christentums'" (The end or the return of religion? on Bonhoeffer's controversial prognosis of a "religionless Christianity"). In *Die Präsenz des verdrängten Gottes* (The presence of the God driven out), 27–49. See Gremmels and Tödt, 1987.

———. "Zur Problematik der gegenwärtigen Renaissance des Religionsbegriffs" (On the problematic of the present renaissance of the idea of religion). *Studien der Zeit* 99 (1974): 672–88.

Floyd, Jr., Wayne Whitson. "The Search for an Ethical Sacrament: From Bonhoeffer to Critical Social Theory." *Modern Theology* 7, no. 2 (January 1991): 175–93.

———. *Theology and the Dialectic of Otherness: On Reading Bonhoeffer and Adorno.* Lanham, Md.: University Press of America, 1988.

——— and Clifford J. Green. *Bonhoeffer Bibliography: Primary Sources and Secondary Literature in English.* Evanston, Ill.: American Theological Library Association, 1992.

Gerhardt, Paul. *Paul Gerhardt's Spiritual Songs.* Trans. John Kelly. London, 1867.

Godsey, John D. "Barth and Bonhoeffer: The Basic Difference." *Quarterly Review: A Scholarly Journal for Reflection on Ministry* 7, no. 1 (Spring 1987): 9–27.

———. "The Doctrine of Love." In *New Studies in Bonhoeffer's Ethics*, 189–234. See Peck, ed., 1987.

———. "The Legacy of Dietrich Bonhoeffer." In *A Bonhoeffer Legacy*, 161–69. See Klassen, ed., 1981.

———. *The Theology of Dietrich Bonhoeffer.* Philadelphia: Westminster Press, 1960.

Godsey, John D., and Geffrey B. Kelly, eds., *Ethical Responsibility: Bonhoeffer's Legacy to the Churches.* New York/Toronto: Edwin Mellen Press, 1981.

Green, Clifford J. "Bonhoeffer's Concept of Religion." *Union Seminary Quarterly Review* 19, no. 1 (November 1963): 11–21.

———. *The Sociality of Christ and Humanity: Dietrich Bonhoeffer's Early Theology, 1927–1933.* Missoula, Mont.: Scholars Press, 1975.

———. "Two Bonhoeffers on Psychoanalysis." In *A Bonhoeffer Legacy*, 58–75. See Klassen, ed., 1981.

——— and Wayne Whitson Floyd, Jr. *Bonhoeffer Bibliography* (See under Floyd).

Gremmels, Christian, ed. *Bonhoeffer und Luther: Zur Sozialgestalt des Luthertums in der Moderne* (Bonhoeffer and Luther: on the social form of Lutheranism in the modern era). Munich, 1983.

Gremmels, Christian, and Ilse Tödt. *Die Präsenz des verdrängten Gottes: Glaube, Religionslosigkeit und Weltverantwortung nach Dietrich Bonhoeffer*

(The presence of the God driven out: faith, religionlessness and responsibility for the world according to Dietrich Bonhoeffer). Munich, 1987.

Grunow, Richard. *Dietrich Bonhoeffers Schriftauslegung* (Dietrich Bonhoeffer's interpretation of the Scripture). In *Die Mündige Welt* 1:62–76. Munich: 1955.

Günther, Walther. "Dietrich Bonhoeffer und die Brüdergemeine" (Dietrich Bonhoeffer and the Church of the Brethren). In *Unitas Fratrum: Zeitschrift für Geschichte und Gegenwartsfragen der Brüdergemeine* (Unity of brothers: Journal for the history and contemporary questions of the Church of the Brethren), no. 7, ed. W. Erbe, D. Meyer, and H.-B. Motel, 62–70. Hamburg, 1980.

Harrelson, Walter. "Bonhoeffer and the Bible." In *The Place of Bonhoeffer*, 115–42. See Marty, ed., 1962.

Iserloh, Erwin. "'Existentiale Interpretation' in Luthers erster Psalmenvorlesung?" (Existential interpretation in Luther's first lecture on the Psalms). In Iserloh's *Kirche–Ereignis und Institution: Aufsätze und Vorträge* (Church–event and institution: Essays and lectures), 2:205–21. Munich, 1985.

Iwand, Hans-Joachim. *Von der Gemeinschaft christlichen Lebens: Zwei Reden zur Feier der Beichte und des Heiligen Abendmahls* (On the community of Christian life: Two talks on the celebration of confession and the holy supper). Munich, 1937.

Jungmann, Josef. *The Early Liturgy to the Time of Gregory the Great.* South Bend, Ind., 1976.

Kelley, James Patrick. "The Best of the German Gentiles: Dietrich Bonhoeffer and the Rights of Jews in Hitler's Germany." In *Remembering for the Future*, vol. 1, ed. Yehudi Bauer et al., 80–92. New York, 1989.

Kelly, Geffrey B. "Bonhoeffer's Theology of History and Revelation." In *A Bonhoeffer Legacy*, 89–130. See Klassen, ed., 1981.

——. "The Influence of Kierkegaard on Bonhoeffer's Concept of Discipleship." *Irish Theological Quarterly* 41, no. 2 (April 1974): 148–54.

——. *Liberating Faith: Bonhoeffer's Message for Today.* Minneapolis, 1984.

——. "The New Edition of *Life Together* and Bethge's 'Afterword' to the 1979 Edition of *Gemeinsames Leben.*" *Newsletter*, International Bonhoeffer Society, English Language Section, no. 57 (1994), 2–7.

——. "The Prayerbook of the Bible: Dietrich Bonhoeffer's Introduction to the Psalms." *Weavings* 6, no. 5 (September/October 1991): 36–41.

———. "Revelation in Christ: A Study of Bonhoeffer's Theology of Revelation." *Ephemerides Theologicae Lovanienses* 50, no. 1 (May 1974): 39–74.

———. "Sharing in the Pain of God: Dietrich Bonhoeffer's Reflections on Christian Vulnerability." *Weavings* 7, no. 4 (July/August 1993): 6–15.

Kelly, Geffrey B., and John D. Godsey, eds. *Ethical Responsibility: Bonhoeffer's Legacy to the Churches*. New York/Toronto: Edwin Mellen Press, 1981.

Kierkegaard, Søren. *Concluding Unscientific Postscript to Philosophical Fragments*. Vol. 12/1 of *Kierkegaard's Writings*. Ed. and trans. Howard V. Hong and Edna H. Hong. Princeton: Princeton University Press, 1992.

Klassen, Abram J., ed. *A Bonhoeffer Legacy: Essays in Understanding*. Grand Rapids: Eerdmans, 1981.

Kuske, Martin. *The Old Testament as the Book of Christ: An Appraisal of Bonhoeffer's Interpretation*. Trans. S. T. Kimbrough. Philadelphia: Westminster Press, 1976.

Leibholz-Bonhoeffer, Sabine. *The Bonhoeffers: Portrait of a Family*. Ed. and expanded by F. Burton Nelson. Chicago: Covenant Press, 1994.

Lange, Ernst. "Kirche für andere: Dietrich Bonhoeffers Beitrag zur Frage nach einer verantwortbaren Gestalt der Kirche in der Gegenwart" (Church for others: Dietrich Bonhoeffer's contribution to the question concerning a responsible form of the church in the present times). *Evangelische Theologie* 27 (1967): 513–46. Also in R. Schloz, ed., *Kirche für die Welt: Aufsätze zur Theorie kirchlichen Handelns* (Church for the world: essays on the theory of church action), 19–62. Munich/Geinhausen, 1981.

Lovin, Robin W. "Biographical Context." In *New Studies in Bonhoeffer's Ethics*, 67–101. See Peck, ed., 1987.

———. "Dietrich Bonhoeffer: Responsibility and Restoration." In Lovin's *Christian Faith and Public Choices: The Social Ethics of Barth, Brunner and Bonhoeffer*. Philadelphia: Fortress Press, 1984.

Luther, Martin. "Two Kinds of Righteousness." *LW*, 31: 297–306.

Marsh, Charles R. *Reclaiming Dietrich Bonhoeffer: The Promise of His Theology*. New York: Oxford University Press, 1994.

Marty, Martin E., ed. *The Place of Bonhoeffer*. New York: Association Press, 1962.

Matthews, John W. "Responsible Sharing of the Mystery of Christian

Faith: *Disciplina Arcani* in the Life and Theology of Dietrich Bonhoeffer." *Dialog* 25, no. 1 (Winter 1986): 19–25.

Miller, Patrick D. "Dietrich Bonhoeffer and the Psalms." *The Princeton Seminary Bulletin* 15, no 3 (New Series, 1994): 274–82.

Müller, Gerhard L. *Für andere da: Christus–Kirche–Gott in Bonhoeffers Sicht der mündig gewordenen Welt* (There for others. Christ–church–God in Bonhoeffer's view of the world come of age). Paderborn, 1980.

Müller, Hanfried. "Stationen auf dem Wege zur Freiheit" (Stations on the way to freedom). In *Die Präsenz des verdrängten Gottes* (The presence of the God driven out), 221–41. See Gremmels and Tödt, 1987.

*Nachlaß Dietrich Bonhoeffer* (Dietrich Bonhoeffer's literary estate: a bibliographical catalogue). Archiv–Sammlung–Bibliothek (Archives, collections, library), arranged by Dietrich Meyer in collaboration with Eberhard Bethge. Munich, 1987.

Nelson, F. Burton. "Bonhoeffer and the Spiritual Life: Some Reflections." *Journal of Theology for Southern Africa* 30 (March 1980): 34–38.

———. "God's Guest on Earth: A Model for Sojourning Discipleship." *Sojourners* 13, no. 5 (May 1984): 27.

———, ed. "A Bonhoeffer Sermon (on a Psalm of vengeance, Ps. 58; 1937)." *Theology Today* 38 (January 1982): 465–71.

*New Revised Standard Version Bible*. Division of Christian Education of the National Council of the Churches of Christ in the United States of America. New York: Collins, 1989.

Peck, William J. "The Role of the Enemy in Bonhoeffer's Life and Thought." In *A Bonhoeffer Legacy*, 345–61. See Klassen, ed., 1981.

———, ed. *New Studies in Bonhoeffer's Ethics*. Lewiston, New York, and Queenston, Ontario: Edwin Mellen Press, 1987.

Pelikan, Herbert Rainer. *Die Frömmigkeit Dietrich Bonhoeffers: Ausserungen–Grundlinien–Entwicklung* (The piety of Dietrich Bonhoeffer: comments–foundations–development). Freiburg, 1982.

Peters, Tiemo Rainer. *Die Präsenz des Politischen in der Theologie Dietrich Bonhoeffers: Eine historische Untersuchung in systematischer Absicht* (The presence of the political in the theology of Dietrich Bonhoeffer: a historical research into a systematic aim). Munich, 1978.

Phillips, John A. *The Form of Christ in the World: A Study of Bonhoeffer's Christology*. New York: Harper and Row, 1967.

Pieper, Josef. *About Love*. Trans. Richard and Clara Winston. Chicago: Franciscan Herald Press, 1974.

Rasmussen, Larry, with Renate Bethge. *Dietrich Bonhoeffer–His Significance for North Americans.* Minneapolis: Fortress Press, 1990.

Rochelle, Jay C. "Introduction." In *Spiritual Care*, 7–29. See Bonhoeffer, 1985.

*The Service Book and Hymnal.* Ed. Joint Commission on the Liturgy. Minneapolis: Augsburg Publishing House, 1970.

Sierink, Kornelis. *Pastoraat als wegbereiding: De betekenis van Dietrich Bonhoeffer voor het pastoraat* (Pastoral ministry as preparing the way: the significance of Dietrich Bonhoeffer for pastoral ministry). Gravenhage, 1986.

Tentler, Thomas N. *Sin and Confession on the Eve of the Reformation.* Princeton: Princeton University Press, 1977.

*The Text Book of the Moravian Church: Being the Scripture "Watchwords" and Doctrinal Texts.* Bethlehem, Pa., 1936–44.

Thomas Aquinas, Saint. *Summa Theologica*, 2.2. New York: Benziger Brothers, 1947–48.

Wedemeyer-Weller, Maria von. "The Other Letters from Prison." *USQR*, 23, no. 1 (Fall 1967): 23–29. Also in *LPP*, 412–19. See Bonhoeffer, 1972.

West, Charles C. "Ground under our Feet: A Reflection on the Worldliness of Dietrich Bonhoeffer's Life and Thought." In *New Studies in Bonhoeffer's Ethics*, 235–73. See Peck, ed., 1987.

Winkworth, Catherine. *Lyra Germanica: Hymns for the Sundays and Chief Festivals of the Christian Year.* New York: James Miller, 1861.

———. *Lyra Germanica.* Second Series: The Christian Life. London: Longman, Brown, Green, Longmans and Roberts, 1858.

Zerner, Ruth. "Dietrich Bonhoeffer's Views on the State and History." In *A Bonhoeffer Legacy*, 131–57. See Klassen, ed., 1981.

Zimmermann, Wolf-Dieter, and Ronald Gregor Smith, eds. *I Knew Dietrich Bonhoeffer: Reminiscences by His Friends.* Trans. Käthe Gregor Smith. New York: Harper and Row, 1966.

## 3. Bibliography of Other Literature Related to
### *Life Together* and *The Prayerbook of the Bible*

Altenähr, Albert. *Dietrich Bonhoeffer–Lehrer des Gebets: Grundlagen für eine Theologie des Gebets bei Dietrich Bonhoeffer* (Dietrich Bonhoeffer—

teacher of prayer: Dietrich Bonhoeffer's foundations for a theology of prayer). Würzburg, 1976.

Bethge, Eberhard. "Gottesdienst in einem säkularen Zeitalter—wie Bonhoeffer ihn verstand" (Worship in a secular era—as Bonhoeffer understood it). In Bethge's *Ohnmacht und Mündigkeit: Beiträge zur Zeitgeschichte und Theologie nach Dietrich Bonhoeffer* (Powerlessness and maturity: essays on contemporary history and theology according to Dietrich Bonhoeffer), 114–34. Munich, 1969.

Bethge, Eberhard, Renate Bethge, and Christian Gremmels, eds. *Dietrich Bonhoeffer: A Life in Pictures.* Trans. John Bowden. London/Philadelphia: Fortress Press, 1986.

Buber, Martin. *I and Thou: A New Translation.* Trans. Walter Kaufmann. New York: Scribner, 1970.

Dudzus, Otto. "Discipleship and Worldliness in the Thinking of Dietrich Bonhoeffer." *Religion in Life* 35, no. 2 (Spring 1966): 230–40.

Glenthøj, Jorgen. *Was hat Dietrich Bonhoeffer zur Frage des Gottesdienstes im säkularen Zeitalter gesagt?* (What has Dietrich Bonhoeffer said on the question of worship in a secular age?). Copenhagen, 1969.

Halkenhäuser, Johannes. *Kirche und Kommunität: Ein Beitrag zur Geschichte und zum Auftrag der kommunitären Bewegung in den Kirchen der Reformation* (Church and community: a contribution to the history and the task of the communitarian movement in the churches of the Reformation), 182–209. Paderborn, 1978.

Hampe, Johann Christoph. "An Interpretation." In *Prayers from Prison*, 37–89. See Bonhoeffer, 1979.

Kanitz, Joachim, Wolfgang Büsing, and Erwin Sutz. "Finkenwalde." In *Wie eine Flaschenpost: Ökumenische Briefe und Beiträge für Eberhard Bethge* (Like a bottled message cast on the ocean: ecumenical letters and essays for Eberhard Bethge), 48–53. Munich, 1979.

Kemp, Walter H. "Polyphonous Christian Community of Dietrich Bonhoeffer." *Lutheran Quarterly* 28, no. 1 (February 1976): 6–20.

Kuske, Martin. *Weltliches Christsein: Dietrich Bonhoeffers Vision nimmt Gestalt an* (Being a worldly Christian: Dietrich Bonhoeffer's vision takes shape). Munich, 1984.

Lehmann, Paul L. "Piety, Power, Politics: Church and Ministry Between Ratification and Resistance." *Journal of Theology for Southern Africa* 44 (September 1983): 58–72.

Meier, Jörg Martin. *Weltlichkeit und Arkandisziplin bei Dietrich Bonhoeffer*

(Worldliness and discipline of the secret in Dietrich Bonhoeffer). Munich, 1966.

Meuss, Gisela. "Arkandisziplin und Weltlichkeit bei Dietrich Bonhoeffer" (Discipline of the secret and worldliness in Dietrich Bonhoeffer). In *Die Mündige Welt* 3, 68–115. Munich, 1960.

Moltmann, Jürgen. "The Lordship of Christ and Human Society." In *Two Studies in the Theology of Bonhoeffer*, ed. J. Moltmann and Jürgen Weissbach, trans. Reginald and Ilse Fuller, introduction by Reginald H. Fuller, 21–94. New York: Scribner's, 1967.

Müller, Gerhard L. *Bonhoeffers Theologie der Sakramente* (Bonhoeffer's theology of the sacraments). Frankfurt, 1979.

———. "Wiederversöhnung in der Gemeinde: Das streitbare Engagement Dietrich Bonhoeffers für die Erneuerung der Einzelbeichte" (Repeated reconciliation in the community: Dietrich Bonhoeffer's aggressive commitment for the restoration of personal confession). *Catholica* 33 (1979): 292–328.

Müller, Hanfried. *Von der Kirche zur Welt: Ein Beitrag zu der Beziehung des Wortes Gottes auf die societas in Dietrich Bonhoeffers theologischer Entwicklung* (From the church to the world: a study of the relationship of the Word of God to society in Dietrich Bonhoeffer's theological development). Leipzig, 1961; Hamburg-Bergstedt, 1966.

Ott, Heinrich. *Reality and Faith: The Theological Legacy of Dietrich Bonhoeffer*. Trans. Alex A. Morrison. Philadelphia: Fortress Press, 1972.

Peck, William J. "A Proposal Concerning Bonhoeffer's Concept of the Person." *Anglican Theological Review* 50, no. 4 (October 1968): 311–29.

Pfeifer, Hans. "The Forms of Justification: On the Question of Structure in Dietrich Bonhoeffer's Theology." In *A Bonhoeffer Legacy*, 14–47. See Klassen, ed., 1981.

Pohl, A. "The Service of the Pastor in a World Come of Age." *Foundations* 18, no. 2 (1975): 1020–1106.

Rades, Jörg Alfred. "Kierkegaard and Bonhoeffer," second draft. University of Saint Andrews. Photocopy, unedited ms. Bonhoeffer Archive, Union Theological Seminary, New York.

Reist, Benjamin A. *The Promise of Bonhoeffer*. Philadelphia: Lippincott, 1969.

Reynolds, Terrence. "Dietrich Bonhoeffer's Encouragement of Human Love: A Radical Shift in his Later Theology." *Union Seminary Quarterly Review* 41, nos. 3–4 (1987): 55–76.

Robertson, Edwin H. *Bonhoeffer's Legacy*. New York: Collier Books, 1991.

Schinjdel, H. J. J. van. *Religie, Geloof, Disciplina Arcani* (Religion, faith, discipline of the secret). Kampen, 1979.

Schoelles, Patricia. "Discipleship and Social Ethics: Defining Boundaries for the Church of the Diaspora." *The Annual of the Society of Christian Ethics* (1989): 187–205.

Schönherr, Albrecht. *Lutherische Privatbeichte* (Lutheran private confession). Göttingen, 1938.

———. "Bonhoeffers Satz 'Unser Christsein wird heute nur in zweierlei bestehen: Im Beten und Tun des Gerechten unter den Menschen': Versuch einer Auslegung" (Bonhoeffer's phrase, "Our being Christians today will consist of two things: prayer and action for justice on behalf of people": A tentative explanation). In *Kirche für andere: Vorträge und Ansprachen im Bonhoeffer-Gedenkjahr 1970 in der DDR* (Church for others: lectures and addresses in the Bonhoeffer commemoration year 1970 in the German Democratic Republic), ed. W. Pabst, 19–37. East Berlin, 1974.

Schroer, Hennig. "Besteht Christsein heute nur im Beten und Tun des Gerechten? Uberlegungen zu einem Liturgie und Diakonie verbindenden Grundmotiv der Theologie Dietrich Bonhoeffers" (Does being Christian today consist in prayer and action for justice? reflections on a liturgy and diaconate integrated into the fundamental motif of the theology of Dietrich Bonhoeffer). In *Solidarität und Spiritualitäat. Diakonie. Gottesdienst als Menschendienst. Ein ökumenisches Symposion* (Solidarity and spirituality. diaconate. worship as serving people. An ecumenical symposium), 13–25. Stuttgart, 1971.

Shriver, Donald W. "Faith, Politics and Secular Society: The Legacy of Bonhoeffer." *Word and World* 1 (Summer 1981): 239–51.

Smolik, Josef. "The Church without Privileges." *The Ecumenical Review* 28, no. 2 (April 1976): 174–87.

Visser 't Hooft, Willem A. "Dietrich Bonhoeffer and the Self-Understanding of the Ecumenical Movement." *The Ecumenical Review* 28, no. 2 (April 1976): 198–203.

Wendel, Ernst Georg. *Studien zur Homiletik Dietrich Bonhoeffers. Predigt–Hermeneutik–Sprache* (Studies on Dietrich Bonhoeffer's homiletics: preaching, hermeneutics, language). Tübingen, 1985.

Wilcken, John. "Bonhoeffer: Church and Ecumenism." *The Heythrop Journal* 10, no. 1 (January 1969): 5–25.

———. "Bonhoeffer: Church in Conflict." *The Heythrop Journal* 10, no. 2 (April 1969): 162–79.

# INDEX OF
# SCRIPTURE REFERENCES

# INDEX OF NAMES

# Index of Subjects

Absolution, 116–17
*Act and Being*, 6–8, 41, 116, 130–31, 163
Admonition, 94, 105
Agape, 8, 39–40
Alien Righteousness, 31, 62
Alone
  in community, 28, 82–86, 91–93
*Anfectungen. See* Temptation
Angels, 28, 29, 79, 118
Angelus, 30
Anthropology, 130
*Arkandisziplin. See* Discipline of the
  Secret
Aryan Clause, 71
Association of piety. See *Collegium*
  *pietatis*
Authority, 106–7
  of the Bishop, 106–7
  of the Word, 107

Berlin University, 9
Bible
  and liturgy, 61–63
  reading of, 58–65
  and Reformers, 63
Bishop
  New Testament description, 106
  authority of, 106–7

*Book of Concord,* 45, 72, 110, 183
Bread
  breaking together, 72, 78
  daily together, 71–74
  for today, 59–60
  sharing, 73–74
  sustaining brotherhood, 124
  petition in the psalms, 168
Brethren
  Bohemian, 67, 68
  Church of the, 15
Breviary, 77
Brotherhood
  Christian, 52 et passim
Brothers and sisters
  as Christ, 94, 132, 138 et passim
Brothers' House, 3, 6, 14, 17–20, 119, 120
*Bruder*
  translation of, 22–23, 30

Care
  pastoral, 15–17, 98–99, 109, 115, 121–22
  of the weak, 11, 45–46, 93, 96, 101
  of the poor, 11, 45–46, 79, 100
Catholicizing
  defense against, 14–17, 20, 138, 146–47

# EDITORS AND TRANSLATORS

WAYNE WHITSON FLOYD, JR. (M.Div., Ph.D., Emory University) is visiting professor and director of the Dietrich Bonhoeffer Center at the Lutheran Theological Seminary at Philadelphia. An Episcopal layperson, he also serves as Canon Theologian for the Episcopal Cathedral of St. Stephen in Harrisburg, PA. He is the author of *Theology and the Dialectics of Otherness: On Reading Bonhoeffer and Adorno* (University Press of America, 1988); he co-authored the *Bonhoeffer Bibliography: Primary Sources and Secondary Literature in English* (American Theological Library Association, 1992); and he co-edited *Theology and the Practice of Responsibility: Essays on Dietrich Bonhoeffer* (Trinity Press International, 1995). In addition to his other various published essays on modern Jewish and Christian thought, Dr. Floyd's articles on Bonhoeffer have appeared in *Union Seminary Quarterly Review, Dialog, The Lutheran, Modern Theology,* and *Christian Century.*

GEFFREY B. KELLY (S.T.D., the University of Louvain, Belgium) is professor of systematic theology, chairperson of the Department of Religion, and director of the graduate program in theological, pastoral, and liturgical studies at La Salle University, Philadelphia. Elected president, Dr. Kelly is the author of *Liberating Faith: Bonhoeffer's Message for Today* (Augsburg Publishing House, 1984). He has co-edited *Ethical Responsibility: Bonhoeffer's Legacy to the Churches* (The Edwin Mellen Press, 1981) and *A Testament to Freedom: The Essential Writings of Dietrich Bonhoeffer* (HarperSanFrancisco, 1995). He has written numerous articles on Bonhoeffer appearing in such journals as *Dialog, Union Seminary Quarterly*

*Review, Ephemerides Theologicae Lovanienses, Princeton Seminary Bulletin, The Irish Theological Quarterly,* and *Weavings.*

DANIEL W. BLOESCH (M. Div., North Park Theological Seminary; M.A., University of Illinois [Chicago]) is the pastor of the Community Church (Conservative Congregational Christian Conference) in Round Lake, Illinois. His translations of sermons by Dietrich Bonhoeffer have appeared previously in *Theology Today, Sojourners,* and *A Testament to Freedom* (HarperSanFrancisco, 1995). He also translated Christof Gestrich's *The Return of Splendor in the World: The Christian Doctrine of Sin and Forgiveness* (Eerdmans).

JAMES H. BURTNESS (Ph.D., Princeton Theological Seminary) is professor of systematic theology at Luther Seminary in St. Paul. Elected vice-president of the International Bonhoeffer Society, English Language Section, in 1992, Jim is presently on the editorial board of *Dialog.* He translated the first English-language edition of *Psalms: The Prayerbook of the Bible* (Augsburg Publishing House). Dr. Burtness is the author of *Shaping the Future: The Ethics of Dietrich Bonhoeffer* (Fortress Press, 1985).